ALGERIA:
A REVOLUTION
THAT FAILED

ALSO BY ARSLAN HUMBARACI

Middle East Indictment, Robert Hale, London 1958.

ALGERIA:
A REVOLUTION
THAT FAILED

A POLITICAL HISTORY SINCE 1954

ARSLAN HUMBARACI

FREDERICK A. PRAEGER, *Publishers*

New York · Washington · London

FREDERICK A. PRAEGER, *Publishers*,
111 Fourth Avenue, New York 10003, N.Y., U.S.A.,
77-79 Charlotte Street, London W.1, England

Published in the United States of America in 1966
by Frederick A. Praeger Inc., Publishers

Library of Congress Catalog Card Number: 66-21783
© 1966 ARSLAN HUMBARACI, London, England

Printed in Great Britain

DEDICATED TO

ABDELHAFID BOUSSOUF
TAWFIK BOUATOURA and MOHAMMED HARBI
wherever they may be, in power, gaol or exile

CLAUDE CHEYSSON and JEAN-PIERRE GAULT
two sincere and idealistic Frenchmen who did so much to
restore the values of France in Algeria

ABDERRAHMAN YUSUFI of Morocco
as a mark of respect for his wisdom and silent courage

ACKNOWLEDGEMENTS

My warm thanks are due to Nadine Fendley for her efficient help in preparing the typescript for the publishers, and particularly for her valuable advice in matters of style. I am grateful to Michael Young for devising the Maps from my specifications.

I owe a special debt to Patrick Seale for his friendly encouragement.

CONTENTS

ABBREVIATIONS

AAPSC: Afro-Asian Peoples' Solidarity Committee.

AGCA: Association Générale des Commerçants Algériens. Created in France in 1956 under the auspices of the FF-FLN.

AGTA: Amicale Générale des Travailleurs Algériens en France.

ALN: Armée de Libération Nationale. Founded October 10, 1954 at a secret meeting of chiefs of Wilayas. Reorganised and given full juridical status as a belligerent army at the first Soummam Valley meeting of the CNRA on August 24, 1956.

ANP: Armée Nationale Populaire. The title of the ALN since the liberation.

APS: Algérie Presse Service. Official news agency. See Appendix IV.

BCA: Banque Centrale d'Algérie.

CCE: Comité de Coordination et d'Exécution. Established in August 1956 by the CNRA meeting at Soummam Valley.

CNRA: Conseil National de la Révolution Algérienne. Founded in August 1956 at the Soummam Valley meeting, this supreme body of the revolution acted as a parliament. See Appendix I and Appendix II for details.

CNS: Compagnies Nationales de Sécurité. These special security forces (equivalent to the French Compagnie Républicaine de Sécurité—CRS) were created when Algeria became independent.

COM-EST (-OUEST): Commandement-Est (-Ouest)—Eastern Command, Western Command—the two supreme military commands of the CCE. The first was in charge of Wilayas I, II and III and the second of Wilayas IV, V and VI. COM-EST was based at Ghardimau in the part of Tunisia known as Bec de Canard which penetrates Algerian territory. COM-OUEST was based at Oudja in eastern Morocco. Later, following the formation of the EMG-ALN, these two commands were known respectively as 'la Base de l'Est' and 'la Base de l'Ouest'.

CRUA: Comité Révolutionnaire d'Unité et d'Action. Founded in 1954 by members of the Organisation Spéciale.

EMG-ALN: Etat Major Général-ALN. This, the general staff, was formed in 1959, taking over supreme military command from COM-EST and COM-OUEST of the CCE. Its first and only chief was Colonel Houari

viii

Boumedienne, who had his GHQ at Ghardimau in Tunisia. His two permanent assistants were Ahmed Kaid, better known as Commander 'Slimane', and Commander Ali Mendjli.

FCDRL: Front Commun pour la Défense et le Respect de la Liberté. Founded in 1951 by the temporary association of the UDMA and the MTLD with the *Ulama*.

FF-FLN: Fédération de France-FLN.

FFS: Front des Forces Socialistes. Formed in September 1963 by Hocine Ait Ahmed to oppose Ben Bella.

FLN: Front de Libération Nationale. Founded in 1954, this became the main national revolutionary front during the war and the only official party after independence.

GPRA: Gouvernement Provisoire de la République Algérienne. The first Provisional Government was established in exile at Cairo and Tunis on September 9, 1958. See Appendix I and Appendix II for details.

JFLN: Jeunesse FLN. A post-independence attempt by Ben Bella to regroup youth after the style of the European Jeunesse Communiste.

JORA: Journal Officiel de la République Algérienne.

MNA: Mouvement Nationaliste Algérien. A bitter rival of the FLN, this body was created by Messali Hadj on November 5, 1954.

MPS: Magasins Pilotes Socialistes. A shortlived attempt to control prices and prevent speculation by the establishment in Algiers of socialist shops during the Ben Bella era.

MTLD: Mouvement pour le Triomphe des Libertés Démocratiques. Founded by the PPA of Messali Hadj for the purpose of entering the legislative elections of 1946.

OAU: Organisation of African Unity.

ONACO: Office National Algérien des Coopérations Ouvrières. Created on December 13, 1962.

ONAMO: Office National de la Main-d'Oeuvre. Established in May 1963 under the authority of the Ministry of Social Affairs to handle the emigration abroad of Algerian workers.

ONAT: Office National du Tourisme. Created on August 25, 1962.

ONC: Office National du Commerce.

ONRA: Office National de la Réforme Agraire.

OPA: Organisation Politico-Administrative. Formed to serve as an auxiliary to the ALN, its members, who did not wear uniforms, were known as *mussabilin* and *fidayin*.

OPL: Organisation Politico-Logistique. A branch and variant of the OPA.

ORU: Organisation Rurale et Urbaine. Another branch and variant of the OPA.

OS: Organisation Spéciale. The first secret organisation which initiated the revolution of November 1, 1954. See Appendix I.

PCA: Parti Communiste Algérien. Founded in 1936.

PCF: Parti Communiste Français.

PPA: Parti Populaire Algérien. Founded by Messali Hadj in 1937.

PRS: Parti Révolutionnaire Socialiste. Founded by Mohammed Boudiaf in September 1962 to oppose Ben Bella. It has always remained clandestine, with perhaps more adherents among Algerians in France than in Algeria itself.

SNATC: Société Nationale Algérienne des Transports Communs.

UDMA: Union Démocratique du Manifeste Algérien. Created by Ferhat Abbas for the purposes of the 1946 legislative assembly.

UEA: Union des Ecrivains Algériens. Created in Algiers on October 28, 1963 following a meeting of twenty prominent pro-FLN Algerian writers, many of whom wished nevertheless to prevent the total submission of culture to the party.

UGCA: Union Générale des Commerçants Algériens. An organisation based in Algiers.

UGEMA: Union Générale des Etudiants Musulmans Algériens. The only pro-FLN body among Algerian students, it operated from Lausanne in Switzerland after being banned from France during the war. It became the UNEA after independence.

UGTA: Union Générale des Travailleurs Algériens. Established by the FLN on February 26, 1956, it remained the only trade union of workers in independent Algeria. Before its formation, the Algerian workers were enrolled by the French Confédération du Travail (CGT) which, in Algeria, tried to group both muslim and christian workers in the CGTU.

UNEA: Union Nationale des Etudiants Algériens. This was the successor, in Algeria itself, of the UGEMA.

UNFA: Union Nationale des Femmes Algériennes.

UNFP: Union Nationale des Forces Populaires; the main leftwing opposition party in Morocco.

UPA: Union Populaire Algérienne. Established in 1938 by Ferhat Abbas to oppose the PPA of Messali Hadj.

USTA: Union des Syndicats des Travailleurs Algériens. Established on February 18, 1956.

ZAA: Zone Autonome d'Alger. The zone created by the wartime FLN during the summer of 1962. Promoting a communal way of life, it played a prominent part in the events of that year.

PREFACE

—∿∿∿ᴕᴕᴕᴠ/⊙/ᴕᴠᴕᴕᴕᴠ—

IN THE LAST DECADE, three major events have aroused world-wide interest and emotion: the war in Vietnam, the Cuban revolution, and the Algerian revolution—the subject of this book.

I have personal experience of many of the events described in the following pages, for I have closely followed developments in Algeria since 1959: first from Morocco and Tunisia—the French authorities not allowing me to enter occupied Algeria—and then, after Independence, from inside the country.

Even the closest observer of the Algerian scene has his task complicated by two facts in particular. In the first place, the Algerians, and especially the revolutionaries (who are mostly French-educated), interlarded their Arab verbosity with a very unoriental cartesian logic and, since independence, with a good deal of communist phraseology. Secondly, the nervous temperament and anarchical tendencies of the Algerians, together with the lightning speed of events, produced a situation of bewildering confusion. After only a few weeks' absence from the country, returning observers found they had to start again from the beginning. The faces had changed and, with this, the whole character of the scene, for Algerian affairs are conducted according to personal whims rather than by general principles. It was difficult to recognise the essential, to discard the banal incident, without also discarding the apparently trivial factor which turns out to be profoundly significant. The history of the Algerian revolution consists largely of anecdotes and personal incidents: what the French call 'la petite histoire'. The Algerians have put out an abundance of official statements and texts, but unfortunately these have nearly always been dictated by personal ambition, expediency or merely the desire to adopt revolutionary phraseology. An understanding of the basic facts of history and of agrarian problems is more useful than the study of these texts, which were so soon to be thrown to the winds.

There is another, more sentimental, difficulty. Like most other members of the 'Maghrib circus', I became emotionally involved in the Algerian revolution. I not only reported on this last great colonial venture of France: I militated against it. The 'Maghrib circus' was the collective name given to international press correspondents, mostly based on Tunisia, who had made of the Algerian struggle with France an ideological conflict in which they were personally involved. The tensions and emotions of the Algerian war were further cemented by a very peculiar camaraderie, that of being based on the extraordinarily beautiful and peaceful Tunisian village of Sidi-Bou-Said, where many years earlier André Gide had found shelter. To many of us, and to our families, Sidi-Bou-Said is for ever associated with some of the most memorable years of our lives.

There has been no 'Algerian Dien Bien Phu', and the victory over the French was more political than military. It is in this political field that the 'Maghrib circus' came to play an important part in alerting and moulding world opinion on pro-Algerian lines. Many of us went to rather unjournalistic lengths to give the Algerian revolutionaries a hand. Yet is is hard to think of a single one of those of us who displayed active sympathy for the Algerian cause who has not since been disillusioned, often suffering in some way at Algerian hands. Life has proved difficult for the Algerians, and they have not been slow in making it difficult for themselves and for their best foreign friends.

The Algerians were perhaps right at times in accusing leftwing French journalists of trying to tell them how to run their revolution. Both communist and non-communist elements of the French left did, consciously or unconsciously, try to achieve in or through North Africa what they had not been able to do in their own country. Algerian ingratitude must have hurt them the more in that during the war they had, as Frenchmen, a heavier burden on their consciences than the truly 'foreign' correspondents.

For Algeria, an era of foreign oppression and exploitation has closed. The *Allah Akbar* chant of the muezzin is no longer accompanied by the bugle notes of the Légion Etrangère. May the *shuada* —those who made the supreme sacrifice that their country might be mistress of her own destiny—rest in peace.

Even if it were possible, I would not wish to turn back the wheel of history; and I beg my Algerian friends not to read malice and uncharitableness on my part when I advert to their weaknesses and lack of national unity. Like others of the 'Maghrib circus', I had told them that, once the war was over and independence won, the sympathetic observer would no longer turn a blind eye to Algerian failings but reclaim the right to criticise. Algeria is now independent, and it is to be hoped that, one day, an Algerian who has been able to detach himself from partisan views and narrow nationalism will write what is really needed: a serious and objective book by an Algerian on the Algerian revolution.

There have been many upheavals in Algeria. The anti-French insurrection has been successful. But the revolution which the Algerians claimed to be a 'Socialist Revolution' has so far been a failure—as this book seeks to demonstrate.

A.H.

Rome, January 1966.

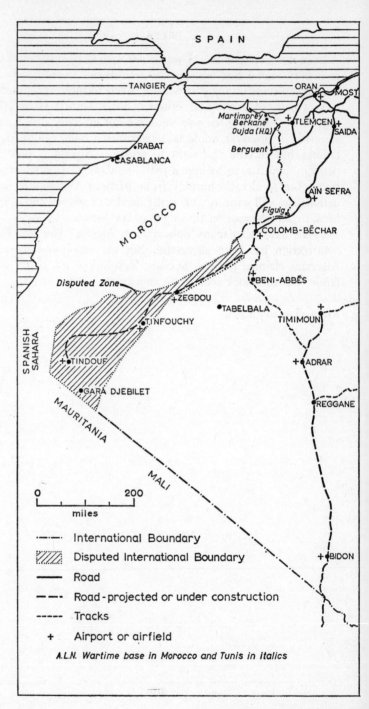

I. POLITICAL, WITH ROAD AND AIR

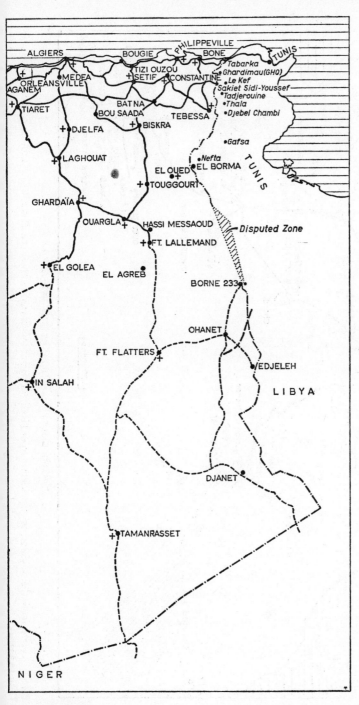

COMMUNICATIONS

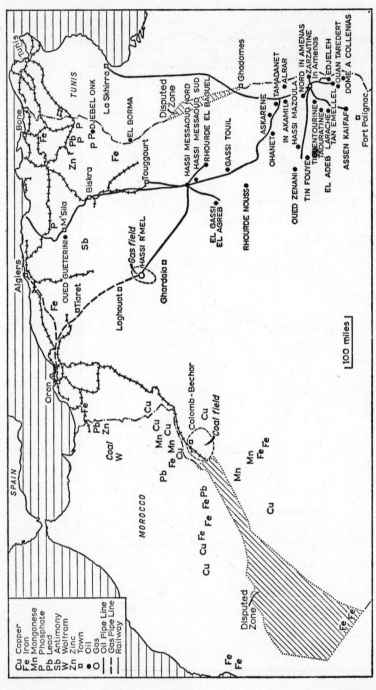

Note: In early 1966, the westernmost oil pipeline from Hassi Messaoud was completed between Hassi R'Mel and the port of Arzew near Oran (Annaba).

2. NATURAL RESOURCES, WITH PIPE LINE AND RAIL LINKS

ALGERIA:
A REVOLUTION
THAT FAILED

INTRODUCTION:
ENEMY BROTHERS

WHEN TRYING to piece together the Algerian puzzle, there are three closely connected factors to bear in mind which, determining the shape of modern Algeria, can only be understood with reference to its history. They are: the lack of unity among Algerians; the scars left on the country by long periods of Arab, Turkish and especially French domination; and Islam.

So diverse have been the influences at work in Algeria over the past centuries, and so disruptive their effects, that it is not surprising if people still ask: are the Algerians in fact a nation? One convulsion of history is sometimes enough to weld different elements into a viable nation, often in defiance of their earlier traditions. What was Pakistan before Jinnah, or Tunisia before Bourguiba? Algeria is the supreme example of a nation born out of one traumatic experience: the fight for independence. Until the struggle revealed the Algerians to themselves, they could hardly have been called a nation in the serious sense of the word—whatever the nationalists may now claim.

It has been said, with reference to the 'nations' mushrooming in Africa, that the only things needed to become a nation are ministers and ambassadors with Cadillacs, a flag, a national anthem, a seat in the United Nations, an airline and a USIS library to wreck. Truth is stranger than fiction, and there are indeed countries in Africa which answer to this description. North Africa, however, is very different. It has benefited from a muslim culture for centuries and has been associated with the civilisations of the Mediterranean from its earliest history. Algeria may be a young nation in years— it may indeed be a nation still in process of formation; but it has the strong foundations of an ancient, if chequered, history on which to erect the edifice of a modern nation-state.

The necessity of knowing something of Algeria's past to understand its present condition has often been overlooked. As a result, many countries equated Algeria with Ben Bella, and only Ben Bella. When he was overthrown, they had to rethink the whole Algerian question. The French, so much better acquainted with the country's history, were able to see his overthrow simply as an 'episode'. (De Gaulle's word for it was 'une péripétie'.) Without this knowledge, it is quite impossible to understand the constant struggle of Algerian against Algerian. 'Disunity has been the one constant factor on the tumultuous Algerian scene', Serge Bromberger has written.[1] A French leftwing intellectual, Gilles Martinet—an ardent supporter of Algerian independence and revolution—even went so far as to coin the phrase 'enemy brothers' to describe the feuding Algerians.[2] By midsummer 1962 it was already clear that these feuds would be the undoing of revolutionary Algeria.

When one Maghribine meets another, there is a prolonged handshake and a fraternal 'accolade'. The concept of brotherhood is so strong in Algeria that *akh*, 'brother' (plural *ikhwan*) is the recognised form of address. During the war against France, even a cynic well acquainted with the Middle East would not have questioned the sincerity of the greeting. The *ikhwan* were engaged in a bitter, unequal struggle with one of the leading NATO powers: a power which had amassed the greatest expeditionary force ever formed for a colonial war. There was, as any close observer will testify, a remarkable discipline among the *ikhwan*: a sense of duty almost sublime. They paid a very high price for their liberty; in the seven and a half years of war, nearly one million Algerians died. Still visible today are the ruins of some 8,000 *meshta* (small villages), destroyed by napalm, artillery or, under the threat of French bayonets, by the very hands of the inhabitants themselves before they were herded into concentration camps. There were some 500,000 war widows, 300,000 orphans and 2,500,000 'regroupés',*

---

* The policy of 'regroupement' was initiated by General Ducorneau, a parachutist colonel when he arrived in Algeria from Indochina in 1955. Influenced, like many French officers serving in Vietnam, by Mao Tse-tung's teachings on warfare, Ducorneau's policy was to lead to the uprooting of well over two million Algerian men, women and children. Taken from their native villages, they were herded into vast concentration camps.

people who had been forced to abandon their *meshta* and who accounted for a quarter of the country's total population. There were over a million jobless; cripples and beggars by the thousand; and as many more rendered half-witted by horror. For years, 300,000 stagnated as refugees in Tunisia and Morocco.

It was no case of independence on a silver platter. Algeria is the only country in Africa or in the Arab world that has achieved independence through a genuine war of liberation. (Nor is it irrelevant to mention that, cruel as it was, the Algerian war of independence did not sink to the depths of the Yugoslav war of liberation or the war of independence in Turkey; and certainly not to those plumbed in the present war of liberation in Vietnam.) The *ikhwan*, everyone agreed, were almost a race apart, outstanding in Africa and the Middle East: a race formed in the toughest of all schools. They deserved respect and support—and received both from practically the whole world, so great was the enthusiasm for their cause and their conduct in fighting for it. Their intellectuals, many of whom had fought in the Algerian maquis before taking up the struggle on the civilian front, were brilliant. Any country would be proud to claim them.

When these young men, backed by the *fellah* turned soldier—'with gun in one hand and pick in the other'—began thinking in terms of revolution, there were many who trembled. The regimes in the Maghrib—republican in Tunisia, monarchical in Morocco—looked shaky indeed; and there was consternation among the big Anglo-American companies exploiting oil in nearby Libya. The Quai d'Orsay and Whitehall took hurried steps to meet the threat of this revolutionary spirit in Africa. Moscow, Peking and their allies rushed to exploit it, each to his own end. There were repercussions even in distant Latin America, where nationalists sought Algerian advice and assistance the better to fight the banana fruit companies. In Quebec, the French separatists appropriately adopted the FLN sickle. At the time of the cease-fire and of the Evian agreements—under which France recognised the full sovereignty of its former colony—the Algerians were regarded almost as supermen by the radical nationalists of the Third World.

This world-wide regard, however, soon evaporated with independence. In less than a year for observers on the spot, in less than two for those outside, the Algerian revolutionaries had exhausted

3

their credit. Even in Black Africa, Algerian delegates at the various gatherings of the Organisation of African Unity were no longer the cynosure of all eyes. In the Middle East, as we shall see later, the Arabs—including Nasser—were bitterly disappointed after private talks with the Algerian leaders. Only the communists and Nasser's propaganda machine continued to applaud 'Ben Bella's' Algeria. Yet it emerged from private conversations with diplomatists and journalists from communist countries that even they were having doubts—although they never expressed them publicly and continued to maintain the official line that all was rosy in the Algerian garden. With the overthrow of Ben Bella (which resulted, among other things, in the tragi-comic failure of the projected Second Afro-Asian Conference due to take place in the Algerian capital in June 1965), even these last tactical supporters withdrew, bitterly disappointed. They even began to attack Algeria.

Ben Bella's overthrow came three years, almost to the day, after independence. During those three years, Algeria had come to such a pass that one can only echo the words of Gautier, the French historian, who, when discussing the inability of the early Berbers to form a nation, asked: 'By which concatenation of fiascos did the total fiasco come about?'[3] Why indeed did the first phase of Algerian independence end so disastrously? One reason is that the Algerians failed to face up to the enormous and complex problems confronting them after liberation—and these were certainly colossal.

The Algerians inherited the most valuable of all possible assets from the colonialists: highly developed economic structures. It was indeed a rich heritage in many ways and it was handed over quite intact. In spite of the efforts of the Organisation de l'Armée Secrète (OAS), the French government did not set out to wreck the country it was giving up. There was no repetition of the withdrawal from Sékou Touré's Guinea after the rejection of General de Gaulle's referendum, when even telephone lines were torn out of the walls. The very richness of the legacy, however, presented a great problem: the Algerians, untrained and inexperienced, were completely unprepared for the task of running a complicated administrative and economic system. It would need volumes to describe the chaos which resulted from the abrupt transfer of power. To cite only one example, the 800,000 departing Frenchmen had formed nine-tenths of the country's administrative and technical personnel. As we shall see later, the Algerians were themselves greatly to blame in that they made no effort to prepare for the take-over of their country. Indeed, they were so unprepared that it seemed as if the Provisional Government (GPRA), while waging an excellent war, never really expected victory.

Another, and more fundamental, reason for the failure of the Algerian revolutionaries was their lack of unity. With the liberation, the Algerian political and military clans allowed their thirst for power to overcome all other considerations. It was this terrible rivalry more than the inherent complexities of the post-independence task which brought about the downfall of the revolution. Even during the war observers had already noticed feuds among the Algerians but, not wishing to impede them in their struggle, most had drawn a voluntary veil of silence over the matter. Serge Bromberger, however, observed: 'These [internal quarrels] reappear at every phase of Algerian history and must be regarded as inherent in the Berber character. . . . In this Berberia can be likened to Corsica, where every village is divided into two clans, clans as old as the island itself, clans to which one belongs even before being born.'[4]

The sort of intrigues which were rife even while the struggle with the French was being waged may be illustrated from my own experience. In 1962, a few weeks before independence, I wanted to get into Algeria but, being persona non grata with the French authorities, I had to sneak over the Tunisian frontier through the Meurice and Challe lines in the company of an officer of the National Liberation Army (ALN). My companion was very apprehensive of the French security organisation, and especially of a parachute unit then withdrawing from the southern part of Algeria, well and truly beating up the country as it moved north. We got to Constantine safely enough, but here my luck ran out and I landed in gaol. My captors were not the French 'paras', however, but the chief of the Wilaya of Constantine, Saout el Arab—then a bitter foe of Boumedienne, now a member of the latter's Council of National Revolution. The charge was of having entered Algeria 'with the ALN'. In vain I protested: 'But the ALN is your own army of liberation!' All the protection I had was a document requiring that 'assistance be granted to our Turkish brother journalist'. So, at last arrived in Algeria, these 'brothers', who only a few weeks before

5

had been pressing me to join them in their 'Zone Autonome d'Alger', were now peremptorily confiscating my papers merely because they bore the stamp of the GHQ of the ALN at Ghardimau. After various adventures and intrigues I managed to get back to Tunisia—though I owe small thanks to the Provisional Government for this; at its request the French had closed the Meurice and Challe lines to keep the ALN out of Algeria!

The sequel to all this came a few days later, on July 3, 1962, when Ben Khedda (head of the Provisional Government) was to leave Tunis for his official entry into Algiers. Lunching with Dehiles, alias Colonel Si Sadok—later to become well known as the resourceful leader of an anti-Ben Bella maquis in Kabilya—I was telling of my disillusioning adventures when Mohammed Boudiaf, also present, leaned over the table and said: 'Well, you can count yourself lucky to be alive to tell the tale. I had personally given orders that all the ALN brigands and their friends should be rounded up and shot if necessary.' Since Boudiaf was one of the great men of the Algerian revolution and a founder of the ALN, the best I could do was choke back my feelings and apply myself to my lunch. (In his *Où va l'Algérie?*, 1964, Boudiaf tells how he was arrested by Boumedienne's security organisation. He complains bitterly of his treatment as a prisoner. But, as he is still alive and well in Paris, it would seem he got rather better treatment from Colonel Boumedienne than he would have meted out to the present writer.)

If wartime discipline did not prevent the Algerians, as we can see, from pursuing their quarrels, it did at least secure a certain cohesion. Internal disputes were not allowed to become too disruptive while the struggle with the French was still on. But, the war over, even this tenuous solidarity was abandoned in the race for power. Violence and treachery were the order of the day. It is easy to imagine Ben Bella, on the night of his arrest, turning to some trusted 'brother', now holding him at pistol-point, and asking with Caesar, 'Tu quoque, frater mi?' But how many have had occasion to ask the same question of Ben Bella himself?

In the struggle for power, the Algerians not only arrested, exiled and murdered each other: they resorted to the basest of all crimes— torture. They lost no time about this. No sooner had the infamous DOP (Division de l'Organisation Psychologique) evacuated the 'villas spéciales' than the Algerians were inside them, applying electric wires and other refinements to each other.* They had hitherto regarded the use of torture as the vilest crime of the colonialists. And in this they had not been alone; there had been a world-wide outcry against the French use of torture during the Algerian war. Frenchmen themselves were ashamed. Men like H. Beuve-Mery, director of *Le Monde*, in articles signed by the pen-name of 'Sirius', went some way to redeem the honour of France by persistent denunciation of such methods, pointing out that Frenchmen would never again be able to condemn with a clear conscience the atrocities of the Gestapo. The conduct of the Algerians unfortunately proves that their wartime indignation against torture was only tactical.

During the first FLN congress, on April 1, 1964, in Algiers, Colonel Boumedienne took the floor. 'Some', he said, 'have asked that the party should be pure and not include anyone with a crime on his conscience. But which of us in this assembly has a clear conscience?' He looked around and deep silence fell. 'Certain things belong to the past', he concluded.

The wish for Algeria must certainly be that such crimes be relegated to the past. But at present, the divisions among Algerians are so deep-rooted that, not only has the revolution suffered a serious setback, but the very existence of the new state is threatened. This will not surprise anyone familiar with Algerian history.

---

* In *Jeune Afrique*, No. 240, July 1965, Dr Ahmed Taleb reveals how he had been tortured on Ben Bella's express orders because he had refused a ministerial post, which led the Algerian leader to believe him part of the Boudiaf opposition group. (Son of Mohammed Rachid Brahimi, president of the organisation of Algerian *ulama*, Dr Taleb became minister of Education under Colonel Boumedienne.) Jean Daniel, the well-known French journalist, recounts in *Le Nouvel Observateur*, June 1965, how he was kidnapped in full daylight in the heart of Algiers, blindfolded and taken by car to a former villa spéciale of the DOP (believed to be on the heights of Algiers itself). Only in the nick of time was he released—with many apologies: 'So sorry! It's another journalist we're looking for. There has been an error of identity.' This took place just after the overthrow of Ben Bella. Torture continued under the Boumedienne regime.

7

I

THE IMPRINTS OF HISTORY

—————∿∿∿∿∿∿(o)∿∿∿∿∿∿—————

NEWLY EMERGING STATES are adept at distorting history. Algeria, whose past has been so bitter, has not been an exception. Algerians have rarely been objective about their lack of nationhood. This is perhaps understandable, for the inability to unite—an effect of Berber particularism, manifesting itself mainly in Kabilya—was distorted into 'separatism' by the French and repeatedly given as a reason for refusing independence.

Italy has existed as a modern nation-state for over a century, but the Italians still openly discuss the weaknesses in the structure of their national unity, and can do so without being branded fascists. No Belgian would dream of denying—quite the contrary—the deep cleavage between the Flemings and the Walloons. In Indonesia, the nationalists have always readily admitted that their lack of national unity contributed to their long period of colonial subjugation. The Algerian leaders, on the other hand, have totally ignored the ethnical divisions of the Algerian population. They simply dismiss as 'colonialist' anyone not accepting the officially sponsored fallacy that modern Algeria is the continuation of a unified Algeria of the past. It may have been excusable to use such a misrepresentation during the independence war,[1] as a psychological weapon, but it is pointless now.

A sense of national unity is of the greatest importance to a new state. Understandably enough, the opening section of the Algerian nationalists' most solemn manifesto, the 'Charter of Algiers', affirms:

The falsification and simplification of the history of our country by historians and publicists politically and ideologically linked

9

with colonialism have acted as a brake on the influence of the national liberation movement. . . . The Algerian people are an arabo-muslim people. The Arabisation and Islamisation of our country, which began in the eighth century, have given to our country the visage she has preserved to the present day. But one has to go further back to see the dawning manifestations of the contribution of the Central Maghrib to civilisation. This contribution, over three thousand years old, flowered particularly in the all-powerful Numidian kingdom of the third and second centuries BC, especially under Massinissa.* . . . The sovereignty of the caliph of Constantinople over this state [of the deys of Algiers] was purely nominal.[2]

The term 'Central Maghrib', medieval in origin, relates to the region between Hodna and the Moulaya and corresponds more or less to modern Algeria. There has been much controversy over the correct name for the region loosely referred to as 'the Maghrib'. 'North Africa' is now generally accepted, although the Arabs use *Jezira al-Maghrib* for the territories west of Egypt and *Maghrib al-Aqca* for Morocco. 'Maghrib' (the-land-where-the-sun-sets) as distinct from 'Mashrik' (the-land-where-the-sun-rises) is now current in Europe. During French colonial times, North Africa was also referred to as 'L'Afrique Française du Nord' and 'Pays d'Atlas' by the French, and as 'Africa Minor' by the Germans. Earlier still it was known as 'Berberia'. Professor Charles-Auguste Julien prefers this latter term since, although there are Berber populations outside North Africa, the inhabitants of this area are almost exclusively Berber. The Roman name for these populations was 'Barbari', from which are derived the European name 'Berbers' and also the Arabic names: *Brâber*, *Berâber* (singular) and *Berberi* (plural). These same Berbers, however, refer to themselves as *Amazigh* ('free men'). In the works of Ibn Khaldun and in other medieval writings there are references to 'Afrikiyya'—derived from the Latin 'Africa'—applied first to north-eastern Tunisia and later to the whole continent. To the ancient Greeks, North Africa was 'Libya'.

The world owes its knowledge of the intricate history of the part of North Africa now known as Algeria mainly to the work of French historians. The Algerians themselves have had to turn to the work of

---

* A famous Berber king, ally of the Romans.

these scholars for their sources. It is noticeable that the form 'Constantinople' used in the Charter of Algiers is neither correct Turkish nor Arabic but the name current until Ataturk in the christian West. The authors of the Charter have dismissed French historians as 'colonialist-minded'—which is ungrateful to say the least! Certainly some of them may have been biased, but Professor Julien, for one, does not merit such a charge. His works (providing the main source of the material for this chapter) have won him the respect of all scholars, Algerians included.[3] If he is to be criticised, it is for being too sympathetic to North Africa. A socialist, he has long argued in favour of Algerian independence. In 1945, when Guy Mollet, following the line of the French socialists at that time, was complaining in Le Populaire that North Africans would be able to read the Atlantic Charter in Arabic, Professor Julien, in the same paper, was denouncing the 'fascism which is invading North Africa'.

The part of the Charter of Algiers from which our extract is taken has all the features of hastily written political propaganda: a criticism which applies also to most of the other documents drafted by the nationalists during and after the war. It is sad to have to say this of a document intended as a declaration of principles for the founding of a new nation. It certainly cannot be regarded as an example of the 'scientific' approach, for all that the Algerians at this time were claiming Ben Bella's policy to be one of 'scientific socialism'.

French historians take a view of North Africa's contribution to civilisation very different from that of the authors of the Charter. Professor Jean Despois wonders whether 'it is not this spirit of diversity' of the Berbers which is behind the 'inability of these populations, who entered the stage of history some 3,000 years ago, to unite and create. . . . Is it this spirit of diversity which has prevented North Africa from contributing to the magnificent blooming of Mediterranean civilisation?' Despois concludes that 'North Africa, which has received and assimilated much, has given little of herself in return'.[4] It is difficult not to draw an analogy between the failures of the past and those of present Algeria. The same historian also notes that 'the principal states formed in ancient times were in Tunisia and the Moroccan plains' and that the ones created in Algeria 'were always fragile. . . . At no time was there, in these kingdoms, a real fusion or lasting association between the different groups: nomads and farmers, townsmen and countrymen.

Fragmentation is one of the permanent characteristics of the Berbers. . . . Union is only achieved temporarily, against foreign domination or princes whose power threatens to increase and establish itself.'[5] Once again the parallel with modern Algeria is clear.

North Africa had well-established trading relations with Rome and other Mediterranean states during the era of Mauritania Caesare. Modern Algiers was then Icosium, Bougie was Saldea, Bône was Hippo Regius, Constantine was Cirta and Cherchell was then the capital, Caesarea. Historians note, however, that even during this Roman period there was very little unification among the Berbers. A Moroccan historian, Professor Abdelaziz Benabdellah, observes that at the time of the invasions by the Phoenicians, Carthaginians and Romans, the Maghrib lived in 'indescribable chaos'.[6] In the fifth century AD the Vandals invaded North Africa, and in 647 the first of the many Arab invasions started.

Before considering this period, crucial in the history of the Maghrib, it may be as well first to consider briefly the Berber, the *Amazigh* or 'free man'. Who is he? Despois speaks of the Berber 'enigma'. When the Phoenicians landed in North Africa in the year 1200 BC, the Berbers were the first people they found. Apparently one of the oldest races in the world, no one seems able to trace their origins. The Berbers, one gathers, have been the victims of a 'geographical curse' in the form of incessant foreign invasions. Thus says Julien, who goes on to observe that there is certainly no evidence of any 'ethnical inferiority'. Historians of the past referred to the 'vitality' and 'personality' of the Berbers: characteristics which are still evident today. In spite of centuries of invasion and long periods of Arab and Turkish subjugation, the Berbers were still spirited enough to cause the French considerable trouble. More recently still, they asserted their independent spirit once again when Kabilya refused to ratify Ben Bella's dictatorship. But, says Professor E-F. Gautier, 'this race which has such persistent vitality has no positive individuality. An autonomous civilisation, art . . . a people conscious of its existence, an organised state, all these are costly capitalist luxuries which the Berbers have never been able to allow themselves. . . .'[7]

The dominant characteristic of the Berber is his passionate love of independence, pursued, even in modern Algeria, almost to the point of anarchy. As a result, the Berbers have never been completely assimilated by any of their conquerors. Following an ancient and very democratic tradition, a Berber unit is controlled, not by the authority of a single chief, but through the advice and control of the *jemma*, the tribal or village assembly. This still applies today. For example, the French discovered, a little late in the day, that all the civilian and military officials (the *caïds*) appointed to run Kabilya were quite useless, the Berbers continuing to follow the dictates of the *jemma*.

They have even maintained their physical characteristics of very pale skin, fair hair and blue eyes. While the rest of North Africa adopted Arabic, there still remain today large pockets of Berber-speaking people. In Tripolitania (Libya) 23 per cent of the population speak Berber, and in Tunisia 1 per cent. In the Algerian departments of Constantine, Algiers and Oran the percentages are 27, 34 and 1 respectively, while in Morocco the proportion is as high as 40 per cent.*

Arab Invasions

There was a good deal of resistance to the Arabs but none to the religion they brought with them. Islam was accepted by the whole of North Africa as a superior philosophy with advanced social implications. However, as it spread it changed, and today the Islam of North Africa differs from the Islam of the Middle East just as the Arabic of the one region differs from that of the other: the inhabitants of the two areas can understand one another only with difficulty.

French historians, including Julien, have criticised the 'audacity' of calling North Africans 'Arabs'. Only a small minority of the pop-

* Though a neighbouring country, Morocco is in a different category from Algeria. There has been a kingdom of Morocco since the fifth century AD, and the customs and traditions of this land are very old. Morocco and Ethiopia are the only two countries in Africa which are also 'nations'. The Berbers of Morocco were largely protected from the invading Arab nomads by the Atlas mountains, and also by the fact that the Arabs were more interested in moving northwards into Spain, skirting Morocco. As a rule, the mountainous regions of North Africa resisted the Arab invasions. Similarly, in Algeria it was the mountain areas which offered the greatest resistance to the French and later to Ben Bella.

ulation of North Africa is truly 'Arab' in the racial sense; the rest are Berbers. The fact that over the centuries they have adopted the muslim religion and the Arab tongue does not make them 'Arabs'. North Africans, generally speaking and with the exception of some Moroccans and a few Algerians, dislike being called 'Arab': 'We are Berbers', they maintain. The term 'Arab' has been accepted largely because of the common language and religion which North Africans share with Arabs of the Middle East, and because the North African nationalists found it convenient to consider themselves Arab. (With the exception of some christian minorities among them, Arabs are muslims. But 'muslim', of course, is not synonymous with 'Arab', and in fact the great majority of the inhabitants of the muslim world are non-Arab.)

It is not intended here to try to solve the problem of whether the North Africans are 'Arabic-speaking muslim Berbers' or 'Arabs', but merely to draw attention to a controversy which has had important political repercussions. When Ben Bella, freed at last from French prison, visited Tunis officially after the Evian Agreement, he aroused great emotion in the Maghrib by proclaiming: 'We are Arab! We are Arab! We are Arab!' Many Berbers resented this and —the real cause of their resentment—saw in it the hand of the Arab nationalists of the Middle East, particularly Nasser. North Africans are sufficiently Arab to dislike Nasser! They admire him in many ways, but are content to do so from a distance.

There is no doubt, however, that the Arab invasions of North Africa revolutionised the area and left a permanent imprint. In spite of strong resistance for a century and a half by the Berbers in the Aurès and Kabilya regions, the Arab invasions of the seventh century established the muslim religion and the Arabic language, first in the towns, then in the country. Greek and Latin died out and customs became oriental. By the ninth century, this new Arab civilisation was in full flower. The Qairawan of today in Tunisia was the first town built by the oriental muslims who later invaded Sicily. The Alhambra in Granada (*Kasr al Hamra*, 'The red citadel') is another great monument to the brilliant Arab culture of the time.

Two centuries later, a different type of Arab invasion swept over North Africa: one which destroyed where previous incursions had created. This was the nomadic invasion, first of the Beni Hilals, then the Beni Solayms. The great Maghribine historian, Ibn Khaldun, says they advanced 'like a cloud of grasshoppers, pulling down and destroying everything which stood in their way'. They mingled with the nomadic Berbers and together they razed towns and villages. A period of anarchy set in: the *razzia*. The glittering Arab civilisation of earlier days crumbled and the region returned to pastoral life. Only the Berber kingdoms of Morocco escaped the havoc. In spite of the destruction, however, the Arab characteristics assimilated in the preceding centuries endured, to reappear at the root of modern Tunisian, Algerian and Libyan nationalism.

At the beginning of the sixteenth century, Spain turned its attention to North Africa. Under Charles V and his admiral, Andrea Doria, and under Philip II, the Spaniards invaded the coasts of Morocco and were only prevented from turning eastwards by the Turks, who then held Tunisia and Algeria.

Turkish Dominance

At the height of its greatness—during the reign of Suleiman the Magnificent—the Ottoman empire stretched eastwards to Persia, southwards to the Yemen and Aden, and westwards as far as Tlemcen, on the borders of Algeria and Morocco.* By 1566, the Arab world was solidly under Turkish rule, without a break, from east to west; and this remained the state of affairs until the end of the eighteenth century. In North Africa, the Turks concentrated mainly along the coasts although they must occasionally have penetrated deep into the southern areas, for there are Turkish remains to be found even in the capital of the Algerian Touaregs at Tamanrasset in the Sahara.

To what extent did the Turks really rule Algeria? This has become a vexed question which has greatly preoccupied the Algerian nationalists. All the official nationalist documents are adamant on this point, and we quote once more from the Charter of Algiers. 'The sovereignty of the caliph of Constantinople over this state was purely nominal.' In this the nationalists agree with Julien, who says that at one stage 'the regencies of Algiers and Tunis (ruled by deys

---

* It is the boast of the 'Lions of the Mahgrib', as the Moroccans are known in legend, that the Turks were never able to go further than Tlemcen. Even today, nightwatchmen in the Maghrib are always Moroccan—because they are the most courageous and reliable.

whose appointments had to be approved by the caliph) disengaged themselves from the authority of the Sublime Porte. . . . Algeria had internal autonomy and was tied to Turkey by a moral link only: the caliph of Islam. She was more mistress of her own destiny than is a British dominion today in relation to Great Britain.'[8] The distinguished French historian's concept of dominion status may be questioned, but the point he makes about Algeria's relationship with the sultanate is sound. In practice, the local military Turks would choose a dey, sending a delegation to the sultan in Istanbul for ratification of their candidate. The dey in turn appointed beys, who were responsible under him for the various districts of the Algiers regency.

The latest Algerian contribution to the discussion appeared in *Révolution Africaine*, the Algerian ideological weekly, on December 26, 1964. In a review of Julien's new book, the first volume of *Historie de l'Algérie Contemporaine*, the reviewer (an assistant to th French professor) respectfully drew his attention to the fact that, while one 'would not pretend that in 1830, on the eve of French aggression, Algeria was a nation in the sense given to this word in the twentieth century . . . Algeria was, at the beginning of the nineteenth century, an independent state'. In another of Julien's books, there is indeed a chapter entitled "The Algerian State", but he begins it by explaining that this was a state of the 'Turks of Algiers', who at that time were known as 'Algerians'.[9] It was not a state of the indigenous inhabitants. These were ruled by the Turkish soldiery of the time—the *yoldachs*—through an institution called the *odjak*, fighting or combining with the *raïs* and their *taïfas* according to the needs of the moment. They imposed their own rule, paying only nominal allegiance to the distant sultan. Robert Mantran says of the situation:

This internal autonomy was in no way to result in a rupture with the government of the Turkish sultan. The Turkish character of the personnel running the administration and the army remained unchallenged until the French took over the destiny of the two countries. [Algeria and Tunisia.] For three centuries, for Algeria as for Tunisia, subjection to the Ottomans was effective, and this subjection was not only in the political field but in the administrative field as well.[10]

The famous Barbary pirate, Khair ad-Dinn Barbaros, provided the 'Algerian state' with a military base which lasted until the French conquest. Inevitably, the nationalists have claimed the Barbaros brothers—there were four of them—as 'Algerians'; but in fact they were born at Mytilene. (Khair ad-Dinn's tomb is at Beshiktash, Istanbul, and is still piously visited by Turkish sailors.)

According to Othman Kaak, the Turks contributed greatly to the development of the Algerian economy.[11] Areas of the country which had fallen back into primitive waste following the nomadic invasions began to deploy again the rudiments of civilised life. Until the coming of the Turks, for example, the use of the wheel in such areas had been quite forgotten. Jean Despois wondered why the Algerians were so slow in adopting wheeled transport, clinging to the use of pack animals for so long. The answer is that the first wheeled vehicles they knew of were the *araba* brought to the country by the Turks. The first bridges (*keupru*) to be built in the Maghrib since Roman times were also the work of the Turks. With the *araba* and *keupru* to facilitate communication and Turkish patrols to keep order inland, it became possible to create the first large farms.

Turkish influence on the cultural life of the country was equally profound. There are still today many buildings, mainly mosques, that are Turkish in style. The outstanding example is perhaps the 'Mosque of the Fishery', the former arsenal of the Barbary pirates on the Algiers waterfront. Many Turkish palaces and houses survive, particularly in Algiers. There is also a strong Turkish strain detectable in Algerian music, the basic character of which reflects both the Andalusian tradition and the purer Arab music traceable to the Abbasid styles of ninth and tenth century Baghdad.

The Turks in Algeria and Tunisia were more socially advanced and more cultured than the indigenous inhabitants. Through extensive intermarrying, they became the ancestors of the modern North African bourgeoisie. Some of their fighting spirit also rubbed off onto the people they ruled. On one occasion during the war, when bivouacking with an Algerian unit in a cave on the Moroccan border, I was awakened by a sturdy member of the unit. After making sure that the political commissar of the ALN was asleep, he said in a whisper, but with the unmistakable tones of Turkish superiority: 'That soldier sleeping there and I—we are Turks! Our fathers were Turks from Tlemcen. The others', he gestured disdainfully at the more Arabic Algerians, 'are weaklings. We do the real fighting while they quarrel among themselves.'

On the whole, the Ottoman yoke fell lightly on Algerian shoulders. Although the Turks were not usually popular with the peoples whose territories they occupied (in most of the Middle East, where Turkey was closer and its yoke heavier, they are still disliked today), in Algeria and Tunisia they got on well with the inhabitants. This was largely because, in addition to the common religion, distance gave lenity to the rule of the Sublime Porte. Even Karl Marx took a tolerant view of the Turkish occupation of Algeria, stressing the common religion.[12] There was certainly little friction, and it is significant that Turkish popular literature still echoes the laments of Algerian folksingers and poets over the fall of *Mozghanna*, 'Algiers the White', into the hands of the infidel French. President Bourguiba of Tunisia, though speaking specifically on behalf of his own country, expressed the feelings of North Africans of today when, addressing the Turkish National Assembly on March 25, 1965, he said:

The [christian] world wanted to convince us that we suffered under the Turkish yoke, but we knew well enough that this campaign of persuasion was not particularly disinterested. In actual fact, the yoke was only a form of allegiance and, in a certain sense, an alliance. Today we would call it a commonwealth. Furthermore, in so far as your sultans were the suzerains of our deys, we looked on them as a possible refuge, as a court of appeal. At the time, neither you nor we had the administrative means or the material power for such a system to be effective. Had they been available to us, the history of the Maghrib would probably have taken a different turn, and the colonial parenthesis would not have darkened our recent past. . . .

As far as my own memories go back, I note that Turkey holds a privileged position among them. On the flyleaf of one of my school exercise books at Sadiki College, I wrote: 'Down with colonialism! Long live Turkey!' This was an expression of refusal and hope. And Turkey represented hope. Later on, in autumn 1918, you entered upon a period of bitterness. The conditions imposed on you at Mudros awoke the same painful echo in our hearts as our baneful Twelfth of May 1881 and the

Treaty of Le Bardo, under which our sovereignty lay buried for three-quarters of a century. It was a most grievous sight to see this ancient muslim bastion lower its flag and undergo in its turn a scarcely less harsh form of domination than that undergone by Egypt and North Africa. Was hope going to become a luxury out of reach to oppressed peoples? We thought so for a moment. It seemed to us that the only way to triumph over an occupying power was to attack it with greater force than it had used in the first place. But once again you showed how wrong this oversimple view of history was. Your proof took the form of a miracle: of a man—Ataturk. . . .*

Tragedy came to Algeria with the switch from Turkish to French rule. 'The white and happy crowd of the *fellah*, immaculate in *ghandura* and *burnous*, became a ragged and sombre stream of luckless poor, now dressed in the tawdry style of the Marseilles flea-market', observed Dr Khaldi,[13] a veteran Algerian nationalist still striving to achieve real unity in his country.

The French were jealous of the Turkish influence in Algeria, although curiously they tolerated Arabism—at least, until Nasser appeared on the horizon. It was dormant and in no way a threat so long as it remained a pro-French Arabism, divorced as far as possible from Islam. To this end they encouraged the *marabu* and others with heretical tendencies, while fighting Islam proper. One of their first actions, in Tunisia as well as Algeria, was to ban the Turkish language. Similarly, most—if not all—French historians ignored Turkish documents when writing North African history. Robert Mantran comments:

> Knowing the care with which the Ottomans ran their administration, it would indeed be astonishing if no single trace of this domination should have remained in any file of archives. . . . Who ever bothered to enquire after such archives in Algiers, Tunis and Istanbul, and especially who bothered to use them? At whom should one cast the stone? At the historians, too easily satisfied

---

* President Bourguiba is a man who does not hesitate to speak his mind, and in the same address he embarrassed the Turkish parliament when he remarked that, in spite of ancient links and Ataturk's legacy, Turkey in 1952 had joined the USA and the UK in opposing at the United Nations Security Council a Pakistani proposal to discuss Tunisian independence.

with European sources, with diplomatic reports, with tales and descriptions of merchants and traders?[14]

In Algeria, until the end of their occupation, the French showed films on television with an anti-Turkish bias. In French eyes the Turks constituted a greater threat than the Arabs, both because they were staunch muslims and because their association with Algeria had been more recent and happier than the Arab rule there. With the end of the first world war and the emergence of Ataturk, the threat became more acute. The Turkish war of independence was a dangerous example for North Africa.

However, when the Algerians eventually embarked on their own war of independence, Ankara was too concerned for its relations with France and its NATO obligations to give overt support to the FLN, and recognised the Algerian national government only at the end of the war. Yet, if Turkey was late in formally endorsing the nationalist cause, she was paradoxically the first non-Arab muslim country to give military assistance to the ALN. This aid remained a well-kept secret during the war and is here made known for the first time as a result of information from a friend in the Turkish diplomatic service, confirmed by Abdelhafid Boussouf, the Provisional Government's minister for Arms and Communications, and by Tunisian officials. Under the cover of military assistance to Libya, a Turkish cargo boat, the *Ardahan*, on November 17, 1957, unloaded at Tripoli arms and ammunition for the ALN. A Turkish military mission, headed by General Nadji Sezen, disembarked and after a planned delay of a few months, intended to deceive the French into thinking that the arms were genuinely sent for the Libyan army, supervised the transfer of the shipment to the Algerians. On discovering Turkish arms among captured equipment, the French made strong, secret protests to Ankara. Anxious for French economic aid, the Menderes government gave a vote favourable to France at a UN debate on Algeria. In subsequent UN voting, however, Turkey abstained, its delegation arguing that 'If France is our ally, the Algerians are our brothers'. A year after the first 'abstention', a second Turkish shipment of arms was sent (November 1959), this time to Tunis, disguised as military assistance to Tunisia. Franco-Turkish relations were again strained when the French blockade intercepted a vessel (non-Turkish) containing arms and ammunition of Turkish origin and intended for the ALN. This was the sum total of the secret military help given by Turkey, where the official attitude throughout the war continued to be friendly to France. But the official attitude did not reflect the feelings of the Turkish public. After the revolution of March 27, 1960, there were strong pro-Algerian demonstrations in front of official French establishments in Ankara and Istanbul. Colonel Ouamrane, the Provisional Government's representative in Ankara, was treated as an ambassador. Colonel Alparslan Turkesh, head of the fourteen 'free' Turkish officers (the 1960 revolutionary committee) and now a civilian political leader, disclosed to me that one of his first actions after the coup had been to give instructions that Turkey should recognise the GPRA and start full-scale military aid to it. Events in Turkey, however, prevented Colonel Turkesh from carrying this out.

The first military contingent to parade in independent Algiers (and the only one to date) was, appropriately, a unit representing the traditions of the Barbaros brothers: the cadets and ratings of the *Savarona*, the Turkish navy's training ship.

French Occupation

'L'Affaire d'Alger'—culminating on June 14, 1830 with the landing of a French expeditionary force at Sidi Ferruch (now a popular holiday resort famous for its oysters)—sprang from very trivial causes. Trivial, that is, in the light of the ensuing century and more of occupation, and of the great problems this was to create in Europe and its later repercussions on the third world.

As French history books describe it, the Algiers Affair was provoked by two unscrupulous Jewish merchants—Bacri and Busnach —who refused to pay their debts. (Echoes here of Don Pacifico and Palmerston!) The pair had the highly profitable monopoly of supplies to the French armies in Italy and Egypt, and they were backed by influential political and financial circles in the great port of Marseilles—then, as now, the main 'Algerian' port. What was called by the satirists of the time *La Bacriade* ended with the dey, Hussein, slapping Deval, the French consul, in the face with an ostrich-feather fan! There are many engravings of this incident, which took place on April 20, 1827. They show the dey with his fan, behind him his *yoldachs* (heavily moustached, in baggy trousers and wielding curved scimitars) and facing him the outraged consul, flanked by Frenchmen in tight trousers, frock coats, double-pointed cocked hats and swords. In the background an Algerian servant pulls back a curtain for the Frenchmen to leave. Deval had come to see the dey on behalf of the two Jews, but the fan incident was regarded in Paris as an insult to the French empire. During the subsequent history of Algeria, Franco-Algerian relations reflect this curious combination of flag-waving and commerce, and the ubiquitous North African Jew reappears time and time again in the role of French businessman or Algerian communist.

To tell the story of the French occupation of Algeria, even in outline, would need volumes. And such volumes already exist in plenty. We need do no more than touch on two of the main effects of the occupation—effects which were to cause many headaches after independence on July 5, 1962. First, the French occupation changed the character of Algeria. Secondly, in consequence of this long period of colonial rule, the Algerian and French economies became so entwined that Algeria could not hope for economic survival on her own. The extent of Algeria's economic dependence on France is discussed in Chapters 5 and 9. Here it is the first of the main effects which merits attention.

A true story is told of an English journalist arriving in Tunis for the first time from the Middle East. So 'un-Arab' did the country appear to him that he exclaimed in amazement: 'But where are the Arabs?' When visiting Algeria for the first time, I similarly had some severe shocks. It was astounding to observe the extent to which France had developed the country both in the northern region and, as was to appear later, in the Sahara. Indeed, in comparison with Algeria, Tunisia (so 'un-Arab' to the English journalist) seemed positively 'muslim' and 'Arab'.

The disappearance of many of Algeria's Arab and muslim characteristics resulted in a grievous loss of identity. Perhaps if the Algerians had had dark skins and a distinctively 'eastern' appearance, they might have had more of a chance of retaining a personality of their own. As it was, with their tanned white skins they looked like any other Mediterranean race. Only their religion saved them from complete loss of identity. Islam was to prove strong enough to prevail against French influence. It may be

22

difficult for an Anglo-Saxon reader to understand how a country could lose its identity in this way. But he should bear in mind how differently the French and British set about the task of colonisation. Britain's liberal conservatism, its dislike of set ideas, led the British to establish in their colonies and protectorates a decentralised form of government. Self-government soon became the ultimate aim, and local customs and traditions were respected. The British, that 'nation of shopkeepers', went abroad in search of trade. And still today, when conditions in their colonies become chaotic to the point of disrupting trade, a member of the royal family is sent out to lower the Union Jack and raise a new flag that the people may be pacified and trade resumed.

The French approach is altogether different. Full of cartesian logic and superiority, and mindful of 1789, the French set out on their 'mission civilisatrice'. They established centralised governments everywhere and their unmistakable intention was the complete assimilation of the native. Colonisation was a patriotic, intellectual, religious and emotional adventure; business implications were there too, of course. (One indication that this missionary zeal still exists is that the French still send more teachers abroad than any other nation—and in doing so render a great service to humanity.)

One incident illustrates just how emotionally involved the French were in Algeria. The decision to grant independence taken, the French lost interest in the million settlers for whom Algeria was home; sacrificing acre upon acre of rich land, and property of every type, the government in Paris began to pour more money into independent Algeria than Britain has probably ever spent on all its African colonies together. But . . . At Rocher Noir—the big satellite town, built by the French to house the administration, which was taken over by the Exécutif Provisoire after independence—there was a magnificent flagpole. The Algerians naturally wished to hoist their red-crescented white and green flag there on Independence Day. The French, learning this, and unable to face the prospect, crept out by night and attempted to saw down the flagpole!

The policy of assimilation went further in Algeria than any other French colony. The country was very nearly wholly absorbed into France. This was partly because of its proximity—only 395 miles from Marseilles. It was not distant Indochina. At first, France imposed her policies by force—later by the sheer strength of her technical and cultural superiority. The original character of the conquered land was completely obliterated. The French were ruthless. Although not every French historian will admit it, the Algerians are certainly correct in claiming that their colonial masters were at least partly animated by the desire to 'crusade' against Islam.

Officially the policy was one of religious tolerance. At the beginning of the occupation, General de Bourmont declared: 'The mohammedans will remain free to practise their religion; the freedom of the inhabitants of all classes, their religion, their properties, their trade and their industries will be respected.'[15] This was the charter of the 'mission civilisatrice'—but only in theory. The practice was very different.

On December 17, 1831, by order of the Duc d'Orléans, 'the cross and the banner of France hoisted on mosques will be saluted by shore and naval guns'.[16] The duke did even better: he rode to official balls on the back of an Algerian. 'By the operation of the Sequestered Properties Act of 1871 alone, Kabilya tribes lost 2,639,000 hectares of their most fertile land. By 1900, 2,250,000 hectares had been sequestered from the Arabs.'[17] Education was denied for a long time. It was only at the time of the first world war that the French began to think of educating the Algerians; 85 million francs were then allocated to the education of several million native children, as against 700 million francs provided for about 90,000 European children.[18] Well before Hitler imposed the yellow star on the Jews, General Bugeaud ordered the Algerians to wear an inscription reading 'submissive Arab'. The insults and massacres seemed never-ending. Montagnac, a French colonial officer who founded the 'Voltigeurs de la Mort', wrote to a friend in France:

In a paragraph of your letter you ask me what happens to the Algerian women we capture. Some we keep as hostages and the rest are auctioned to the troops like animals. . . . Among these women are some very beautiful ones; there are also some charming children. The poor little things are pathetic. In the operations we have carried out during the last four months, I have witnessed scenes that would melt the hardest heart—if one had time to let them! Eh bien! I witnessed it all with a frightening indifference. Kill all men above the age of fifteen; take all the women and children and put them on a ship for the Marquesas Islands or some other destination. In one word: annihilate all those who will not crawl at our feet like dogs.[19]

'But', says Dr Khaldi—and it is a very big 'but', for it explains why France, in spite of many crimes, managed to retain such a big corner in Algerian hearts—'on the other hand, the French people have throughout their history so often manifested their attachment to the highest humanitarian principles ... that daily contact with them reveals the most beautiful disposition of heart and mind.'[20]

Here we have a different aspect of French colonisation. The brilliance and spiritual vigour of France were magnetic, attracting the Algerians in spite of themselves. This was the secret of French success, and if France had only allowed the Algerians to become true citizens—instead of second or third-rate ones—the existing problems would probably never have arisen. How else can we explain why, during the seven-and-a-half years of war, the overwhelming majority of Algerians co-operated with the French? Some, it is true, did so passively rather than actively, some out of fear or ignorance; but, nevertheless, the French were able to enrol no less than 200,000 Algerians as officials—*harkis* or *goumiers*—to help them in the struggle against the revolutionary minority.* The nationalist maquis and the ALN were never able to muster anything like so much support. Their purely military force never exceeded 50,000 men, as we shall see later.

The paradox is, however, that those Algerians who best learnt the lessons France had to teach were the first to turn against French rule. Not really against France itself, but against France as the occupying power in Algeria; for it was France which had imparted to them the modern concept of national consciousness.

The case of Ferhat Abbas, although well known, can hardly be omitted here, for it illustrates only too well the Algerian 'national

* It is true that a number deserted to the maquis and that others remained in the French ranks on specific ALN instructions. But the high figure of 200,000 still speaks for itself. At the time of independence, no less than 70,000 *harkis* sought asylum in France. By March 1966, under the terms of the Evian Agreements, 55,000 muslim Algerians had obtained French nationality.

tragedy'. Ferhat Abbas spent the greater part of his long political career in working to obtain the honourable integration of France and Algeria. As late as 1936, he did not believe in an Algerian 'nation', and wrote: 'I have interrogated history; I have interrogated the living and the dead; I have visited cemeteries—no one spoke to me of it.'[21] It was only in 1942-3 that he became converted to 'bourgeois nationalism'. In 1946, in his daily paper *La République Algérienne* he was militating for no more than a federated republic 'within the French Union'. Only in 1953 did he become convinced that the time had come for the guns to speak. He joined the FLN in 1956. Ferhat Abbas is not a nobody. He has been a president of the Provisional Government, was the first president of the first Algerian parliament, and today he is still one of the best-known leaders of his country, inside as well as outside Algeria.

Islam: The Saviour

If France sowed the seed of national consciousness, Islam cultivated it. When *Révolution Africaine* proudly announced in 1964: 'Three hundred and forty-seven new mosques in Algeria. Sixty thousand illiterates following Koranic courses'[22]—there were some ironic smiles among leftwing supporters of the revolution, both Algerian and foreign. But, although Algeria at this time was still under Ben Bella, the country was already turning to the right. Mohammed Harbi, the most lucid of Algeria's young marxists and for a time Ben Bella's closest adviser, had just been dismissed as editor of this ideological weekly. Ben Bella was allowing himself to be swayed by the opinion of the army, which considered that the regime, under Harbi's influence, was swinging too far left. The words we have just quoted appeared in an article entitled "Islam and Socialism". When mohammedanism tangles with socialism, chaos results. The young leftwing intellectuals cannot be blamed for failing to appreciate, in the confusion, the strength of Islam's hold on Algeria. They failed not only because they were confused but because of the 'Frenchness' of their very European outlook. It is natural for Europeans to underestimate the strength of Islam. To progressive intellectuals, Islam is only the 'opium of the people'—as indeed it is at times. But in adopting this attitude, they are, all unconsciously, reflecting the arrogance of the christian towards a 'pagan' religion. European communists do not dismiss their own 'opium' so lightly!*

The French missionary explorer, Fr Charles Foucauld, wrote in 1916: 'If we cannot succeed in making Frenchmen of these [North African] people, they will drive us out. The only way to make them into Frenchmen is to make them christians.' Foucauld, who was eventually assassinated in Tamanrasset, was right; for the only armour the Algerians had against the French was their own creed: Islam. The French were well aware of it. They attacked Islam as hard as they could and from all angles. The colonial administration itself appointed the *muezzin*. It also turned mosques into churches by the hundred; it destroyed those that were left or even turned them into bars for the troops. Although in metropolitan France the church is disestablished, the French state took over the control of religious affairs in Algeria in order to have a better hold on Islam. Thus, in 1892, a French parliamentarian was able to attack the fact that in Algeria's official budget for religious affairs, muslims had been attributed 'seven times less money than Israelites, twenty-two times less than catholics and . . . a hundred times less than protestants' (sic!).[23]

Islam, the only force militating against the complete absorption of the country by the French, became the driving force in the resurgence of national consciousness. The legendary Emir Abdelkader, the great warrior who resisted the French so successfully (it took France seventeen years to 'pacify' Algeria), opposed them on religious rather than nationalist grounds. Anti-muslim propaganda had been particularly virulent in the region of Miliana, Emir Abdelkader's birthplace, which the French had converted into a military stronghold.

When I had occasion to visit some Koranic schools in backward parts of Algeria—the parts which had resisted the French most persistently—I could not help remembering how, in my own country, I had criticised similar schools in Anatolia. But Turkey is

* In Italy, where this book has been written, not only has the communist party refrained from tackling the issue of legal divorce but it has lately started a remarkable flirtation with the Vatican. Large numbers of Italians keep their party card next to their holy pictures in their wallets. In southern Italy, in 1965, the local section of the communist party invaded a church to force a recalcitrant priest to give their dead leader a christian burial. What price Don Camillo?

an old independent nation. How different was the spirit in these schools! It cannot be denied that they were backward and primitive —so backward that many of them lacked slates and chalks. The pupils had previously been learning to write by tracing letters on the ground with stones. But for all their backwardness, these schools had formed, together with the mosques, the backbone of the resistance movement inside Algeria. They had a sense of discipline and they were proud of having maintained the ancient traditions and sense of values of the land in the teeth of the invader.

The more reliable Algerian scholars (those who do not try to explain history by clichés) state that the 'renaissance' of Algeria began in 1922 with Ben Badis, the famous sheikh who initiated the *islahiya* (reform) movement. Malek Bennabi, the great Algerian scholar, says that Sheikh Ben Badis and his movement to reform Islam introduced a 'sense of community' among Algerians. When Islam came to North Africa, it was distorted by the Berbers who adopted heretical forms, very near to idolatry. The best known of these heresies is that of the *marabu*, fostered by the ill-famed Bureaux Arabes (French department of native affairs) in order to undermine true Islam. Sheikh Ben Badis set out to purge Algeria of religious abuses, such as the use of amulets. His *islahiya* was also a social movement, and the climax came when the *ulama* held their Islamic Congress in 1936. 'But, alas!' observes Bennabi, 'even the *ulama* took the road to Paris'—where they got involved with politicians. 'What did they go to find in Paris? Is the key to the problem, the Algerian soul, to be found there?'[24]

In 1925, as a result of the reforms of Ben Badis, 'the Algerian people reappeared in the pageant of history equipped with a few words of Arab syntax and a few verses of the Koran. The first *madrasa* appeared: humble as the first schools of Charlemagne.'[25] Yet it took some ten years for the French to perceive the nationalist implications of the *islahiya*. The préfet of Algiers in 1933, in a circular which has remained famous to this day, refused the islahist *ulama* entry to the mosques on the grounds that they were rousing the 'apathetic people'. The French colonial administrators were not the only ones who were slow to recognise that Islam was the fostering agency of nationalism in Algeria. The left, from the non-communist progressives in Paris to the strategists in Moscow, also missed the point.

This is not to say that Islam is now the answer to Algeria's problems. Even a scholar like Bennabi, who believes that in a reformed Islam his country will find the cohesion and force it needs, agrees that Al Azhar (Cairo) and Zeitun (Tunis) have been unable to 'rethink' Islam 'so enormous is the weight of decadence'. But the key role of Islam in the resurgence of Algerian nationalism is unquestionable. It is likely to maintain this role until Algeria discovers her own identity and religion there becomes, as it ought to be, a matter of individual conscience.

Young Algerian nationalists greatly object to the *ulama* thesis that 'to be colonised, one must be colonisable'. It is not proposed to enter this debate on either side. Let the word pass to one of the most respected elders of contemporary Algerian nationalism. In his rather flowery language (it is a great pity that his book, *Les Conditions de la Renaissance Algérienne*, is now out of print), Bennabi says that, with each phase of history, 'the drama of every race is essentially that of its civilisation'.

One race succeeds to another: each has its appointed task; each is a cog in the time-piece which strikes out the solemn hours of history.

The sun only rises for peoples awake: for those asleep there is only twilight. Blessed dawns of the renaissance: luminous thresholds of dawning civilisations. Sullen twilights: the sun setting over a dying civilisation. . . .

By 1830, the sun was sinking over Algeria: when this happens, a race no longer has a history. A people asleep has no history, only nightmares, dreams . . . through which pass the figures of terrible tyrants or legendary heroes.[26]

Bennabi's brother-writer, Dr Khaldi, thinks that what Algeria needs most 'is to have her feet set once more on the path of her own destiny, which has been blocked by an accident of history'.[27] Both these men were writing immediately after the second world war, inspired by the hopes the Allies' cause had aroused in the breasts of the underprivileged.

Algeria's struggle for independence started on November 1, 1954. It has now been won, or at least one phase of it has been won. Algeria has regained her national and territorial independence. She has yet to become a nation.* The fight waged by the FLN-ALN accelerated the process, for there is no greater accelerator than war to move nations. But it has yet to be completed. It takes a long time for a nation to form. At the moment it is impossible to see what type of nation Algeria will become, or even to describe what is an Algerian. In their search for a national personality, Algerians have claimed to be 'Arab'. But how French can one be and still remain an Arab? This is a question which the Algerians will have to face.

A little while after independence, I was waiting for my wife to arrive from Tunis at Dar-El-Beida airport in Algiers. At the control point, those with French identity papers were able to pass through quickly; but my wife, with Turkish papers, was delayed while the official scrutinised them. She was then told to wait on one side. I went to the chief of security and complained of the delay. 'I thought we were friends of Algeria. My wife has a Turkish passport and a courtesy visa from your embassy in Tunis. This is her first visit to Algeria. Is it still necessary to have French papers in order to pass through Algerian airport control?' Rather red in the face, the chief of security went to investigate. He returned all smiles. 'Brother, we have nothing against your wife. The trouble is that our embassy in Tunis issued the visa in Arabic, and the police are still looking for an interpreter!'

Though trivial, the incident is significant. Algeria—urban Algeria, at least—speaks French. In parliament, in the ministries, in the streets, the language is French. Books, magazines and news-papers are in French, and Algeria's own publications are in the same language. Algerians think in French; their minds and reflexes are French. The country they know and love is France. When a fashionable Algiers restaurant with a floorshow tried to introduce sugary Egyptian music, the clients clamoured for "Les Feuilles

* The view that there is not yet an Algerian nation in the sense that the word is used in Europe is also taken by the German jurist, Thomas Oppermann, in his *Die Algerische Frage*, 1951—a work undertaken at the suggestion of the Political Institute in Hamburg. It is worth noting that in the French edition of this book (*Le Problème Algérien*, 1961) the publisher, François Maspero—a man of the left and well known for his pro-Algerian views—says that most of the French publications on Algeria are 'militant' in attitude. 'It is perhaps to be expected', adds Maspero, 'that the most serious work on the subject should be by a foreigner.' Opperman's book is, indeed, one of the most balanced analyses of the period of the Algerian war.

Mortes". As well as French music, they like French food, French drinks and the French approach to making love. Out of any ten foreign women married to Algerians, nine are Frenchwomen. Offer ten young Algerians a free holiday anywhere in the world; what will their choice be: Cairo, Moscow, Peking, London, New York, Rome, Jiddah? Most of them will undoubtedly choose Paris. It is difficult to think of two other peoples as closely linked as the Algerians and the French.

At this point it may rightly be remarked that things could change with Boumedienne's more muslim and Arab-orientated regime. This is certainly possible. Colonel Boumedienne never speaks French. He is perfectly fluent in the language, but he never uses it in public. He is the only Algerian leader who does not make use of *Le Monde*—the French paper which has played, and continues to play, a prominent role in Algerian affairs— for important statements. He prefers a Cairo or Damascus paper.

But, as we shall see later, the Armée Nationale Populaire (ANP)— the post-independence successor of the ALN—has more French cracks in its 'Arab' armour than it would like to admit. Shortly after Ben Bella's overthrow, Cdr Slimane (Ahmed Kaid) was spokesman at a press conference. A tall and handsome Syrian journalist, with all the fire of the Ba'athist, asked whether 'we Arab journalists may see Ben Bella?' (a rather naïve question, revealing that the journalist understood little of Algeria). The answer came: 'Oui, certaine- ment.' Overjoyed, the Syrian replied: 'Thank you, my Colonel.' Unfortunately, he had not realised that neither Commander (not Colonel!) Slimane nor his interpreter understood Arabic as spoken in the Middle East. The interpreter had translated the Syrian's question as: 'Will Algeria continue to support Arab unity?'

To be fair, the commander had warned the Syrian journalist repeatedly that 'here in Algeria we speak French'. A warning, we may add, which was at variance with Article 5 of the First Algerian Constitution (adopted on August 28, 1963, under Ben Bella), which reads: 'The Arabic language is the national and official language of the state.' Were those who took part in the Soummam Congress of 1956, which decided on the war of liberation, perhaps a trifle more realistic? They declared that 'French will be the official language of the Revolution'.

31

2

KASSEMAN:
THE GLORIOUS YEARS

IT IS DIFFICULT to remain unmoved when telling of battles fought by men, whatever their race or creed, for liberty, the dignity of their women and the future happiness of their children. The Algerians fought a highly unequal struggle with the greatest courage, resourcefulness and dedication. In the words of "El Djezayir", an old patriotic song of the Parti Populair Algérien and at present the national anthem:

> Par le fer et la mitraille,
> Par les flots de sang pur et sans tache,
> Par les drapeaux de nos aînés,
> Sur les djebels inviolés,
> Nous jurons nous être révoltés,
> Pour vivre et pour mourir
> Pour que vive l'Algérie:
> *Kasseman, Kasseman, Kasseman.*

Kasseman! We swear it!*

* Because of the PPA-origin of this song, the Cultural Section of the FLN announced in February 1965 that there was to be a competition for a new national anthem, in literary Arabic and not exceeding sixteen verses. It was to be inspired by traditional Algerian music. 'The music as well as the words must convey a sense of the richness of our national heritage on which we will build our future.' The announcement concluded by saying that Ben Bella would personally remit 10,000 dinars to the winner: no longer possible, of course. As this book goes to press it is not clear what the attitude of the Boumedienne regime is to this project.

The Algerian revolution began on November 1, 1954. The French were determined to maintain their hold on Algeria. A few patriots therefore decided that, since all other measures had failed, they would resort to a war of liberation. The intransigence of the French had made a peaceful solution impossible. Any doubts on this score were cleared up by Mohammed Yazid's letter to the *New York Times* on November 13, 1958. The paper had criticised the Algerians for rejecting an offer of 'amnesty to the rebels' which de Gaulle had made at a press conference on October 23. Yazid, after explaining that to accept this offer would mean abandoning the struggle and accepting a solution 'within the frame of the French legal system', added: 'In 1948, there were 59 nationalists standing as candidates for the Algerian Assembly. We then hoped to reach our objective by French constitutional means. The result? Some 30 of us were arrested during the electoral campaign and kept in gaol for years. The list of candidates arrested is more or less identical with that of the leaders of the Algerian revolution.'

Late on the night of November 1, at Batna in the wild province of the Aurès, home of the tough Chaouia tribe, two sentries of the 24th Artillery Regiment were killed. There were similar episodes throughout the province and in Kabilya. To the west, in the department of Oran, a French farm was attacked, traces being purposefully left to show it was the work of the FLN. Many things went wrong on that night.[1] What was intended to be a spectacular onslaught on the French all over the country petered out in a series of isolated incidents. For instance, a bomb which was exploded on the Algiers waterfront, though it succeeded in waking up the whole neighbourhood, quite failed to blow up the oil tanker for which it was intended. The toll of Frenchmen on that historic night was not more than half a dozen killed and a dozen or so wounded. The reason for this failure is very pertinent. The Algerians were desperately short of equipment. Some of the revolutionaries did not even possess firearms. Colonel Ouamrane has more than once told me that the revolution was begun with less than fifty obsolete shotguns. This is certainly not far from the truth.

Nevertheless, the revolution was well and truly begun on that night of November 1, 1954. Before the general staff of the Tenth Military District (responsible for Algeria) realised what was afoot, a broadcast from Cairo's *Sawt al Arab* ('Voice of the Arabs') radio station triumphantly proclaimed to the Arab nations and the world:

> Brothers! Today Algeria launched her sublime struggle for free-
> dom and for Islam. Today—November 1, 1954—Algeria has once
> again begun to live with honour. A powerful elite of the sons of
> Algeria have begun the struggle to rid themselves of the tyranny
> of French imperialism.

Coming as it did from Cairo and from the demagogic 'Voice of the
Arabs', this broadcast helped to convince the French that it was all a
plot engineered by the Egyptians. This was not the case, for all that
Cairo provided immensely valuable help. Egypt's later efforts to
steer the course of the Algerian revolution failed, even under Ben
Bella. It was not true that the fight, as the announcement stated, was
'for Islam'. As we have seen, Islam certainly was responsible in
large measure for the resurgence of national consciousness in Algeria.
But it was not the primary cause of the revolution. Though Cairo
sought to exploit pan-Islamic feeling, the Algerians both in theory
and practice always refrained from waging the *jihad* or 'holy war'.

The Mujahidin: An Army is Born

Understandably, the French thought at first that their army in
Algeria, numbering in 1954 some 70,000 men, would easily and
quickly quell this insurgency. Even so, as a precaution, France's
forces there were increased by three parachute regiments. Ironically
this decision was taken by one of the most progressive of French
premiers, Mendès-France. The French were anxious to crush
the *fellagha** swiftly for fear that the movement would link up with
Cairo and an international struggle begin. For this reason Paris was
careful to refer to 'outlaws', and was determined to keep the Algerian
struggle a purely 'French domestic affair'.

On November 5 of that year, when the Armée de Libération
Nationale was officially set up by the Algerian revolutionaries, its
strength was not more than a few hundred. The highest figure ever
quoted is 500, with at least 300 of these concentrated in the Aurès,
the birthplace of the revolution. How did these miserably equipped
few achieve such great things?

* The term was first applied to the Tunisians who had taken up armed
resistance against the French.

It is true, of course, that later on the Algerian fighters obtained a great deal of outside help, both material and moral: more than any other insurgents had obtained before. When visiting an Algerian unit during the war, I noticed that the men were much better sheltered, fed and equipped—and certainly better treated—than ever I had been in the Turkish army of the 'forties. (Clearly, the Algerian soldier benefited from the adherence to French rather than to Turkish standards!) But however much help they received from abroad, the Algerians owed their victory to their own efforts. The fearlessness, the discipline and sense of duty they displayed during the war compensated for their material inferiority, and led them to a well-deserved politico-military success over their powerful opponent.

France spent something in the order of a billion* (old) francs a day to suppress the despised *fellagha*. At the height of the war there were 800,000 French troops in Algeria, including a full NATO unit (the Division Lorraine), armoured vehicles of every description, aircraft and radar detection networks. French war craft patrolled the western Mediterranean by sea and air. Libya and Tunisia were the main transit routes for supplies of arms coming to the revolutionaries by land, but there was also a heavy sea traffic, especially of arms destined to enter through Morocco. For years, France acted like a pirate in the Mediterranean, stopping any shipping she considered suspect. In December 1960, for example, there was a serious crisis with Western Germany after France had stopped no less than seventeen German ships. In 1959, the number of ships 'controlled' by France in the western Mediterranean reached the record figures of 41,300 reconnoitred, 2,565 stopped and investigated, and 84 rerouted under escort to French ports. The most spectacular air interception occurred on February 9, 1961 when French Vautours buzzed a Soviet IL-18 which contained no less a person than Brezhnev, then head of the presidium of the Supreme Soviet, on his way to Morocco for an official visit. French pilots fired warning shots. The incident took place some 130 kms north of Algiers over international waters. Gromyko branded it as 'international banditry perpetrated by the armed forces of France'.

The French employed psychological warfare to the point of

* Billion throughout is used in the French (and American) reckoning of a thousand million—not a million million as in British usage.

using torture as a regular means. They had at their disposal their vast intelligence services and—last, but not least—the powerful diplomatic influence of the Quai d'Orsay. An old and strong country, France had all these weapons, and many more, at her disposal, yet she was not able to prevail. The Algerians proved then, as the Vietcong did later, that a few ill-equipped men dedicated passionately to their cause can work miracles. An Order of the Day, sent out by Belkacem Krim, then minister of War, to the ALN commanders in Algeria in 1959, gives an idea of the scale of French operations in the military field. (Author's comments in italics.)

At the end of September 1958, the colonialists introduced 35,000 men, under General Faure, into Greater Kabilya, in the Upper Sebaou and the Akfadou and, at the end of October, in the upper section of Oran province. In the Saida-Frenda mountains, there are nearly 20,000 men—the 1st REP and the 5th Airborne REI—under General Gilles, who has air cover. From October to end of November, operation *Brumaire* was carried out from the Akfadou towards the Soummam Valley and Guergau: 10,000 men, under General Faure himself, pursued Colonel Amirouche.

From 20th to 30th November, there were operations south of Palestro under the orders of General Massu. [*The famous parachutist had just arrived from the Indochinese theatre of war.*] Commander Azzeddine was wounded and made prisoner by the French for the second time. [*He escaped on both occasions.*]

January 1959: French operations from 14th to 21st on the western slope of Tizi-Ouzou [*chief town of Kabilya*] and Dra-El Mizan [*a region of great maquis activity*].

Beginning February 1959: operation *Couronne* in the Ouarsenis; 30,000 men under General Gambiez with Bigeard [*another famous parachutist officer from Indochina*] operated in the Guillaumet-Tiaret region, near Saida-Frenda.

February: operation *Eclair*: 10,000 men swept Djelfa.

March: Operation K 21 in the Sidi ali Bounaf range of mountains; 50,000 men under General Camas.

March-April: operation launched to find the Cesaro family [*kidnapped by the Algerians*]; this involved 10,000 men in the Bibans mountains as far as Tazmalt. General de la Maison Rouge was unable to trace the [*kidnapping*] Kabyles who eventually released their prisoners on the orders of the GPRA. [*The Provisional Government did not want French civilians to be kidnapped.*]

30th April: 6,000 men sent into the Bou-Saada mountains. Heroic death of Colonels Amirouche and Haouès after 48 hours of combat.

July: operation *Etincelle* in the Hodna range of mountains under Generals Challe and Gracieux.

20th July to September 1959: operation *Jumelle*. 40,000 men under Generals Challe and Faure attempted to dismantle Wilaya III. [*One of France's most brilliant young officers, General Challe is still in a French gaol for his share in a plot against de Gaulle by a group of officers out to prevent peace in Algeria.*]

End of August: south of Aumale, 5,000 men operate under General Max Briand.

In all these encounters, the ALN emerged victorious. She has won in the field and in the hearts. I entrust to you the task of transmitting the Government's congratulations to the officers, non-commissioned officers . . . of the ALN.

Long live Algeria.[2]

Like most war communiqués, this one exaggerates—as the reader has probably noticed. While 'hearts' were certainly being won, the ALN did not 'emerge victorious' in the sense that it defeated these huge numbers in the field. It was victorious only in the sense that its own forces were not annihilated by the superior numbers of the French. This was, of course, a guerrilla war.

By 1960–61 the French had unquestionably established their military superiority, forcing the ALN to withdraw to mountain redoubts in order to save its men and equipment. From now on the Algerians had to rely increasingly on political warfare. But even so, the French were never able to discount the ALN 'of the interior' completely. They had to admit that there were a number of areas under complete FLN–ALN control: Greater Kabilya and the Soummam Valley in Kabilya; the Collo peninsula, the Aurès-Nément-chas range of mountains and the Hodna mountains in Constantine province; the Nédromah region; the towns of Marnia and Tlemcen and the areas surrounding the Traras and Tlemcen mountains in the province of Oran; the Dahra range of mountains between Oran and Algiers; the area between the sea and the plain of Chélif; and, south of this, the huge area of the Ouarsenis mountains. The Algerians claimed to have added many more strongholds to these. They were probably right for, after all, the French eventually declared the whole of Algeria 'insecure'.

Although the ALN was destined to fight a largely guerrilla war, the leaders of the revolution did not want it to consist merely of groups of partisans. They struggled to mould it into a regular fighting force, with a legal status such as to belie the French description of the revolution as an 'outlaw' movement. A little over a year after its formation, the ALN had a uniform, with the distinguishing red crescent and star worn on the cap, and regular ranks which are unchanged today.* Colonel was the highest rank. It is significant that there was no rank of general, ostensibly to avoid the 'cult of personality'. Officers and men drew the same pay: 20 francs a month. Everyone was entitled to five days of leave a year and a regular tobacco ration. The only exception to the rules was made in favour of Colonel Boumedienne, the chief of the general staff. He was a chain-smoker and was allowed a double ration of cigarettes. Officers and men both wore the US type of olive-green battledress and were required to fight in uniform. Military service was voluntary and for a minimum period of two years. Only once, in February 1961, did the GPRA order mobilisation, and this was confined to Algerians resident in Morocco. The aim was to bring the Moroccan bases of the ALN up to the strength of the Tunisian.

Internally, Algeria was divided into six *Wilaya* (provinces), each of which was subdivided into *Mintaka* (zones); each zone into *Nahia* (regions); and each region into *Kism* (sectors). The fighting units of the ALN were grouped as follows:

---

* *Djound* (*djounoud* in plural): private. *Djound el-aouel:* corporal, wearing reversed red V on sleeve. *Aarif:* sergeant, with two reversed red Vs. *Aarif el-aouel:* sergeant-major, with three reversed red Vs. *Moussaad:* adjutant, with one red V underlined in white. *Moulazem:* officer-cadet, with one white star. *Moulazem ethani:* second lieutenant, with one red star. *Dhabet el-aouel:* lieutenant, with one red and one white star. *Sagh el-aouel:* major, with two red stars, one white. *Sagh ethani:* colonel, with three red stars.

Note: French transliteration of the Arabic is retained here, and for the ALN units described below, since it is in this form that they occur in current Algerian military usage. In the majority of other cases (place-names and personal names apart), Arabic terms are transliterated in an English form (*cf. ulama, fidayin*).

Faoudj :   group—11 men under a corporal;
Ferqua :   section—made up of 3 *faoudj* under a section head and his assistant: 35 men all told;
Katiba :   company—made up of 3 *ferqua* under 5 officers: 110 men all told;
Failek :   battalion—made up of 3 *katiba* under 20 officers: a total of 350 men.

A colonel would be in charge of a province with the *idara*—a politico military staff of six—under him. A major would be in charge of a zone, a captain of a region and an adjutant of a sector. Thus an ALN adjutant faced a French full colonel, and a captain no less than three French generals.

Each ALN unit had a political commissar and a military adviser ranking with the officer in charge. Decisions were taken collectively by the three. The institution of political commissar underlined the revolutionary character of the ALN; but public opinion also connected it with the political commissars of the Red Army: a false interpretation which the Algerians did nothing to contradict at the time because it suited their book. In fact, such political advisers are necessary to any army which fights a revolutionary war and has to deal largely with civilian populations. It is, however, true that these political commissars of the ALN were responsible for the 'Castroite' and Chinese ideas which followed independence, particularly the commissars attached to the Ghardimau (Tunisia) and Oujda (Morocco) headquarters of the ALN 'of the exterior'. These were responsible, among other publications, for the review *El Djeich* ('The Army'). They played a key role in the shaping of Algeria after independence.

The famous Wilayas played such an important role after independence, and indeed still do, that they merit listing here, together with the best-known officers from each one. (Those whose names are marked with a dagger died in the struggle.) Personality has been such an over-riding consideration in Algerian politics that some emphasis on individuals is inevitable.

Wilaya I: Aurès-Némentchas. Colonels: Mostefa Ben Boulaid,† Cherif Mahmoud,† Belkacem Krim, Mohammedi Said, and Tahar Zbiri (now chief of general staff of the ANP). Zones: 1 Batna; 2 Khenchela; 3 Biskra and southern territories; 4 Southern Constantine province; 5 Tébessa; 6 Soukh-el-Ahras.

Wilaya II: North Constantine. Colonels: Mourad Didouche,† Youssef Zighout,† Mostefa Ben Ouada, Ali Kafi, Si Larbi and Saout el Arab (a member of the Revolutionary National Council since the coup of June 19, 1965). Zones: 1 Western Constantine; 2 Constantine-Philippeville; 3 Bône-Sedrata.

Wilaya III: Kabilya. Colonels: Belkacem Krim, Mohammedi Said and Mohand ou El-Hadj (currently a member of the Revolutionary National Council). Zones: 1 Ménerville-Les Issers; 2 Tizi-Ouzou; 3 Bougie; 4 Sétif.

Wilaya IV: The Algérois. Colonels: Rabah Bitat, Amar Ouamrane and Slimane Dehiles, alias Colonel Sadok. For the ZAA (Zone Autonome d'Alger): Commander Azzeddine, Commander Si Taib, alias Omar Oussedik, and Si Mokhtar. Zones: 1 Aumale; 2 Blida-Médéa; 3 Orléansville.

Wilaya V: The Oranie. Colonels: Larbi Ben M'Hidi,† Abdelhafid Boussouf (who became a member of the GPRA responsible for arming the ALN and for communications and intelligence), Si Lofti,† and Boumedienne, alias Si Houari, Si Othmane. Zones: 1 Tlemcen; 2 Marnia; 3 Oran-Mers el Kebir; 4 Inkermann; 5 Southern Oran; 6 Mascara; 7 Tiaret.

Wilaya VI: Southern Sahara Territories. Colonels: Si Hassan, Ali Mellah, Ahmed Ben Abderrazek, alias Si Haouès,† and Chaabani (executed after independence for rebellion). Zones: 1 Bou-Saada; 2 Reibell; 3 Djelfa-Laghouat; 4 Aflou. This province, ironically referred to by the French as the 'phantom Wilaya' was never very active because movements on the vast surfaces of the barren Sahara were easily spotted by the intensive aerial reconnaissance of the French.

At first, the command of the ALN rested with the Comité de Coordination et d'Exécution, which had created two bodies for this purpose: COM-EST, in charge of Wilayas I, II and III; and COM-OUEST in charge of Wilayas IV, V and VI. Later, with the formation of the first Provisional Government in 1958, this authority was transferred to the Ministry of Armed Forces of the provisional government. In 1959, the Etat-Major Général of the ALN was appointed. By 1960, the minister of the Armed Forces (for political reasons, as we shall see later) was replaced by an interministerial Committee of Three, which then became known in newspaper argon as the 'powerful trio': Belkacem Krim, Abdelhafid Boussouf and Lakhdari Bentobbal. But already the general staff under Boumedienne was turning its back on the Provisional Government. The 'ALN of the Wilayas', as the army 'of the interior' was also called, drew its main strength from a paramilitary organisation of which little was known during the war: the Organisation Politico-Administrative (OPA). It was sometimes also known as the Organisation Politico-Logistique (OPL), or Organisation Rurale et Urbaine (ORU). This was the basic organisation, the ordinary people in the countryside acting as auxiliaries of the ALN. It consisted of many different groups which assisted the ALN by sheltering it, scouting for it, spying for it, sabotaging and when necessary fighting. The *mujahidin* (meaning 'those who combat for the faith') were the regular officers and men of the ALN, fighting in uniform. These auxiliaries, called the *mussabilin*, were the civilian guerrillas, and the smallest Algerian *duar* (hamlet) had its group, a few of whom were always armed.

There was a second category of non-uniformed fighters: the *fidayin*. These operated as saboteurs in the towns, and it was they who were entrusted with the task of killing French torturers—and Algerian traitors. To stop terrorist activities, particularly in Algiers, the French commissioned the famous General Massu and his parachutists to investigate the Casbah, door by door and window by window. But terrorism dies hard, especially if it is motivated by aims such as those of the Algerians. In fact, the French never stopped it.

To return to the course of the war. Although the French army was clearly superior, the huge well-equipped operations they launched only resulted in the capture of a few 'suspects' and the killing of a few Algerian soldiers. These massive operations, mounted regardless of expenditure and very ably conducted by General Challe, were not by any means the only cause of the Algerian retreat. This was brought about largely by the closure of the Tunisian and Moroccan borders. The ALN's supply of arms was cut off, and members who had been undergoing intensive training courses at camps in Morocco and Tunisia were prevented from returning. A first line of fortifications—the 'Meurice line'—was completed on September 15, 1957, and General Challe later doubled it with another complete line which was named after him. A good part of these 'barrages' still stands today. The lines consisted of a wide and intricate network of electrified barbed wire, alarm systems, pillboxes, gun emplacements, observation posts, electricity generators and searchlights (at 30-metre intervals), the whole liberally interspersed with a variety of mines and detection devices. The French also used a comprehensive radar system, permanent air surveillance and, by night, a hundred armoured cars constantly patrolling behind the searchlights. There were, in fact, so many detection systems that even a passing rabbit could send French units into action. Along the Tunisian border, the 'Meurice' and 'Challe' lines extended from La Calle, near the Mediterranean, to El-Ma-el-Abiod, north-east of Negrine, where the Sahara begins.

Once the frontiers were closed, another phase of the war began: the 'battle of the barrages'. It was a battle of wits between the Algerians trying to evade every obstacle to send men and materials into Algeria and the French troops assigned to the lines (about 40,000 men all told). Not many Algerians succeeded in crossing and those that were successful were able to cross only with light equipment. Once the French had perfected the systems, the Algerians found they could cross only in groups of twenty to a hundred. One of the highest Algerian officers concerned (who wishes to remain anonymous) gave me some very interesting information on this phase of the war—though much of it is not relevant here. According to him, in 1958 the Tunisia-based ALN lost close on 4,500 men over a six-month period in attempts to cross the lines. After this hard lesson, the ALN decided that no more attempts to cross the lines would be made before the men were well prepared and the necessary equipment gathered. By 1960, though the French had perfected their detection systems, the Algerians had also perfected their own techniques and were once more able to penetrate into Algeria.* The Algerians concentrated their attempts at penetration

* An OAS leader has revealed what the French military authorities would not divulge. Jean-Jacques Susini reveals in his *Histoire de l'*OAS, Vol. I, 1961 that, according to the confidential Daily Information Bulletin of the French general staff on August 21, 1961, the ALN had managed, using bangalores, to open up 'twelve breaches in the barrages from 5 to 18 metres wide'. The same bulletin noted for that day: 'Rebels still in recrudescence. An increasing number of deserters [muslim Algerians in the French army] breaking away with their arms. Military losses of French army: 34 killed, of whom 6 officers; 51 wounded. Main repressive action [by French forces against civilian population]: 800 *gourbis* set on fire; 4,000 left roofless.'

particularly between Soukh-el-Ahras and Mondovi, for this area gave access to the Djebel Edough mountains, which were particularly suitable for guerrilla action. Soukh-el-Ahras still bears the gloomy aspect of a town which for years has been completely encircled by fortifications of all kinds, including a dense belt of electrified barbed wire. In 1961, as senior an officer as Tahar Zbiri, then a Wilaya commander, managed to cross the lines.

Exploits were also possible inside the country. In theory, the French army had every square kilometre of the country (except for the acknowledged maquis strongholds) under surveillance. Nevertheless, in 1959 Colonel Boumedienne, then head of COM-OUEST, managed to transfer large quantities of supplies from Oran to Constantine, by way of Figuig down in the desert along the Moroccan border. And this in spite of the fact that the French were keeping a special watch on the Sahara with the aim of not allowing a single convoy across.

Inevitably, the ALN came to be divided into the 'forces of the interior' and the 'forces of the exterior': a division which was to have important political consequences. The French received confirmation that an efficient force was being created outside the country during General de Gaulle's visit in 1959, when some ten battalions of the ALN, supported by modern heavy artillery, launched a spectacular attack on the barrage from Tunisia during the night of September 27–28. It is not known how many Algerians died that night, or how many succeeded in crossing the border, but it was made abundantly clear that the ALN 'of the exterior' was just as much a 'force in being' as the British Home Fleet during the first world war.

According to the prominent Algerian mentioned earlier, in 1962 the ALN issued rations for '40,000 men' in Tunisia and Morocco. This would seem to be the maximum figure for the strength of the ALN, including much-reduced auxiliary services. It is difficult to obtain accurate figures for the ALN 'of the interior': Wilaya commanders give various figures for various times. But it is generally accepted by Algerians that the number of *mujahidin* inside the country was between 5 and 10 thousand. This means that the total number of *mujahidin* never exceeded 50,000.

The situation was not static, as the French civilian leaders realised only too well. The ALN 'of the exterior', far from being idle, was going from strength to strength, and sending experts for training in Arab military schools and communist countries. These men, who included airmen, returned as instructors to the Tunisian and Moroccan camps, some even managing to sneak back inside Algeria.

Moscow has always shown a wary regard for de Gaulle. Russian recognition of the GPRA de jure came late in the day, but in 1960 Moscow did at last decide to help the ALN indirectly by supplying military equipment, at first through Bulgaria and Czechoslovakia. Having once taken the plunge, Russia became the ALN's biggest supplier, providing the heaviest equipment. Yugoslavia was the first European communist country to come to the assistance of the ALN, selling them a great deal of equipment, though part of it fell into French hands when two Yugoslav ships failed to break the French blockade of the Mediterranean. China started to help—and officially recognised the GPRA—before Russia. Although Peking's assistance was handicapped by distance, Algerian officials have always emphasised that China gave 'the most genuine' assistance. I have seen myself the great quantities of Chinese equipment in the hands of the ALN: storm lanterns, underclothes, food and drugs, and even anti-aircraft guns. By 1961–62, the ALN 'of the exterior' was receiving so much foreign help that the ugly spectre of an international struggle began to rear its head. Several foreign military missions were known to have visited the ALN camps. The question of 'foreign volunteers' was very much in the air: a cause of acute anxiety to the Moroccan and Tunisian governments. The Yugoslavs, too, lived in fear that the ALN would play its trump card, the Peking ace, calling for Chinese soldiers in the form of a military mission. And what of Cairo, which would be only too glad to despatch whole battalions? The question worried all the great capitals: Paris, London, Washington and Moscow.

But here we come to the broader question of what the Algerians were achieving on the political front whilst the ALN were active in the field. To appreciate this we must return to November 1954.

The FLN is Born

The decision to attack on November 1, 1954, was not made overnight. It was the culmination of long years of anguish and doubt. Observers of Algerian affairs generally agree that nationalist feeling crystallised in May 1945, after the French massacres at Sétif and Constantine. By 1947, individual groups of Kabyles under such leaders as Belkacem Krim and Amar Ouamrane (once corporals in the French army) were forming resistance units. By 1952, the first members of the Organisation Spéciale (OS), formed from the Mouvement pour le Triomphe des Libertés Démocratiques (MTLD), were pressing for action, although at the time the majority of their future companions still hoped to achieve their ends by 'legal' means.

The massacres at Sétif and Constantine in 1945 were particularly bloody. According to official French sources, 15,000 Algerians were killed at Sétif alone; but the Algerian estimate is 45,000. The bloodshed was provoked by the Algerian demonstrations at Sétif on May 1, 1945. Anticipating a speedy Allied victory over the Nazis, the Algerians paraded with slogans reading 'Long Live the Victory of the Allies!' and—the real crime—a solitary Algerian flag. The French immediately started fierce and barbaric reprisals all over the Constantine region, and with particular intensity between Bougie and Sétif, Bône and Soukh-el-Ahras. Algerians were shot and buried en masse in quicklime pits in the ruins of Heliopolis and Millesimo. 'Never', says Charles-Henri Favrod, 'was a colonial country struck so savagely, at such an hour'—the hour of victory for the Allies whose promises to those still under colonial domination contrasted so sharply with the savagery of the French. Tens of thousands of North Africans had fought for the Allied cause at Cassino. Tens of thousands of Algerians were the recipients of French gratitude for this. There is little doubt, continues the Swiss journalist and writer, that 'it was these events of 1945 which decided the revolution of 1954'. He quotes many Algerians met in Cairo, Tunis, Bonn, Rome and Geneva in support of this. One of these, the well-known writer, Kateb Yacine, he reports as having said:

My humanitarian feelings were first outraged by the ghastly sights at Sétif in 1945. I was sixteen years old and I have never forgotten the shock of that merciless butchery which took thousands of muslim lives. There at Sétif the iron of nationalism entered my soul. There have been, it is true, other factors: the economic and political alienation of my people in their own country, for instance. But it was particularly this betrayal of the values which the French had given us which opened my eyes.[3]

The contemptible rigging of the elections held by the French in Algeria after the war was a further revelation to those still hoping to win their freedom by 'legal' means. The elections for the Algerian Assembly, and the municipal elections, were so heavily rigged that it is not worth going into the figures.*

In the spring of 1954, twenty-two men met secretly in the rue de Chartres in Algiers to create the Comité Révolutionnaire d'Unité et d'Action (CRUA). Nine of the men associated with this meeting eventually earned the title of 'historic chiefs': Mohammed Boudiaf; the late Mostefa Ben Boulaid; the late Mourad Didouche; the late Larbi Ben M'Hidi; Belkacem Krim; Rabah Bitat; Hocine Ait Ahmed; Ben Bella; and Mohammed Khider. The three last-named were fellow conspirators although in Cairo at the time. The meeting decided on a date for the revolution and began the work of organisation by dividing Algeria into Wilayas. The Front de la Libération Nationale (FLN) was born. It rapidly grew into a national party, joined by all except the Mouvement Nationaliste Algérien (MNA) and the Parti Communiste Algérien (PCA). (More details on these can be found in the chart, 'Origins and Development of Algerian Nationalism' in Appendix I, pages 272-3.)

Why exactly did the revolutionaries create the FLN, and what were they fighting for? These questions were answered in a proclamation made on the first day of revolution. It will be noticed that the aims are not very different from the terms of the agreement achieved at Evian after seven-and-a-half years of war.

TO THE ALGERIAN PEOPLE,
TO ALL WHO FIGHT FOR THE NATIONAL CAUSE,

You have the right to pass judgement on our actions (the first group in a general way, the second in a more particular way); we are, therefore, making the present proclamation so as to make clear our motives, and so that you may understand why we have been forced into action and what we are trying to achieve: our reasonable aim of National Independence within a North African framework. We wish to spare you the doubts which imperialism will try to implant in you through its administrative agents and other corrupt political rabble.

* The French held elections in Algeria in April 1948 for the Algerian Assembly; in March and October 1950 for district officials; in June 1951 for legislative purposes; in April 1953 for municipal purposes and again for the Algerian Assembly in February 1954.

We consider that after long years of struggle our National Movement is entering the final phase of the battle—the phase of achievement. As the aim of any revolutionary movement is to create conditions favourable to the fight for freedom, we consider the moment propitious. Within the country, the people are united in their desire for independence and action; outside, the relaxation of international tension will allow the rest of the world to direct its attention to the solution of lesser problems, of which ours is one. We hope for the diplomatic support of our Arabo-Muslim brothers. The events in Morocco and Tunisia have been very significant and are important milestones on North Africa's road to freedom. We may say here that we, so long in the vanguard, were the first to urge joint action—unfortunately never realised—among the three countries.

Today, the other two have already set out on their journey to freedom whereas we, who have been overtaken, are already suffering the fate of those who are left behind. Our national movement, weakened by years of routine and inactivity, badly directed, deprived of the indispensible support of public opinion and overtaken by events, is gradually disintegrating to the great satisfaction of the colonialists who think they have achieved, in the defeat of the Algerian avant-garde, the greatest victory of the struggle. The danger is serious!

Determined to act before the situation becomes hopeless, a team of young men and active supporters, after careful and due consideration, has joined forces with other groups of true and active supporters in order to take advantage of this propitious moment and rescue our nationalist movement from its impasse—an impasse into which it has been dragged by clashing interests and personal rivalry. We shall launch it once more into the true revolutionary struggle at the sides of our Moroccan and Tunisian brethren.

We wish to make it quite clear that we are completely independent of either of the two factions which are struggling for power. According to true revolutionary principles, we place the interests of our nation above petty and misguided personal disputes or considerations of prestige. Our only enemy is the hostile and blind colonialism which has always rejected our demands for freedom, when presented by peaceful means.

We consider we are justified in presenting our new movement under the title of:

Front de Libération Nationale

We hope thereby to avoid association with any particular group, and to provide all Algerian patriots, from all social levels and from all truly

Algerian parties and movements, with an opportunity of joining in the fight for freedom, unhampered by any conflict of loyalty.

For your information, we here give a broad outline of our political programme:

Aim : National independence:

1. By restoring the sovereign, democratic Algerian state within the framework of the principles of Islam.

2. By respecting the basic rights of man without distinction of race or creed.

Internal Objectives :

1. Political renewal through redirecting the national revolutionary movement onto its true path and by removing all traces of corruption and revisionism—the causes of our present downfall.

2. To assemble and organise the efforts of the Algerian people to liquidate the colonial system.

External Objectives :

1. To make the Algerian problem one of international concern.

2. To bring about union in North Africa within the natural Arabo-Muslim framework.

3. Within the limits of the Charter of the United Nations to emphasise our active sympathy with all nations who support our struggle for freedom.

Means of Combat

According to revolutionary principles, and taking into account the internal and external situation, we shall continue the fight by every means until we realise our aims.

To achieve these ends, the Front de Libération Nationale will have two highly important tasks to carry out simultaneously: internal action, both general and political; and external action, to bring our problem before the eyes of the world with the help of our natural allies. This will be a heavy task which will necessitate mobilising all our energies and all our national resources. The struggle will be long but the outcome is certain.

Lastly, in order to avoid misinterpretation, to show our sincere desire for peace, and to avoid unnecessary bloodshed and loss of life, we suggest honourable negotiations to the French authorities if they are willing to act in good faith and accept once and for all the right of the peoples they rule to selfdetermination.

1. Let them recognise the Algerian nation by an official declaration abrogating all edicts, decrees and laws which make Algeria French soil in the teeth of her history, geography, language, religion and customs.
2. Let them open negotiations with authorised representatives of the Algerian people accepting the sovereignty of Algeria as one and indivisible.
3. Let them give proof of good faith by releasing all political prisoners, relaxing their emergency laws, and ceasing to prosecute the combatants.

We give our pledge :
1. That French interests, cultural and economic, which have been honestly acquired, will be respected, as will individuals and families.
2. That all Frenchmen wishing to remain in Algeria will be allowed to choose between their original nationality, continuing which will entail legal recognition as foreigners, and adopting Algerian nationality, in which case they will be considered as such in right and duty.
3. The position of Algeria as regards France will be defined and will be the subject of an agreement between the two powers, based on equality and mutual respect.

Algerians! We invite you to ponder on this Charter. It is your duty to associate yourselves with it so that we may save our country and regain our freedom. The fight of the Front de Libération Nationale is your fight, and its victory is your victory.

As for ourselves, we are resolved to carry on with the fight. Confident of your anti-imperialist sentiments, we shall give of our best for our country.[4]

The FLN attracted the support of the working classes immediately. By February 26, 1956, they had formed the Union Générale des Travailleurs Algériens (UGTA), forgoing their former allegiance to the French Confédération de Travail (CGT). The middle-class nationalist leaders of the Union Démocratique du Manifeste Algérien were slower to come forward. They pledged their support secretly in 1955, but did not make open avowal until they were outside Algeria. Ferhat Abbas, for instance, joined from Cairo in April 1956. Students were enthusiastic supporters. Extremely active in organising strikes, they joined in the fighting as *mujahidin*, *mussabilin* and *fidayin*. Their union was the Union Générale des Etudiants Musulmans Algériens (UGEMA).

As the fighting intensified in the country and the towns, and the blood began to flow, many of the early partisans were killed. It became necessary to reorganise and make new plans. On August 24, 1956, the members of the CRUA met once more in the valley of the Soummam. The meeting was again held in the greatest secrecy, and the ALN launched diversionary operations to distract the French from this part of Algeria. The meeting created the first institutions of the Revolution: the Conseil National de la Révolution Algérienne (CNRA)—a legislative body—and the Comité de Coordination Exécutif (CCE)—an executive body. The administration of the Wilayas was reinforced both materially and judicially. The first CNRA consisted of thirty-four members, of whom seventeen were 'proxy members', authorised to deputise for full members prevented from attending future sessions by the hazards of war. At a second meeting, held in Cairo in 1957, the number was increased to fifty-four.

The Comité de Coordination Exécutif

The original CCE consisted of five men: Abane Ramdane (a Kabyle who played a great role in the revolution although he never reached the rank of chief of Wilaya, as death cut short his brilliant career), Ben M'Hidi, Saad Dahlab, Belkacem Krim, and Ben Khedda. Each acted almost as a minister, Ben M'Hidi dealing with general strategy, Ramdane with organisation, Ben Khedda and Dahlab with propaganda and foreign relations, and Belkacem Krim with liaison between the CCE and the Wilayas. In Cairo in 1957, membership was increased to nine and the 'ministerial' duties were better defined. The members were now: Abane Ramdane, Abdelhafid Boussouf, Lakhdari Bentobbal, Lamine Debaghine, Ferhat Abbas, Abdelaziz Mehiri, Cherif Mahmoud, Amar Ouamrane and the inevitable Belkacem Krim. The Conseil National empowered the new committee to form a provisional government. The first Gouvernement Provisoire de la Révolution Algérienne (GPRA) was appointed on September 19, 1958. The announcement was made simultaneously from Tunis and Cairo. (See Appendix II for the composition of this and subsequent Algerian governments.)

The same year, 1957, saw both the completion of the barrages, with the consequent formation of the ALN 'of the interior', and also the exodus of the civilian revolutionaries who could no longer operate safely inside the country. Men like Ben Bella and Mohammed Khider had left long before and were already working in Cairo as 'external delegates' of the CCE at the time of the historic Soummam meeting of the Conseil National in 1956. By 1958, all the important figures of the revolution were out of the country.

The GPRA conducted the political war with astounding success. The Algerian government-in-exile was based in Tunis, and from there it gradually won diplomatic recognition, first from the Arab countries, and then from African and Asian states, sending out legations and delegations in its turn. From 1960 onwards, the communist countries also recognised the GPRA and accepted its envoys as official representatives. The following countries recognised the GPRA immediately or within ten months. *De jure :* Tunisia, Morocco, Libya, Iraq (September 19, 1958); Saudi Arabia, Jordan (September 20); United Arab Republic, Yemen (September 21); Sudan, Chinese People's Republic, North Korea (September 22); North Vietnam (September 26); Indonesia (September 27); Guinea (September 30); Mongolia (December 15); Lebanon (January 15, 1959). *Defacto :* Yugoslavia (June 12, 1959; confirmed April 12, 1961).

The revolution in Algeria naturally affected other countries in neighbouring Africa. It is generally accepted that it influenced de Gaulle in granting independence more quickly to the former Afrique Française. It also stood high as a topic on the agenda of the Conference of the Peoples of Africa held at Accra in December 1958. Indeed, the failure of the Lagos conference fixed for January 1962 showed how strongly African feeling supported the Algerians. Seven independent African states refused to attend because the GPRA had not been invited; and although the Nigerians agreed to issue an eleventh-hour invitation in August, the 1962 conference never took place. In 1959, the GPRA was recognised as a full member of the Conference of Independent African States which met at Monrovia.

The Gouvernement Provisoire paid those who worked for it a salary of 28 Tunisian dinars a month (roughly 300 francs), regardless of rank. All the civilian combatants observed a strict discipline. Drinks, women and cinema-going were forbidden, and contacts with non-Algerians severely restricted—on security grounds, not out of puritanism. As we shall see later, the Algerians became fanatical devotees of 'security'. The GPRA became extremely rich. Not only were there generous donations from the Middle East and from Morocco, but the GPRA imposed its own system of taxation on all the Algerians it controlled, inside and outside the country. Furthermore, as it can now be disclosed, the Gouvernement Provisoire forged various currencies in Holland and elsewhere. The greatest expense was the purchasing of armaments.

The Algerians were fortunate in possessing an excellent organiser in Abdelhafid Boussouf. He contributed greatly to their victory, managing the communications and intelligence networks both inside the country and out, and also supervising armaments. Between 1957 and 1960 the time needed to relay information (from Algeria to the HQ in Tunis) about French troop movements was reduced by Boussouf's efforts from 'three days' to 'a couple of hours'—thereby giving the ALN the desperately needed opportunity of sneaking across the border. During the war he was known as 'The Terror': a reflection on his achievements against the French rather than on his character, for he is a jovial-tempered man. He once said to me jokingly: 'I can now confess to you that if we managed to infiltrate the French, they too managed to infiltrate us heavily, in spite of all our precautions. The trouble, or perhaps the advantage, is that we Algerians and French understand each other too well! But we were in a better position to make use of our information—and that was the all-important point.' He added: 'We taught the French how to build barrages, and I'm afraid we were too successful as teachers.' It was, in fact, Boussouf's sense of organisation and competence in communication matters which first obliged the French to erect the barrages along the Moroccan border. In 1957, when he was still commander of Wilaya V, Boussouf equipped his troops with wireless sets, as he did his rearguard in Morocco, and this gave him great mobility. He was a daring man, and once sent a regular ALN unit, fully armed and equipped, into Tlemcen in marching order. Before the astounded French could believe their eyes, the ALN unit blazed away at them and then disappeared.

The Algerian war was also fought on a third front: that of France itself. The Algerians called it Wilaya VII! This third front was also the responsibility of the GPRA. There has always been a large (and cheap) Algerian labour force in France, together with a great number of Algerian students and professional men.* (By early 1966, there were close on 600,000 Algerians resident in France: more than there ever were before independence. In West Germany and Belgium there are about 100,000 more.) It was natural that such Algerians should be organised and enrolled in the fight. The duty was delegated to the powerful Fédération de France (FF-FLN). There were also the Fédération de Tunisie and the Fédération du Maroc, grouping Algerians in the two countries. But these two organisations were closely controlled either by the GPRA or by the ALN, and they never gained the importance, or the autonomy, of the Fédération de France. This body raised funds, enrolled combatants for jobs all over the world, sent specialist workers from the Renault factories to ALN depots, shot traitors and intimidated the French.

The activities of the FF-FLN have been well described by a man who should know all about them: M. Maurice Papon, head of the French police. In a document issued on May 18, 1960, he stated:

Sympathisers, members and combatants of the FLN are grouped in the Fédération de France, which comes directly under the GPRA. The Fédération is divided into six Wilayas covering the whole territory [of France]. The most important ones are: *Wilaya I*—Paris, with 30,000 members, and *Wilaya II*—Greater Paris, with 40,000 members. Wilayas are divided into two super-zones, then into regions, districts, *kasmas*, groups and cells. Each cell has its own 'action group' which controls the workers and students, and raises funds. Each student or worker must pay a minimum due each month of 3,000 [old] francs. In the Seine Département alone, the FLN treasury gains approximately 250 million [old] francs every month.

---

* France first imported Algerian labour during the first world war, when 78,000 were brought in to work in agriculture, transport, mines and war factories. This first batch of official immigrants was repatriated at the end of the war, but many had come to like the life and the higher pay in France, and by 1924, 100,000 Algerians were working in France. Their origins, by administrative regions, were roughly as follows: from Constantine, 60 per cent; from the Algérois, 30 per cent; from Oran, 10 per cent. In France they have settled mainly in five regions: Paris, the East, the Mediterranean coast, the Rhone and the North. According to official statistics, these immigrants sent back some 50 million francs a year to their families in Algeria.

. . . Seventy [French] parliamentarians have to be under protection in the Seine Département, and fifty cars are permanently mobilised to that effect. In 1959, 119,000 muslim Algerians were investigated and 848 fund collectors arrested. Of these, 141 were members of 'action groups', 400 were officials with special responsibilities, 9 were heads of zones, 1 was head of a superzone, and 2 were heads of Wilayas. During the first four months of 1960, 544 members of the FLN were arrested.[5]

In 1962 it was rumoured, very secretly, that the Fédération de France was getting ready to create real havoc in Paris. It was thought that the Algerians were hoping, through increasing the pressure in France, to intimidate the French before the Evian peace talks. This is quite likely. The Algerians would have paid dearly for such tactics later but they have demonstrated repeatedly that they are not of the breed that is deterred by fear of reprisal.

At about the same time, the Algerians were preparing to intensify the military struggle in Algeria should the peace talks fail. When discussing this book with me, Abdelhafid Boussouf disclosed that there were plans for 'pirate' Algerian planes to make surprise attacks on selected targets in Algeria. The first airmen had been trained as night pilots. The only night fighters attached to the Fifth French Air Region were based at Reggane to protect the French atomic installations. Even if the French warning system worked perfectly, the Vautours would take an hour and twenty minutes to reach eastern Algeria and 'by that time the pirate planes would be some twenty minutes away from Algerian territory'. I gathered that the United Arab Republic would have provided the planes, which would have had secret bases in North African countries.

Inside Algeria the GPRA were waging a successful political battle as well as a military one. One important development had been the setting up in 1956 of *La Voix de l'Algérie Combattante*. Its broadcasts played an important role in awakening in the Algerians a sense of nationhood. Listening to the wireless had never been a popular pastime in Algeria, and hitherto the use of the radio for political propaganda had been a French monopoly. But once 'The Voice of Fighting Algeria' came on the air, there was a rush for radio sets and transistors—and a similar rush by the French to try and put a stop to sales. Listening to the broadcasts was soon regarded as an act of defiance. The transmissions came from Tunis, Rabat and Cairo and were in Arabic, Kabyle and French. They helped to make the Algerians conscious of the fact they all belonged to one country, whether they lived in Constantine or Oran.

The GPRA was anxious to show that it had the support of Algerian public opinion and staged various demonstrations to prove this. The most spectacular was that which came to be known as 'the battle of Algiers'. (A film is currently being made about this.) For three days, December 10–13, 1960, the inhabitants of the city demonstrated in support of the FLN and as a counter to the political manoeuvres of the French who were trying to create a 'third force' among Algerians. There were demonstrations in all the main towns but it was Algiers that really counted. Neither the French parachutists, nor the tanks, nor the barbed wire, prevented thousands upon thousands of men, women and children from erupting everywhere chanting FLN slogans. As usual, the French took brutal repressive measures.

The financial cost to France of the Algerian war was enormous: 50 billion francs (new) together with $1·7 million foreign currency spent on arms purchases and to close the gap of Algeria's foreign deficit. Other vast financial losses were incurred which cannot be calculated accurately because of the effect of war-induced inflation. However, in terms of human lives French losses were relatively small. According to official figures, from 1956 to the cease-fire in midsummer 1962, a total of 32,500 French citizens were killed in Algeria. Of these, 18,500 were civilians (2,500 of French stock and 16,000 of muslim North African origin), and 14,000 were military personnel (9,000 of French stock and 5,000 North Africans and members of the Foreign Legion). In metropolitan France, the war brought death to 4,395 French citizens, of whom 4,172 were of muslim North African origin.

We shall not here go into the Algerian fight against the notorious extreme rightwing Organisation de l'Armée Secrète, the OAS, which resorted to the wildest terrorism to keep Algeria French. (On one occasion in Algiers in 1961 they killed 61 muslims and wounded another 110 quite indiscriminately by a boobytrap placed in a car.) Nor shall we go into all the unsuccessful attempts at negotiation— for all the time they were fighting, the Algerians and the French never ceased to probe for a possible peaceful solution. There were contacts between the two sides in Cairo on April 12, 20–21 and 30,

1956. In the same year there were exploratory meetings in Belgrade in July and in Rome on September 2. Negotiations proper began at Melun between June 25 and 29 in 1960. The following year there took place the first of the meetings at Evian, between May 20 and June 13, renewed in July at Lugrin. These attempts failed because the French were still hoping to obtain what the Algerians would never grant: the partition of Algeria.* The strikes, the assassinations, the battles of the ALN and the diplomatic struggles— all the events of the period from 1960 are too well known to need relating again. What counts is that, after a magnificent and courageous struggle against colonialism, the revolutionaries achieved their hard-won success on May 18, 1962. The cease-fire was proclaimed the following day.

The results of the referendum on self-determination, held on July 1, 1962, were a crushing 'Yes' for freedom:

Registered electors	6,549,736
Votes cast	6,017,680
Spoilt ballots	25,565
Votes registered	5,992,115
Yes	5,975,581
No	16,534

But, even as victory appeared on the horizon, the 'brothers' turned against each other.

---

* Each partition proposal put forward by France contained two identical provisions: that the Sahara, with its oil and gas, should remain French; and that part of the coastal strip should also stay under French control as an outlet for the Sahara and to serve as an enclave for the French settlers. Both provisions were eventually dropped, but it is interesting to see how 'French' the Sahara still is, albeit under Algerian jurisdiction. *France-Observateur* on December 21, 1961, published an interesting study of this subject with maps illustrating the six possible divisions of Algeria as suggested by the French. Alain Peyrefitte, now French secretary of state for Information, wrote a book on the question: *Faut-il partager l'Algérie?*, Collection Tribune Libre, Paris 1961.

3

CIVILIAN AND MILITARY 'PRECEDENCE'

SOON AFTER the liberation, it was announced that five of the capital's main thoroughfares, bearing illustrious colonial names, would be renamed after five great dead heroes of the Algerian revolution: Ben M'Hidi, Colonel Amirouche, Ben Boulaid, Mourad Didouche and Abane Ramdane. The Algerians themselves were the first to remark that, of these five, only the first two died in action against the French; the remaining three were assassinated by their fellow-countrymen. Wars and revolutions always breed crime, and political standards are degenerating everywhere. It is generally agreed, however, that the Algerians plumbed new depths.

By the time Algeria achieved her hard-earned independence, the long period of colonial rule had resulted in a general lowering of morals. Moreover, although Algeria had close affinities with Europe, the state of society was undeveloped by Western standards. Only small sections had attained the level where friendship and pleasant, sociable manners are valued. The majority had little respect for the value of human life and the war did nothing to help this. Oddly enough, they appeared to have more respect for French than Algerian lives. Except during actual combat, it was not easy to harm or kill a Frenchman; and even then instructions had been given that French lives should be respected and that French prisoners should not be shot unless strictly necessary, as they might prove useful pawns in the future. In fact the ALN, in its anxiety for international recognition as a regularly constituted fighting force, had given very strict orders that French prisoners should be correctly treated in accordance with international convention—and generally speaking this was observed. In the towns, determined not to provide ammunition for the French propaganda dismissal of the FLN as mere assassins, the Algerians usually selected their targets with care. This attitude gave the French a measure of protection. There were, moreover, other factors in the Algerian respect for French life: the inevitable inferiority complex of the colonised (shared by most Algerians, except the minority which rebelled), and—more important—the very special love-hate relationship of the French and the Algerians.

When about to enter Algeria during the interregnum between the Evian Agreement and independence, I felt sick at heart to think that I would once more see human beings, the French this time, fleeing for their lives, as I had seen others in South-East Asia and parts of Africa. Remembering these sad sights, I was astounded to find that, on the contrary, the enemies who had been fighting so bitterly only a few days before, were not only coexisting but collaborating. It is true that, under General de Gaulle and after the signing of the Evian Agreement, the French army had behaved with exemplary correctness in Algeria; but no one had expected that the Algerians would observe the same standards. Revenge would have been natural; the French, who had themselves taken revenge on the defeated Germans, agreed that if the positions had been reversed, and it had been an Algerian army leaving French soil, 'there would have been hell to pay!'

Such was the bewildering and intricate relationship built up during the hundred and thirty years of French occupation that, directly after the cease-fire, all antagonism seemed to disappear. It was almost a miracle. There were, of course, one or two incidents, but unpleasantness was exceptional. With the end of the war, there straightway began a new phase of understanding and co-operation. It was as if both sides had completely forgotten the long years of dominance by the one and subjection of the other, and the bitter years of warfare.

Why did the Algerians behave so magnanimously? Were they displaying superior moral qualities? In common with many other observers, I came to the conclusion that there was probably another explanation, for the Algerians did not reveal any notable magnanimity of character in their dealings among themselves. The post-independence relationship with France could only be the result of a colonial inferiority complex (centuries of foreign rule are not swept away overnight) and of the loverlike association of the two peoples. Algerian intellectuals have come to the same conclusion. As a good many of them observe: 'Unfortunately for us, we are still the mistress. Otherwise we have no objection to the relationship.'

At Algiers airport, with foreign colleagues equally persona grata with the official administration, one would so often experience irritating searches and delays only to see some pied-noir allowed to slip through with no greater formality than a nod and an exchange of smiles. It had all the appearance of complicity. In front of one counter there were long queues of Algerian workers, dressed in the blue overalls favoured by French workmen, clutching their miserable luggage and pressing sheeplike against each other for fear they might miss the last seat. Before an adjoining counter were a few French soldiers, officers and men. Both counters were ordinary commercial counters of Air Algérie,* manned by Algerian staff. But what a shocking difference in the attitudes displayed to the two sets of passengers!

Once, well after independence, I was walking along the Algerian waterfront with a French officer. We passed a fully armed sentry posted in front of a French military establishment close to the Prefecture and the Hotel Aletti. He stood above street level and dominated the surroundings. I said: 'Could not you Frenchmen have the decency to tell that sentry to stand a few metres further back so that he does not disturb the passers-by?' 'My dear chap, the passers-by! . . . The passers-by don't object. The Algerians have never complained, *you* are the only one who has ever found him disturbing. But come to think of it, you are quite right.'

The discriminating attitude displayed at the airport occasionally became a source of embarrassment to the French authorities in Algeria; foreign observers might conclude that the French occupation had merely assumed a different form. This came to a head when two serious clashes occurred between Algerians and French

* From February 1963, the Algerian government owned 31 per cent of the shares of this company. The other shareholders are: La Compagnie Trans-atlantique, Air France (which provides the pilots and mechanics) and La Compagnie de Navigation Mixte. By 1965, only 45 per cent of the non-technical flying personnel were Algerians.

soldiers. (It is remarkable that these were the only two serious incidents which took place.)

The first incident took place on August 9, 1962 at a desert post named Kasr el Hiran, some 20 kilometres east of Laghouat. Troops of the ALN captured some unarmed legionnaires going on leave and killed four who tried to escape, including an officer. The French protested strongly; so strongly that they later felt they had perhaps gone too far, particularly as the men had belonged to the notorious Foreign Legion. General Brebisson despatched Lieutenant Jean-Pierre Gault, his political aide, to the Algerian Political Bureau (of Ben Bella and Khider). Gault's official report, transmitted to Paris said that: 1. The Political Bureau thinks France is 'scrupulously respecting' the Evian Agreement and does not think that 'any danger of neocolonialism exists'. 2. Far from thinking that the communiqué issued by the French on August 10 to protest at the Kasr el Hiran incident was 'severe', they considered it quite normal. Furthermore, they considered that the French communiqué had rendered a service to the Political Bureau in that it underlined the necessity of the (Boumedienne-controlled) ALN's subordinating itself to the political power (Ben Bella and Khider). The next day the young French officer's interpretation of the situation was confirmed when Khider reiterated all this in a broadcast and televised speech.

The second serious incident occurred at Orléansville in the unruly and turbulent Wilaya IV—a town no one could approach without trouble—on December 8 of the same year. Some armed bands clashed with French soldiers, one of whom was drunk. Two French soldiers and three French gendarmes were killed and two French children wounded. The indispensable Lieutenant Gault went into action once more (he was the only French official in contact with important Algerians at the time), waking up Ben Bella late at night. The Political Bureau was then at daggers drawn with Wilaya IV, and Ben Bella was all the more concerned since France was about to make a much-needed financial loan. In fact he was in despair, and it can now be disclosed that the official Algerian communiqué on this Orléansville incident was drawn up by none other than Lieutenant Gault himself. Ben Bella was at such a loss that he asked him to do 'what he thought best'. Gault was only too pleased. The shy young officer certainly saved Franco-Algerian relations that day for, by writing the communiqué himself, he was able to ensure that it did not sound too pro-French—which he feared it might have done if the Algerians had written it themselves!

Much later, in 1964, Algiers, at Moscow's request, staged an International Conference for the Denuclearisation of the Mediterranean Basin. The show had just begun with the usual fanfare when Ben Bella despatched an emissary (Mohammed Yazid, former minister of Information of the GPRA) among the delegates to warn them that, although they should give full rein to their feelings about all other atomic installations throughout the globe, not a word was to be said about the French atomic installations and tests within Algeria herself. As we shall see later, some Algerian leaders became so biased in favour of the French that their attitude was quite hypocritical.

Unfortunately, the Algerians did not show the same bias towards themselves. Unable or unwilling to vent their spleen on the French, it would seem that the Algerians, all unconsciously, worked out their complexes on each other. They also attempted to sit in judgement on each other, with catastrophic results for their own nation.

This society in formation was subject to another scourge which imparted a greater character of violence and treachery to the endless internal feuds: the adoption of stalinist and trotskyite methods. The communist experience had impressed the Algerians, and they sought to emulate its methods in hope of quick achievements. But they grasped the shadow rather than the substance, adopting the slogans but not the discipline, hard work and deliberate self-denial behind them.

The Algerian nationalists adopted stalinist and trotskyite methods from the very beginning. The first modern Algerian nationalist movement, established in Paris in 1925 was the Etoile Nord Africaine. (See Appendix I.) The father of this movement was Hadj Abdelkader, a member of the Central Committee of the French Communist Party (PCF), but his place was soon taken by that well-known patriarch, Messali Hadj, who also joined the PCF and took part in the Third International in Moscow in 1930. On his return to Paris, Hadj founded the newspaper *El Oumma* (The Nation), but eventually abandoned the communists, who denounced him loudly. Not only did he introduce militant nationalism into Algeria but also the personality cult and, as noted in *Révolution Africaine* of

December 14, 1963, 'the cult of the killer'. His Parti Populaire Algérien (PPA) was the melting-pot of modern nationalism, observed Ch-H. Favrod.[1] Messali Hadj was for many years the embodiment of Algerian nationalism and his mark is still upon it. On August 20, 1965, when celebrating the 'day of the *mujahidin*', marking the anniversary of the Soummam Valley meeting, the prime minister, Boumedienne, said: 'There have been two mistakes in our history: Messali and Ben Bella.'

One proviso must be made in regard to the 'cult of the killer'. At high levels both the GPRA and the ALN acted with restraint. All death sentences, whatever their nature, were given at least a semblance of legality. Boussouf and Lakhdari Bentobbal, who have both retained their terrible wartime reputations, have explained to the author and other observers that the death sentences imposed on Algerians by their Ministries were 'collegial decisions taken by the GPRA after serious consideration', and there is no reason to doubt this. But they also added that this procedure did not apply 'to the small cases'. As far as the army is concerned (and we may point out here that Colonel Boumedienne always acted with great dignity in his dealings—kept down to a strict minimum—with the French military in Algeria), here too death sentences were imposed by regularly constituted courts-martial. How far these were impartial is another matter. Of course, even among those who took part in violent actions, there were plenty of men of great integrity and respectability. They are too numerous to be listed here, but one thinks of men like Lamine Khan (director-general of the Organisme Saharien, until its disbandment in December 1965), of Abdessalam (minister of Energy after Ben Bella's overthrow), and of such parliamentarians as Bouzid and Hocine, and of such young ambassadors as Rheda Malek, Tawfik Bouatoura, Ben Yahia, Benhabyles and Lakdar Brahimi—men who, though serving under Ben Bella, profoundly disagreed with him.

Behind the façade of wartime unity, the Algerian revolutionaries were so divided that there were many groups which escaped the direct authority of both the GPRA and the ALN. As was the case in France after the liberation, the maquis suddenly and mysteriously received a dramatic increase in numbers. In Algeria, with independence, the number of maquisards rose from a true maximum of 10,000 to an official reckoning of 130,000—a figure which worried even the demagogic Ben Bella. The ALN of the borders suddenly swelled from 40,000 to an estimated 120,000. Inevitably in such circumstances, the new influx consisted largely of riff-raff. (If the judgements passed on Algerians in this chapter seem harsh, it must be stressed that they refer largely to this group of so-called 'activists' and certainly not to the overwhelming majority of the Algerian population, which to this day remains an apathetic spectator.) Unfortunately it was this riff-raff that was to form the nucleus of the post-war FLN. It was they who supplied the image of the politically active Algerian. Algerians themselves have been the first to admit that the outcome was ugly and uninspiring.

The result was that the tendency for power to be concentrated in the hands of those with the guns, always the curse of Algeria, became a prevalent characteristic. The more responsible Algerians were only too aware of this traditional danger and they tried to protect the country from the political domination of any one man, and to curb the lust for power. It was to this end that the Congress of the Soummam in 1956, trying in vain to halt the train of events put in motion by Messali Hadj, had emphasised the need for 'collegial' rule—a concept inherited from the *jemma*: the assemblies which rule the small Berber communities—and had decreed there should be no rank above colonel in the revolutionary army. Similarly, to try and prevent the rule of pistol and gun, it had also decreed 'the precedence of the civilians over the military, and the precedence of the interior over the exterior'.* This went to the very heart of the problem. Not only did the Algerians want to prevent the rule of

---

* A propos of the Soummam Valley resolutions: on August 18, 1965, it was announced in Algiers that a file hidden in the Casbah house of Mme Bou' Arab, sister of the minister, Amar Ouzegane, had been produced by her as the first archives of the revolution. The file, disclosed three years after the attainment of independence, was said to contain the following documents: *Algérie d'Abord* (an appeal to the Grand Rabbi of Algiers, asking the Jews to disassociate themselves from colonialism); reports on Frenchmen sympathetic or hostile to the insurrection; minutes of secret negotiations; diagrams of the secret organisation of the FLN; and—most important of all—the first draft of the resolutions of the Soummam Valley Congress in 1956. It was announced that these would be published in *Révolution Africaine*, edited by Ouzegane. But none of them saw the light of day, for the relevant issue of the journal was seized and Ouzegane dismissed by Boumedienne. No reason was given for this: another mysterious incident in the annals of modern Algeria.

force; they also wanted the revolution to remain essentially Algerian. They wanted their own brand of revolution, not one imported by politicians in exile. Hence the precedence of the 'interior' over the 'exterior'.

All the internal feuds among nationalist leaders have centred around this theme. The greatest struggle was that of Ben Bella and Khider (men of the 'exterior') against men, like Boudiaf, who belonged more to the 'interior'. Ben Bella and Khider were not able to attend either the CRUA meeting which decided on the revolution nor the Congress of the Soummam Valley, and their opponents held this against them. In turn, they held that their non-participation at the Soummam Congress invalidated much of what was decided there.

Feuds were the rule. The Wilayas clashed with the 'exterior', and with the GPRA and the ALN. The ALN clashed with the GPRA. The all-powerful Fédération de France, taking advantage of its geographical autonomy, clashed with everyone, with the GPRA as well as the ALN. There were also disputes within these large groups: regional disputes (particularly pro- and anti-Kabyle), clan disputes and personal disputes. These were usually resolved by a règlement de compte: rivals were physically eliminated, with or without a judicial process. To add to the confusion, the Algerians became almost neurotically security-conscious, seeing spies behind every bush—hardly surprising, perhaps, in view of the excellence of the French intelligence service. But this suspicion of everyone, which will probably characterise Algerian political life for a long time to come, became an easy pretext for getting rid of the opponent, a justification for the removal of the rival.

There are no figures available, but the Algerians certainly killed more of their own countrymen than they did French colonial occupiers. (See above, page 55, for French losses.) How many more is anyone's guess. The feud was particularly bitter between the FLN and Messali Hadj's Mouvement Nationaliste Algérien, successor to his Parti Populaire Algérien. These rivals fought each other with more intensity and cruelty—and with more result—than they ever attacked the French. Of course, the French played their part, doing their best to increase the antagonism between the two. The struggle between the FLN and the MNA was conducted with great savagery not only in the backstreets of Paris and Brussels but in

Algeria as well. On June 2, 1957, 300 Messalists were horribly butchered in the village of Melouza. Though the FLN tried to lay the blame on French shoulders, this was in fact their own work. It would need volumes to describe all the feuds, plots and counter-plots among the revolutionaries. Only one thing was clear: although lip-service continued to be paid to the decision of the Soummam Congress, in practice events took exactly the opposite turn. The 'military' took precedence over the 'civilians', and the 'exterior' over the 'interior'. To complicate matters even further, the 'military of the exterior' took precedence over the 'military of the interior'. This second development was to have important repercussions later.

While all this dissension was boiling away, inside Algeria the French were succeeding in cutting off the various Wilayas from each other. Each Wilaya was thrown back on itself and internal divisions assumed greater importance. Even now, the Kabyles still accuse the ALN of the border districts of having supplied arms to the frontier Wilayas at their expense. Colonel Mohand ou El-Hadj said openly that he would never forgive Boumedienne (whose ally he became, however, after Ben Bella's overthrow) for 'parading with arms which we needed to defend ourselves'. What actually happened was that the Wilayas near the frontiers simply helped themselves to the supplies which had to pass through their territories to reach the interior. The snatching of arms coming from Tunisia and Morocco was, indeed, one of the favourite pastimes of the commanders of the border Wilayas. At the same time, outside Algeria the gulf was deepening between the GPRA and the ALN. The split only became obvious to the world when, a few days before entering Algeria, the GPRA dismissed Colonel Boumedienne and his general staff. Close observers, however, had noticed several years earlier that Boumedienne was no longer leaving his Ghardimau headquarters to report to the GPRA in Tunis as he should have done. Only Boussouf, his former superior, could persuade him to come to Tunis. (Later on these two men also fell out.)*

While these many feuds were being pursued with such intensity,

---

* Before taking over the EMG-ALN, Colonel Boumedienne was chief of Wilaya V. He took over the command here from Boussouf, whose assistant he was. In between Wilaya V and the EMG, Colonel Boumedienne headed COM-OUEST.

another phenomenon was emerging—one which was to determine the shape of independent Algeria. The ALN was building itself into the only organised body of Algerians. It is hardly necessary to say that the ALN did not achieve this without much internal strife of its own. On one occasion, during the famous 'plot of the colonels', it even went so far as to call in the Tunisian Guarde Nationale to quell, on Tunisian soil, rebel elements of the ALN. But whereas Boumedienne and his young political commissars eventually achieved a high standard of discipline—and indoctrination—among the Algerian troops, the GPRA became increasingly bureaucratic and 'bourgeois', and the 'interior' increasingly feudal. Critics have said that the ALN was able to achieve greater cohesion because, fighting a static war opposite the French barrages, it had plenty of time to concentrate on other things. It has even been suggested that it was frustration at not being able to fight the French properly which led to the ALN's becoming politically vicious. In reply to the first remark it can be said that at least the ALN used its spare time intelligently: to the second, that although it may contain an element of truth, there would have been no Evian but for the ALN. The fact remains, however, that the ALN as a whole began to reflect the personality of its founder and chief, Colonel Houari Boumedienne. It became self-sufficient and secretive, rarely raising its voice. Later events were to show that it had developed a distinctive esprit de corps—a certain fanaticism, indeed—which set it apart from the Algerian people at large. Today, it is esteemed, respected, feared—but not greatly loved.

The ALN was indeed remarkable in many ways, as I was able to observe, being one of the few to visit it during the war. Discipline was almost spartan and great efforts were made to overcome illiteracy. The attitude to the enemy was extraordinary: simple soldiers were taught that 'the enemy is not France or Frenchmen, but the colonialists—who happen in this case to be the French'. At a higher level, the officers of the ALN gave more thought to post-independence problems than did the GPRA. They even considered the crucial problems of the vineyards and of oil (first mentioned in the army periodicals). The ALN, who wanted their own food supplies, ran two farms in Morocco (called 'A' and 'B'). There I saw young Algerians trying to gain practical experience in agricultural problems. This very down-to-earth, almost Chinese, revolutionary approach resulted in useful advice to the *fellah*. Instead of being instructed in the use of the tractor, which he would never be able to afford, he was shown how to better his lot without extravagance by switching from the sickle (generally used in the Maghrib) to the more practical European scythe. When independence was in sight, the ALN put out such slogans as: 'A cease-fire is not peace—the revolution goes on', or 'An army of the people for the people', or 'The gun in one hand, the pick in the other'.

While the ALN was building itself into a revolutionary group with a strong esprit de corps, the civilians—the GPRA—were concentrating on day-to-day problems to the exclusion of those of the future. They made no attempt to study agrarian reform or the problem of Saharan oil. They gave as little thought to the host of other questions which would confront them the day they entered Algeria. Most surprisingly, they did not even tackle the problem of the FLN itself. It was referred to as a 'party', but it had no basic party structure or common ideology. The question was unresolved at the time of Ben Bella's overthrow, when those in power were still wrestling with the fundamental problem of converting the FLN into a proper political institution.

The question of a political programme was not even considered at the CNRA meetings that followed the Soummam Congress. Ben Bella first began to think of establishing a programme for the FLN only when he emerged from gaol. This was known as the 'Tripoli Programme' because it was supposed to have been adopted at the CNRA's meeting in Libya in May-June 1962—'supposed' because it is known that this meeting took no decisions and ended in complete failure. The Tripoli Programme was a hastily written document, compiled in a few days at Hammamet in Tunisia, written at the request of, but not by, Ben Bella. The first two chapters were written by Rheda Malek and Mostefa Lacheraf—wartime editors of *El Moudjahid*—and the third by Mohammed Harbi and Ben Yahia (ambassador in Moscow and then in London). The document acknowledged all the wartime failings of the FLN.

During the first congress of the FLN in Algiers in April 1964, another analysis of the wartime period was put forward, one which bore the imprint of Mohammed Harbi's lucid brain. This, the Charter of Algiers (see above pages 9–11), was not strictly impartial, for it was designed to consolidate the position of Ben Bella. Moreover, Harbi and his colleagues were anxious to give it a strongly socialist slant. It is not surprising if it therefore takes an unusually harsh view of the GPRA and is slightly equivocal on the subject of the ANP (as the ALN was known after independence) to which Ben Bella and, even more, Harbi, were strongly opposed. But with these provisions, the Charter of Algiers does give quite an accurate analysis of the failure of the FLN.

In short, the FLN entered independence as a national and very patriotic front, successful in having won a war of liberation. But it had very little to offer in the way of social reform, and it reflected faithfully the divisions which bedevil Algerian society. The only group which knew its own mind was the ALN—and it also had the means of enforcing its policies.

4

A SUMMER OF SHAME

THE STORY of how the Algerian nationalist leaders entered their own country does not constitute one of the shining pages of history. While the French were still in power as the colonial occupiers, the GPRA—based on Tunis under the leadership of Ben Khedda—asked them to close the barrages against its own army of national liberation. (A few outlets had been opened after the Evian Agreements to allow refugees and some officials to pass through.) They made this extraordinary request in order to reach Algiers and seize power before the ALN and Ben Bella could get control. Earlier in June, the GPRA had officially dismissed the chief of the general staff of the ALN, Colonel Boumedienne: an empty gesture since the GPRA was in no position to enforce the order. At first the GPRA denied having made such a request to the French, but a few days later, on July 10, 1962, in an interview with a British journalist Ben Bella stated that the opening of the barrages to the ALN constituted the 'acid test of French goodwill towards Algeria'.

I was able to judge matters for myself, for it was when trying to return to Tunisia that I found the barrages sealed again. A companion and I were miraculously able to cross after a French colonel took personal responsibility and ordered the gates to be opened just for the passing of our car. Two French tanks stood by and the gates were immediately closed again. The forces of the ALN were opposite, angry at being stopped. They immediately formed a hostile circle around the privileged beings for whom the barrages had been opened. Luckily, two of them recognised me (I had spent some time in their unit) and shouted '*Naruf*'—We know him!

Under the original agreement, the GPRA were due to enter Algiers on July 10, 1962. The French agreed to accommodate them to the extent of allowing them to enter on July 3. There were still some 500,000 Frenchmen in Algeria, many of them OAS terrorists, and the authorities feared another Congo; they hoped the GPRA would be able to prevent further catastrophes. But de Gaulle was determined to give the Algerians their territorial independence and he was not prepared to go back on the Evian Agreement and take sides in internal quarrels by closing the gates to the ALN—particularly as the French intelligence services expected the combination of Ben Bella and ALN to triumph over the GPRA. De Gaulle indeed saw Ben Bella as a trump card up his sleeve. Ben Bella had been a sergeant in the French army and it has been held that the general liked the idea of helping this man (whom, it is said, he had himself decorated on the Italian front in the second world war) to become the leader of Algeria.* The GPRA's demand was transmitted to Paris by General de Brebisson, the commander-in-chief in Algeria, but it was rejected and the first troops of the ALN entered Algeria from Morocco on July 3. As they reached Oran, the population shouted 'Long Live Ben Bella!' When this ALN column ran short of fuel, tankers of the French army, by some mysterious coincidence, were on the spot in time to refuel them. This gesture of the French was taken as further evidence that Paris was backing the Ben Bella–ALN combination.

The ALN on the Tunisian side entered the next day, but had to advance more cautiously since the Wilayas it had to cross to reach Algiers, were not, unlike Oran, well-disposed to Ben Bella. Colonel Boumedienne had meanwhile disappeared in order to avoid the gangs sent out by the GPRA to eliminate him. He hid in the desert where the first to rally to him was Colonel Chaabani, head of Wilaya VI. (Later, as we shall see, Boumedienne was to order the execution of Chaabani, branding him a 'traitor'.)

The Evian Agreement, in fact, was the signal for the Algerians to abandon restraint and bring their quarrels out into the open. In 1958, the first GPRA had, as a gesture of solidarity, appointed Ben Bella one of its vice-presidents and Boudiaf, Hocine, Khider and Bitat as ministers of state, although they were imprisoned in France. During the Evian talks, the GPRA issued frequent assurances from Tunis that their imprisoned brothers were not being forgotten

* It should be noted that official French sources have neither confirmed nor denied Ben Bella's claim that he was decorated personally by de Gaulle.

during the negotiations. From their comfortable château prison in France, the five 'historic chiefs' denounced the results of their *ikhwan*'s negotiations. Events were to prove that Ben Bella's disapproval was only tactical, for he made the Agreement work more smoothly than the French could ever have hoped. At the time, however, he managed to jeopardise the negotiations by inducing all Algerian prisoners in France to go on a hunger strike until a clause was inserted in the agreement providing for their immediate release. Shortly afterwards the ALN opened fire fiercely from Tunisia, in the Ain-Zana region, and advanced across no-man's land right up to the barrages. They did this as a reminder of their presence and to mark their disapproval of the Evian concessions, regardless of the fact that the army was represented at Evian by Commanders Slimane and Mendjli and a third ALN delegate. But de Gaulle was adamant. The war was to end and a new phase of history was to begin, in which an independent Algeria would maintain close links with France. The salvos of the ALN were ignored both by the French troops manning the barrages and the negotiators at Evian.

To understand the situation, it is necessary to return to the last meeting of the CNRA at Tripoli on May 27 of the same year (1962), the meeting supposed to have approved the Tripoli Programme—the revolution's only document of any value. The session was stormy. After their release from gaol, Ben Bella and his companions in captivity had first rejoined the ALN at Oujda in Morocco. It was quite clear to eye-witnesses that they were astonished to find such a well-organised and disciplined army, for they could only remember the ragged bands of the beginning of the war. Now, in Tripoli, Ben Bella and Boumedienne joined forces in rejecting the Evian Agreement and denouncing the GPRA for having made too many concessions to the French. Ben Bella asked the CNRA to appoint a new government, but this was opposed by Ben Khedda who wanted to remain in power and enter Algiers as head of the government which had brought peace to the country. Ben Bella persisted, suggesting that the CNRA appoint a 'political bureau' to rule Algeria until a national assembly and legally constituted government could be formed. The army tried to arrest Ben Khedda and other ministers in Tripoli, but they escaped to Tunis in time. (It is worth noting here that when Nasser's mediator, Ali Sabri, came to Tripoli to try to smooth the quarrel, the UAR sided with the GPRA rather than with

Ben Bella whom Nasser considered 'obstinate' and a 'loser'.) The meeting broke up in confusion, but Ben Bella emerged maintaining that it had approved the formation of a 'political bureau', although in fact there had been no majority in favour of this or any other plan. In early July, when the GPRA tried to dismiss the general staff of the army, the latter refused to obey, arguing that it had been installed by power of the CNRA and could only be dismissed by the same body. The GPRA retorted that the CNRA had certainly decided on the institution of the general staff, but that the nomination of officers was at the discretion of the GPRA. This legal argument carried little weight in practice since no one could prise Boumedienne from the army he had created with such care.

Thus it came about that, on the day of Algeria's triumph, the GPRA and the ALN entered Algiers as two bitterly opposed factions, each seeking to destroy the other by violent methods. After the Tripoli meeting, Ben Bella himself while at Tunis airport suddenly jumped, by pre-arrangement with the UAR embassy, into an Egyptian plane. Mohammed Khider said at the time that Ben Bella had escaped to prevent being killed or arrested by the Tunisians at the request of the GPRA. The Tunisians denied this, but observers noted that shortly afterwards the chief of security at Tunis's El-Aouina airport lost his job.

What support could the two sides count on? The GPRA had the support of Wilaya III and the Berbers of Kabilya. The ALN and Ben Bella had the support of the Chaoui Berbers of Wilaya I (the Aurès), of Wilaya V, and of the head of Wilaya VI. The province and town of Constantine were divided into pro- and anti-GPRA factions. It was in this Wilaya that Commander Slimane was arrested and put in chains on July 10, accused of inciting the people against the GPRA. There remained the all-important Wilaya IV, which included Algiers. Si Hassan, the colonel in charge of this province, after Evian had increased the strength of his troops from an estimated 8,000 to 35,000 but he did not appear able to control all the revolutionary groups mushrooming around him. He seemed, moreover, to want to play a solitary hand. The situation in Algiers itself was complicated by the existence of the 'Autonomous Zone', comprising the heart of the capital under the command of Colonel Azzeddine and Commander Oussedik: two revolutionaries who had organised the zone on socialist lines. The French press, always on the look-out for analogies with the French revolution, baptised it 'le régime de la Commune d'Alger', pointing out that even the vegetable gardens had been nationalised. The 'Commune d'Alger' had been very successful against the OAS but, the need for action over, it began to look like an amateur experiment in socialism. Nevertheless, there it was: well-armed, well-organised, and in complete control of the Casbah, where it dispensed rough justice through its tribunals.

Ben Khedda attempted to ally himself with the Kabyles of Wilaya III. Ironically, it was a Frenchman* who had last pointed out the dangers of playing off the Berbers against the Arabs, for the capital, although outside Kabilya, had at least 100,000 Berbers settled there as workers. It was known that during the war Wilaya III, under Belkacem Krim, had cast covetous eyes on the capital.

The ALN and Ben Bella redoubled the accusations of high treason they had been hurling at the GPRA after Belkacem Krim recommended that it recognise the truce agreement reached with the OAS by the Provisional Executive, the caretaker body appointed at Evian. The truce agreement had been the idea of the heads of the Provisional Government: Fares, a well-known figure in Algerian life, and Mostefai, a former GPRA ambassador in Morocco. They considered it the only way to avoid bloody encounters between the French rightwing OAS and the incoming ALN, and a means of reassuring Frenchmen and preventing their mass exodus—which they rightly considered would be catastrophic for Algeria. But how to reach an agreement with the killers in the OAS? When Belkacem Krim returned to Algeria, his first visit for many years, he reported that some form of agreement, however unpalatable, was essential, for he too was convinced that a large-scale departure of the French was to be avoided at any price. This was also the opinion of Colonel Azzeddine, the head of the 'Commune d'Alger', who took great pains to prevent the excited bands of Wilaya IV from starting reprisals against French civilians. In the course of his campaign, he was nearly killed himself. The bands missed him but killed his assistant.

While the Algerians were taking up their positions for battle, Ben Bella informed the French that he had, after all, no objections to the

* Colonel Buis, then on the Provisional Executive, now a general, and assistant to the military governor of Paris.

73

Evian Agreement, and Boumedienne issued strict orders to his troops to avoid any contact and, above all, any clash with the French army. The members of the GPRA, busily installing themselves in their new offices, ordered that all pictures of General de Gaulle taken down from the walls should be treated with respect. The ordinary Algerians even took over Bab el-Oued, the notorious stronghold of the OAS, without molesting the Frenchmen remaining there. The revolutionary bands of Wilaya IV, however, had no intention of restraining themselves. They took the law into their own hands and began to pilfer and loot. It was probably these gangs who were responsible for the kidnapping of about 4,000 Frenchmen, who were never heard of again. Ten thousand former French *harkis*, in the police force of the Provisional Executive, had deserted with their arms, and many joined the 'patriots' of Wilaya IV.

The official celebrations on July 5—chosen by the Algerians because it was also the anniversary of the French landing a hundred and thirty years earlier—was probably the only occasion on which the people of the capital truly rejoiced. For the first time in years, the '*you-yous*' of the Algerian women became cries of joy (as they had been at marriage ceremonies in olden days) rather than the cries of defiance they had been under the French. The government wisely forbade the sale of alcohol to Algerians on that day for fear that it might end in disaster. For the first time, the streets of the capital were filled with Algerians, shouting and chanting. (A typical colonialist reaction came from the French owner of a large restaurant in the capital. She said: 'I never knew there were so many Arabs!' She had lived in Algeria for thirty-five years.)

The GPRA used this occasion to make a last bid to retain legal power. In his speech, Ben Khedda said: 'The GPRA will not tolerate any attempt against its authority. The objectives of the revolution can only be gained through the realisation and consolidation of the state.' But even as he was saying this, members of the GPRA were falling out among themselves. Khider resigned to join Ben Bella, who had been touring the Middle East in search of allies, and had arrived triumphantly at Tlemcen on July 12. Others, such as the foreign minister, Saad Dahlab, resigned in disgust and departed for Switzerland. The situation deteriorated rapidly throughout the whole country. A hundred people, including twenty Europeans, were killed during fighting in Oran and two hundred wounded. In this case, order was soon restored by an ALN officer named Bakhti. (He invited the foreign press to witness him threatening to shoot Algerian maquisards caught creating havoc. His action contributed greatly to the ALN's reputation as the upholder of law and order.) There were also two days of fighting in Constantine between pro- and anti-GPRA factions.

It was in Algiers, however, that the situation began to look really ugly. While armed bands were roaming the city, Ben Khedda—by now the sole active representative of the GPRA—was shut up in a house within the compound of the Palais de la Résidence, and other members of the government were wasting with journalists at the Aletti Hotel what time they could spare from their preparations to escape. Mohammed Yazid, minister of Information and spokesman for the GPRA, was in Algiers. Boumendjel had become Ben Bella's spokesman at Tlemcen. Yazid and Boumendjel had been colleagues in the same office in Tunis. Even then each had tended to go his own way; each had had his own group of journalists to whom he fed information; but there had been, at least, a superficial unity. If any-one had dared to hint to them during the war that the Algerians were divided, they would have combined at once to accuse him of fascism. Now they were fighting each other in deadly earnest. In Algiers, lawless activities assumed such proportions that it became dangerous to venture out after five o'clock. The only people who dared to risk the journey between the two main hotels of the capital, the St George's and the Aletti, were the foreign journalists. The nights resounded with shots and cries for help, but no one dared to go out.

Meanwhile, in western Algeria, Ben Bella, with the provinces of Oran and the Aurès solidly behind him, summoned Yacef Saadi to Tlemcen. The wartime organiser of the 'battle of Algiers' was instructed to act as a Trojan horse, prepare his men, and take the Casbah, still under control of Colonel Azzeddine. But before he could carry out these orders, Algiers received a new shock. On July 29, jeeploads of troops wearing the camouflaged uniform and red berets of the French parachutists appeared. The Algerians thought at first that the French, disgusted with anarchy, were reoccupying the city. But it was only the 'justiciers' of Wilaya IV who had come to take possession of the 'commune' and throw its leaders into prison—from which they were quickly released. Yacef Saadi managed to escape while Si Hassan's men were busy removing lorryloads of automatic arms from the Casbah. Once order had been restored, the 'justiciers' settled in to enrich themselves.

In Kabilya, preparations for war were in full swing. The Berbers were getting ready to march on the Arabs of Constantine. Ben Khedda succeeded in preventing this. 'The Algerian people will never forgive us if we start fighting each other now', he said. Similarly, Ben Bella made great efforts to save Boudiaf and Lakhdari Bentobbal, the GPRA minister of the Interior, when they fell into the hands of the ALN. Bitat also interceded in their favour, and both men were released. Five days later the Wilaya chiefs met to discuss the situation at Orléansville, but their decisions were immediately rejected by Boumedienne on the grounds that the ALN had not been represented at the meeting. Finally, on July 22, Ben Bella's head-quarters at Tlemcen announced that the Political Bureau, allegedly instituted by the CNRA at Tripoli, would take over in view of the GPRA's failure to govern since June 12. This announcement was made to outmanoeuvre Ben Khedda who was trying to summon another CNRA meeting, in which Ben Bella and the ALN would probably have been outvoted. But the hour of legal or semi-legal procedure was over. Strength was needed now, and the GPRA had none at all. Boudiaf, who had always maintained that 'the army must not indulge in politics; it must return to barracks', left for Paris—as he was to do over and over again.

Under pressure from Khider, a determined man of action, Ben Bella decided to come to Algiers on August 3. Khider warned Ben Khedda and his colleagues that if they did not come to an agreement with the Tlemcen group, 'the army will rule us all'. When Ben Bella and Ben Khedda appeared on the balcony shaking hands, and Belkacem Krim embraced Ben Bella, the people of Algiers thought that union had been achieved and the nightmare was over. But if Ben Khedda needed Ben Bella, the latter could very well do without the former. That day Ben Bella settled in at the Villa Joly, opposite the summer palace of the former French resident-general. The Villa Joly also housed the Political Bureau. Yacef Saadi, who had re-appeared, kept it constantly guarded by armed men. While the diverse elements were trying to gather support by fair means or foul, there began a period of hard bargaining with Kabyles and Wilaya IV as to the conditions under which the ALN could enter

Algiers. Various agreements were reached but never kept. The main issue was the number of troops Colonel Boumedienne would be allowed to barrack in the capital. But Boumedienne saw no reason why he should be dictated to. He became even less disposed to listen to civilian advice when Ben Bella and Khider, who had his army to thank for getting them to Algiers, began to speak with the voice of Ben Khedda. 'We will establish purely civilian structures. . . . Competent officers and men will be able to join the civilian administration or form the cadres of the future army', Ben Bella said. Khider was even more explicit: 'The national army will be an organ of the state. It will have to derive its means from the state and its authority from the people.' Ben Bella and Khider also added that the Wilayas must abandon their wartime structure and lay down their arms. The Kabyles of Wilaya III, more politically aware, were ready to agree in the hope that their example would restrain the ALN. But Wilaya IV made no attempt to obey. This was not surprising, for there was no one in that Wilaya with sufficient authority to control the armed bands.

These bands of eleventh-hour patriots were responsible for arson and other very ugly crimes. Some professed a 'revolutionary puritanism', and any man and woman seen walking together were likely to be thrown into gaol, if not shot, unless they were married. The secretary of Ferhat Abbas (then president of the Assembly), was nearly married by force to her brother, a Foreign Ministry official, with whom she was walking down the street. Passers-by could only proceed from the sector of any particular band with a pass from that band. Algeria's failure to accomplish the difficult transition from wartime to peacetime mentality is largely attributable to these Wilaya IV bands.

The Political Bureau, protected by Yacef Saadi's men, settled down to build Algeria into a civilian state. Ben Bella was in charge of general administration and liaison with the Provisional Executive. Khider refused a government post, devoting himself to 'building up the party'. His aim was to become its secretary-general. Boudiaf took over Foreign Affairs, Benalla Hadj Military Affairs, and Mohammedi Said Education. Bitat assisted Khider with party matters, trying to organise the party in the different provinces. But while this was happening the ALN was slowly converging on Algiers.

The progress of the troops was slow, not only because they wished to avoid bloodshed, but because they were everywhere establishing their own men and their own administration. The toughest of all the advancing ALN commanders was Colonel Chaabani, head of Wilaya VI (Sahara). His men were equipped with modern heavy arms against which the light arms of Wilaya IV were no match. Better-armed Kabyle units had to come to the rescue. Inevitably the result of these clashes was that, although the country was nominally independent, the French troops, whatever their seclusion and discretion, were still de facto the occupying force. While the Political Bureau argued about who had the right to stand for the National Assembly that was about to be formed—an issue on which Boudiaf resigned because he had not been consulted—fighting broke out between the ALN and Wilayas III and IV. Since some troops of Wilaya II, then commanded by Colonel Saout el Arab, had refused at the last moment to join the ALN's march to Algiers, there were two armed columns progressing towards the city: one coming from the south, from the Sahara; the other from the west, from Oran. Ben Bella and Khider, sensing that Boumedienne would advance come what may, forgot their fears of civil war and appealed to the ALN general staff and to Wilayas I, II, V and VI 'to despatch any troops they deem necessary, and which are under their command, to assist the Political Bureau in establishing order and security, whatever the cost'. Wilayas III and IV retorted 'that they would defend their positions, whatever the cost'. Civil war was beginning.

The roofs of the Casbah were held by hostile groups. Yacef Saadi's men patrolled the harbour in small boats to prevent the Kabyles landing to reinforce their hold on the capital. Civilians swarmed into the Aletti Hotel to plead with the bewildered and powerless ministers of the GPRA to stop the catastrophe. They also broke into Ben Khedda's residence but all he could find to say was: 'You see that I am still here with you. I have not let you down.' The people pleaded with him to intercede and prevent the fighting, but he could only suggest in reply that they should go themselves.

On August 30, the first shots were fired by the troops of Colonel Chaabani at Boghari, some 160 kilometres south of Algiers. Ben Bella, suitably dressed for the occasion in an ALN uniform, went to Tiaret to witness the departure of the ALN troops for the capital. His vehicle was surrounded by people pleading with him to stop the fighting. At Aumale, nearer Algiers, there was a heavy engagement between the forces of Wilaya IV, reinforced Kabyle units, and Chaabani's forces. No one knows exactly how·many were killed in that battle but the numbers were large—3,000 is the generally accepted figure. Fighting also broke out in the Casbah in Algiers after an unknown person had fired into some French barracks. The French soldiers were not involved, and they watched the men of the Political Bureau fight the aggressors. To many Frenchmen, the spectacle avenged their enforced departure from Algiers. Ben Khedda at this point blundered heavily, alleging that French troops had 'perpetrated an aggression'. But the Political Bureau was quick to exculpate the French, placing the burden squarely where it belonged: on the shoulders of the irregulars of Wilaya IV. Around Orléansville, the fighting continued and the bodies began to decay under the burning sun.

While the ALN and the Wilayas were fighting, I was travelling to Algiers by car with a friend, B.M. He was a Moroccan of Mauretanian origin: a fierce Maghribine nationalist, a man of pride and principle, a man of action and of the left, and a correspondent for *At Tahrir*, the main leftwing opposition newspaper in Morocco. We were constantly stopped by hostile patrols and subjected at gunpoint to all manner of threats. We were suspect because travelling from Oran, which was under the control of the ALN. As it grew dark, we became exceedingly apprehensive when a column of soldiers loomed in sight—until they proved to be French soldiers, who let us proceed unhindered. After some hesitation, I said: 'B., let's be honest. I hate to say this, but I'm thankful that those soldiers wore French and not Algerian uniform. I don't wish to hurt your feelings, but that's what I feel.' B. looked stunned for a moment. Then he bowed his fine head and whispered: 'Yes. It is a tragedy, but I feel the same.' In many parts of the world, especially in the Maghrib and the Middle East, others felt the same too. After nearly five generations of colonial rule and seven-and-a-half years of war, Algeria—the paladin of revolutionary nationalism—was rending itself in civil war.

Then suddenly the civil war came to an abrupt halt. Not as the result of political action or any change of heart on the part of Boumedienne (who proceeded to enter Algiers as planned), but because the people of Algiers, among them women bearing children in their arms, threw themselves between the fighting men. 'We want bread. We don't want war', they shouted. '*Baraket, Sabba s'nine, baraket*—Enough, seven years of it, enough!' The ALN officers, ashamed, grounded their troops' arms.

When the Political Bureau, victorious at last, appeared on the balcony of the Forum from which the OAS leaders a little while before had thrilled tens of thousands of French settlers, there were only a couple of thousand Algerians to applaud them. Independence found the Algerian people cruelly wounded and sick at heart.

5

BEN BELLA IN POWER

BEN BELLA took over in midsummer 1962 and was overthrown in midsummer 1965. Events during this period were widely varied, succeeding each other with lightning speed. In a way, this was natural for the country was changing hands after a very long period of colonial occupation, and the Algerians are a dynamic people. But Ben Bella's volatility gave the chain of occurrences a particularly bewildering and chaotic tempo. A man of no established principles, he continually indulged in voltes-face and intrigues of all kinds.

A detailed chronicle of the events of these three years would add little to the reader's grasp of the situation. Arguments of 'this is revolution' failed to convince bewildered observers, trying to make some sense out of the swiftly changing Algerian kaleidoscope. Whereas most revolutionary upheavals and disorders have their own logic, events in Algeria make little sense to those seeking an 'inner revolutionary coherence'. The leaders of the new state tried to explain away the chaos by a phrase which has since become a classic: 'We Algerians are like no other people, and our revolution is like no other revolution.' This reflected a certain pride, fully justified by the immense wartime exertions of the nationalists; but it also indicated their perplexity and their inability to make anything out of the post-war confusion over which they presided.

Economic and Social Problems

There were two different categories of problems and difficulties with which Ben Bella had to contend. The first category was summarised in the Charter of Algiers as follows:

1. Underdevelopment characterised by: weak industry; the employment of the main strength of the population in agricultural work; underemployment and unemployment; illiteracy aggravated by the difficulty of obtaining a reasonable education—a difficulty due to the shortage of teachers; and lack of technical personnel.

2. An economy strongly dependent on the former coloniser—disconnected and vulnerable to begin with, disorganised and paralysed by the departure of French managers and technicians; an economy groaning under the burden of investments made according to colonialist and neocolonialist plans.*

3. Aggravation of our social problems due to: the departure of French doctors and the sabotage of certain medical installations; the rise in unemployment due to the abandonment of projects during the recession; the increase in the numbers of socially dependent persons, e.g. war-widows and orphans and war-invalids; the increasing exodus from the country to the town.

The expression 'underdeveloped', when applied to Algeria refers to the underdevelopment of the land. In fact, the country's main problems—past, present and future—all spring from this land problem. The *fellah* form 70 per cent of the population, and agricultural commodities 38 to 40 per cent of the total value of exports. (See Appendix III, Table 2, on social structure of population, and Table 5 on Algerian exports to France. This latter table indicates clearly the vital importance of agriculture to the Algerian economy.)

According to ALN statistics, the social composition of Algeria during the war of independence was as follows: Algerians 11,000,000; French 390,000; other Europeans 450,000; Jews 160,000. Of the Algerian muslim population, 7,000,000 lived by agriculture (200,000 being classified as 'agricultural workers'); 300,000 were employed in industry and trade, 400,000 were working in France, 650,000 were part-time workers, and there were about 1,000,000 unemployed. In the distribution of the land, 532,000 muslim Algerians owned a total of 7,672,000 hectares, the average holding being 14 hectares, of which an average of 5 were productive. Some 22,000 Europeans owned 2,720,000 hectares, representing an average holding of 108 hectares, 62 of which, on average, were produc-

* I.e., investments aimed at enriching France rather than Algeria.

tive. As regards utilisation of land: in northern Algeria the cultivated surface was 4,400,000 hectares (21 per cent of the total surface); of approximately 400,000 hectares under cultivation for vines, 90 per cent belonged to Europeans, while 93 per cent of the 30,000 hectares cultivated for citrus fruits were European-owned. At this period there were 19,940 tractors in use in Algeria, of which 19,440 belonged to European farmers.

These figures show that 70 per cent of the Algerian population lived in rural areas, and that 60 per cent of the total population derived its livelihood directly from agricultural activities. Some 22,000 French or other European landowners, possessing the most fertile land, produced about 60 per cent of the gross agricultural revenue. In terms of income, this European minority, representing only 4 per cent of the total population, made striking profits amounting to 53 per cent of the total net agricultural revenue and to at least 12 to 15 per cent of the national income. No wonder they tried so desperately to cling to the Algerian soil! Of 580 billion (old) francs estimated as national income for 1954, 800,000 Europeans made 480 billion (old) francs—an annual average per head of 600,000 (old) francs; while 9 million muslim Algerians made 100 billion (old) francs—an annual average per head of 11,000 (old) francs.

Industry was weak, employing a mere 200,000 people (Algerians and Europeans) and absorbing only 15 per cent of the country's agricultural products. In turn, agriculture assimilated only 8 per cent of the country's industrial production. Both sectors got their essential requirements from France.

The agrarian economy was itself divided into two sectors: the modern and the traditional. The French sector, employing up-to-date methods and relatively few people, produced 60 per cent of the country's agricultural goods; the Algerian sector consisted of the mass of the peasants, toiling at subsistence level and clinging to traditional methods. With little to offer and with only minimal spending power, the *fellah* was of no interest to other branches of the economy. In a confidential report in 1964, a UN team of experts estimated the income of a 'typical' family in the Médéa region as follows:

(a) This family has 6 hectares which are used in a two-year wheat-fallow cycle. The yield is 5·2 quintals per hectare [7·748

English bushels per acre]; thus the family produces 15·6 quintals. Ten quintals of wheat are sold at the wholesale price of 50 dinars* per quintal; the remaining 5·6 are home-consumed and are valued—as an absolute maximum—50 per cent higher than the wholesale price.

(b) Forty per cent of gross income is derived from animal production on the 3 hectares of fallow ground.

(c) Costs of production are 5 per cent of gross income. Hence total net family income is about 1,223·60 dinars. This is broken down as follows [figures in dinars]:

Sale of wheat	500	
Home consumption of wheat	420	
Income from wheat		920
Income from livestock		368
Gross income		1,288
Expenses	64·40	
Net income		1,223·60

To the extent that home-grown and home-consumed vegetables and fruits have been omitted, the above figure underestimates net family income. But in any case net income is unlikely to be higher than 1,500 dinars, i.e. about $300. Per capita income, then, is likely to be between $50 and $60. In other areas of the traditional sector, it is officially estimated that per capita income is 200 dinars, i.e. $40.

It is evident that such a unit could be of little economic significance, either as producer or consumer. Moreover, the UN example is that of a fairly well-off rather than of a typical *fellah* family.

The economic tragedy of Algeria is that, though an essentially agricultural country, there is very little good land available for farming. In the ancient past there were large forests and grazing areas, but over the centuries these have largely disappeared, partly because of the remorseless advance of the desert northwards from the Sahara, and partly because of the failure to control erosion. The colonialists also spoiled much good land through the dry farming

* As from April 20, 1964 Algeria, while remaining in the French Franc Zone, changed its monetary unit from the franc to the dinar, 1 Algerian Dinar equalling 1 French Franc. The first dinar banknotes were printed in England.

methods and the mechanised monoculture of the settlers. Neglect and destruction (particularly napalm bombing) during the war have aggravated the land-scarcity problem. It is estimated that the country, with a total surface of 850,000 square miles (seven-eighths of which are desert), possesses only 10 million hectares of cultivable land. The total cultivated surface is between 6 and 7 million hectares, of which 2.5 million each year has to lie fallow. Good, regularly tilled land is reckoned as being between 4 and 5 million hectares only. Since independence, the cultivated area is of the following order: some 4 million hectares are under cereals cultivation; vineyards cover 350,000 hectares, citrus fruits trees 100,000, horticulture 100,000 and fodder-crops 60,000. Most cultivation is done in northern Algeria—in the Constantine, Algérois and Oranie provinces which together constitute some 29.5 million hectares, but of which only 6.7 million are cultivable.

At the beginning of the colonial period (*circa* 1830), Algeria's forests were estimated to cover 4·5 million hectares; today there remain only 2·5 million, and much of the existing forest areas is in an advanced state of deterioration. The war created great destruction of livestock. Before the war, there were reckoned to be 6·5 million sheep, 3 million goats and 1 million head of cattle. In 1963 the figures were: sheep 4 million; goats 1·5 million; cattle 0·3 million. The loss here was the more severe in that it mainly affected the traditional sector of agriculture, wholly muslim, which represented roughly one-fifth of the gross agricultural revenue.

Such was the state of the country's agriculture when Ben Bella came to power. It was the most serious of the many problems facing his regime. Yet agriculture, however vital, was only one aspect of the economic structure created by the French: a structure which any nationalist government would need to amend drastically.

The colonial regime imposed on Algeria a marked economic dualism, leading to the coexistence of two economies: one over-developed (that of the French settlers), the other underdeveloped (that of the traditional muslim Algerians). The modern economic structure left behind by the French was, in fact, composed of various sectors, unconnected and often in conflict. This made economic unification on a national scale very difficult. The economic divisions of Algeria are such that it is cheaper to trade between northern Algeria and France than between Constantine and Oran.

Lines of communication run from south to north—towards France; east-west communication is much more difficult. The French were concerned primarily with linking the Sahara to northern Algeria and the latter to France. Thus, the zones of Bône, Philippeville, Bougie, Algiers and Oran each have close economic relations with France but none with each other. Oran, because of its European population of Spanish descent, also has had closer ties with Spain than with any other Algerian region.* Far from being complementary, the main zones are rivals: vineyards in the region of Algiers compete with those of the region of Oran: iron ore from Ouenza, near Bône, with the iron ore extracted near Tlemcen; vegetables and citrus fruit of the Mitidja against those of the plain of Bône—all being essentially destined for export to France.

The vineyards in the Maghrib present a pleasant sight—to the eye of the visitor; but from the point of view of the muslim populations in this area, they are symbols of colonial economic exploitation, and have become a great problem since independence. The intensive cultivation of vines in Algeria and the rest of the Maghrib dates from the 1880s, following the great damage done to French vineyards by the phylloxera. The settlers took over the best flat lands for vine cultivation, although planting in the hills would have done just as well and would, moreover, have helped to prevent erosion. Although the largest area of cultivable land in Algeria is taken up with cereal production, the value of the wine output is considerably greater. Between 1951 and 1957, wine represented 51 per cent of the value of planned production as against 24 per cent for cereals. (Vegetables represented 10·1 per cent, fruits 12·1 per cent and industrial enterprises 2·9 per cent.) But today these vineyards are nothing but an embarrassment. The 15 to 16 million hectolitres produced annually before independence were absorbed either by purchasers in metropolitan France or by Frenchmen living

---

* In 1856, some 176,000 Spaniards settled in Oran and their number was to grow quickly thereafter. Though they became French by nationality, they retained their Spanish characteristics to the point where, at independence, I was amazed on going to the small town of Rio de Oro to find that even municipal correspondence was conducted in Spanish. During the French occupation, Oran was the liveliest of all Algerian towns because of its Spanish population. As a result, Spanish influence, already historic, went deeper among muslims of the Oran province. A number of Algerians, including Ben Bella and Bouteflika, speak Spanish.

in Algeria. This utter dependence on the French market for wine continues. There is very little local consumption of wine in muslim countries, and alternative outlets are hard to find. (The Moroccans tried to popularise unfermented grape juice as a beverage, but failed. Muslims were suspicious of it, considering grape juice to be much the same thing as wine in the Koranic injunction against alcohol.) Plans to uproot the vineyards were considered, but soon abandoned. Not only would the process be extremely expensive: the land would also have to lie fallow for some years. So Algeria, like Tunisia and Morocco, remains dependent on French willingness to accept her most valuable export, and France is in a position to exert considerable pressure on her former colonies in return for the purchase of the vine-crop. In 1965, Tunisia was in a desperate situation: the depots were full of the previous year's stocks which the French had refused to buy (this was a reprisal for the nationalisation of French-owned land), and there was nowhere to store the new harvest. As for Algeria: although by the end of 1965 a fundamental agreement had been reached with France over oil and gas (see Chapter 9), there was still a great question mark hanging over the Algerian wine trade—would France buy the year's vintage or not?

It is, however, in foreign trade that independent Algeria is most dependent on the former coloniser. Traditionally, Algeria sends 80 per cent of her exports to France, while French goods constitute between 60 and 65 per cent of Algerian imports. The country's export trade is based on four main commodities: oil (45 per cent of total exports); wine (28 per cent); fruit and vegetables (14 per cent); and mineral products (3·3 per cent). All of these go to France. The vulnerability of such a trade is too obvious to require comment. And, as can be expected in a former colonial country, imports consist largely of consumer goods. (See Appendix III, Tables 5 and 6.)

Under the colonial regime, there was practically no internal trade. Algeria was dependent on France financially as well as economically. In 1961 a recession set in, for many Frenchmen, realising that the war was beginning to turn against them, started to withdraw capital from the country. It is estimated that by midsummer 1962 the total of bank deposits had dropped by about 110 billion francs, while unpaid terms amounted to about another

20 billion. Exactly how much capital left the country is anyone's guess. Transfer of funds to France was free, and it is estimated that returning settlers took back to France at least 400 billion francs.

Another great problem was the acute shortage of qualified personnel. This has been a stumbling block to nationalist progress for many countries of the Third World, but the shortage assumed grave importance in Algeria, not only because there was so much to reconstruct, reorganise and create, but because of the highly complex administrative and economic organisation left by the French. The European exodus was catastrophic for Algeria in many ways. Over a million Europeans left and by 1964 there were under 100,000 in Algeria.* Algeria was left almost entirely devoid of professional and technical personnel. Some 300,000 of the Europeans had been engaged in active work: 15,000 had belonged to the higher administrative levels or liberal professions; 33,000 were of managerial level; 35,000 were skilled workers and some 200,000 occupied posts requiring a higher than average technical or general level of education. The sudden departure of the people who were running practically all the small industries and trades, and who together formed the market for nearly all the consumer goods, left the Algerian economy and administration completely paralysed.

It was then that the Algerians began to pay both for the past colonial policies of the French and for their own failure to make some attempt to train the necessary personnel during the war. (This is dealt with more fully in chapter 9.)

In chapter 1, we mentioned that France, perhaps the most cultured nation in the world, deliberately denied education to the Algerians from the time French troops landed in 1830. In spite of all the promises made by the Allies during the second world war, France was still practising educational discrimination in Algeria in 1954. In that year, of a total of 5,146 students of all races at Algiers University, only 557 were muslim Algerians (see Appendix III,

* According to an official French release, there were in Algeria on March 31, 1965, 92,086 Frenchmen of both 'SF' and 'SE' categories (meaning of 'French' and 'Foreign stock'—*Souche française* and *Souche étrangère*) of whom 41,376 were in Algiers, 21,140 in Oran (the zone of French of Spanish origin), 3,816 at Ouargla, 3,317 at Asnam (formerly Orléansville) and 2,825 at Constantine. There were groups of 2,000 to 3,000 French at Blida, Bougie, Colomb-Béchar, Mostaganem and Sidi-Bel-Abbes (former HQ of the Foreign Legion) and groups below 2,000 at Skikda (formerly Philippeville), Tizi-Ouzou, Tlemcen and Batna.

Table 9). As far as the agricultural sciences are concerned, despite the fact that the population is 80 per cent peasant, there were in November 1954 only 381 agricultural students, of whom merely 75 were muslim Algerians. The illiteracy rate was 90 per cent for muslim Algerians and 3 per cent for the European minority.

Ben Bella was furious when Bourguiba criticised the Algerians and stated that they would be unable to carry out their ambitious social schemes because, never having thought of training personnel during the war, they lacked sufficient people with the necessary expertise to plan and administer such schemes. But the Tunisian president was quite right. Extraordinary though it may seem for a movement which, from the start, had claimed its revolution to be essentially agrarian in character, the FLN only made its first study of agrarian reform in 1962—and more by chance than carefully thought-out purpose. Even then, the person commissioned to do the study was a Greek with only a theoretical knowledge of conditions in Algeria.

Such was the economic and social picture when Ben Bella came to power. How did he tackle the country's problems?

Ben Bella's Solution: Dictatorship

'Power tends to corrupt, and absolute power corrupts absolutely.' There have been many illustrations of Lord Acton's maxim throughout history. The case of Ben Bella can certainly be added to the warning examples of modern history.

As he changed his ideology—if, indeed, he ever had one at all—he changed his dress habits, for he wanted his clothes to be 'political symbols'. When first in power, he gave up wearing civilian clothes, adopting the battledress instead in order to identify himself with the ALN which had brought him to power, and also with Fidel Castro. He then discovered a garment even more sublimely symbolic of revolution: the *chung shan*, the Chinese-style tunic. This he adopted after Nkrumah but before Nyerere. It appealed to him as the suitable uniform for a leader of the 'southern hemisphere', such as he aspired to be about this time. However, when at the FLN Congress the army took the line that the leftist adventure had gone too far, Ben Bella not only got rid of Mohammed Harbi and other marxist advisers: he also discarded the *chung shan*. He reverted to civilian clothes, this time evincing a marked preference for spotted silk ties. The Algerians, well aware of the political implications of Ben Bella's wardrobe, were fascinated spectators of his sartorial waverings.

His first preoccupation on coming to power was the 'unity of the Maghrib', but he quickly dropped this for the diametrically opposed concept of Arabism à la Nasser. Then he discovered Black Africa, whereupon the United Arab Republic and its works were abandoned and the 'African vocation of Algeria' became the thing. This, however, eventually proved disappointing and was in its turn abandoned. At this point the internal situation made it expedient to adopt 'socialism'. It was socialism by qualification: first 'Algerian', then 'scientific', and finally 'arabo-islamic'. The political methods used to boost these diverse expedients were of the 'coffee-house' type: mere day-to-day devices, determined largely by the playing off of one individual against another. They proved expensive, and served in the end only to retard Algeria's progress. Ben Bella's chief interest was to maintain himself in power; everything else was secondary and subsidiary—even the formidable task of establishing the Algerian state as a viable undertaking, and of moulding its people into a cohesive society.

Ben Bella took a simple view of life. 'Sincere' or 'convinced' patriots were those men who had joined him at Tlemcen or later in Algiers; those who paid court to him at the Villa Joly, his residence and office. He set out to create a state and a party from the ruins of Algeria guided solely by the simple definition of the good and the true. He recruited 'good patriots' and rejected 'bad patriots' according to a criterion known only to himself. The case of Chanderli exemplifies Ben Bella's procedure. Chanderli was for years the spokesman of the revolution, not from some obscure post but at the United Nations itself. He also represented Algeria at numerous international conferences. For some six months of the Ben Bella regime he was secretary-general at the Ministry of Foreign Affairs. Then—as happens in Algeria—one morning he was unceremoniously rejected. The only explanation given was that Chanderli was 'un faux militant'. Dozens of men in high positions and hundreds in the lower echelons suffered the same fate. Only Ben Bella himself knew what caprice led him to advance or demote any particular préfet, ambassador, minister or head of department.

Nominations, demotions, renominations and redemotions, changes of posts and titles—all became increasingly frequent until the country's administration took on the appearance of some crazy game of general post. With their ready wit, the Algerians called it 'la valse des préfets'. In Oran, the préfet was changed eight times in one year. In the whole of the country, where there are fifteen prefectures, Ben Bella changed préfets two hundred times. There was but one sole qualification required of those in public office: servility. Most high functionaries—after all, one has to live—proved docile careerists. But the effect of Ben Bella's purge of those he didn't fancy was to dissipate Algeria's only available talent. The main responsibility for the rapid transition from revolutionary enthusiasm to petty-minded bureaucracy must be laid at Ben Bella's door.

Under the colonial regime, there was a derisive French term for the 'submissive Arab': *Beni-oui-oui*—'son-of-a-yesman'. Already in the early days of the Algerian National Assembly, pro-government zealots were saying openly that what mattered was not parliament but the party, and one deputy, Zouaoui, even went to far as to use this insulting colonialist expression as a term of commendation for loyal supporters of Ben Bella. As quoted in the *Annuaire d'Afrique du Nord* (Vol. II, page 19), Zouaoui said in a debate: 'What have I come to do here in this Assembly as a member of parliament, as a militant of the party? I have come to defend the decisions taken by the party, just as I do outside this Assembly or in my contacts abroad. . . . Some say here that the militants are *Beni-oui-ouis* in regard to the party, in regard to its discipline. All right: to this I say Yes, twenty times Yes; I am a *Beni-oui-oui*.' The *Annuaire* observes that this statement was made in the chamber 'without raising any protest'.

If the *Beni-oui-ouis* were the 'good patriots', there were certain especial worthies: those belonging to a select band who, with the advice and assistance of Nasser's notorious *Muhabarat* (intelligence), formed the secret police, arresting, imprisoning and torturing the 'bad patriots'. In view of Ben Bella's links with it and of its important role in Arab affairs, a word or two needs to be said here about the activities of the *Muhabarat*. It was to be a factor in arousing resentment in Algeria against Egypt during Ben Bella's regime, resentment which did much to bedevil the pan-Arabist schemes of Nasser and the Algerian leader. Perhaps its most notable effect was its contribution to the collapse of Nasser's greatest Arabist venture: the union with Syria. During the unity talks in March and April, 1963 (the official minutes of which have been made public), the Syrians complained directly to President Nasser that 'there was always the feeling [in Damascus] that the Egyptian government was looking for agents and was not anxious to deal with revolutionaries. . . . To rely on the Secret Service [i.e. the *Muhabarat*] is very dangerous. . . . The Service became dominant. . . . Little confidence was placed in the Syrians.'[1] The story was not different in Algeria where *Muhabarat* agents operated at several levels.

As he rose to power, Ben Bella gradually lost his earlier simplicity of approach and became inflated with a sense of personal pride. The motives that led to his overthrow may have been mixed, but he certainly deserved the charges of 'despotism' and 'dictatorship' levelled against him.

The case of Colonel Chaabani is a good illustration of Ben Bella's devious authoritarian methods. I happened to be present at Tlemcen when Ben Bella privately exclaimed: 'Ah, if only I had seven colonels like Chaabani, there would be no problems whatever.' What he liked in the Colonel was his fanaticism and his 'arabising' tendency (Chaabani 'arabised' his Sahara Wilaya after independence by putting up Arabic signposts in the desert and conducting his official correspondence in Arabic). Before attacking Chaabani, Ben Bella built him up to play him off (with others) against Boumedienne in an attempt to split the monolithic ANP. But Chaabani, a really feudal character, turned against Ben Bella as well as Boumedienne. He and his well-equipped army were captured by Boumedienne after one of Chaabani's companions had betrayed his hiding place. Ben Bella was not allowed to bring Chaabani before one of his 'popular tribunals' nor did Boumedienne allow communication between the nation's leader and the former favourite. Boumedienne was interested in obtaining information from Chaabani about the organisation Ben Bella had created under his direction. Chaabani was questioned, tortured, condemned and executed by Boumedienne's agents. When Ben Bella thought the affair had been closed, he put out the official explanation that Chaabani (and other rebels, such as Hocine Ait Ahmed) were part of a 'counter-revolutionary action linked to foreign interests'.[2]

Though North Africa and the Congo are not to be compared, it is possible to draw a certain parallel between Lumumba and Ben Bella. Both men were far more highly regarded outside their countries than within them. Both undoubtedly had their merits, but neither deserved the reputation accorded them abroad. When officials of the UAR were trying to obtain the release of Ben Bella, they warned Boumedienne that he might become 'another Lumumba'.* The Algerian people, with their long history and their war achievements, deserved something better than a Lumumba!

The era of Ben Bella, however, was not without its bright spot. His regime paid great attention to national education. Algeria became one of the few countries in the world to devote the largest part of its budget (after defence) to education. (See Appendix III, Table 7.) In the school year 1964–65, the number of primary pupils jumped from the pre-independence figure of 750,056 to 1,400,000. In three years, an independent Algerian government had offered schooling to as many young muslim Algerians as colonialism had done in ten years. In the same year the number of university students reached 7,000, of whom over 5,000 were at the university of Algiers (including 809 students from various African countries), and there were also 2,000 Algerians in foreign universities, mainly in France. (Compare these figures with those for 1954, Appendix III, Table 9.) This progress, particularly in the primary schools, was achieved thanks to French teachers who were there in time to start the academic year despite the turbulent midsummer of 1962. This French assistance, however, should not detract from Ben Bella's good work in providing for Algeria's great thirst for education. (See Appendix III, Table 10.)

Under Ben Bella, there was a great effort made to increase the percentage of Algerians in the teaching corps. (See Appendix III, Table 11.) It remains to be seen if there will be an improvement in quality as well as in quantity. In the course of the 'Algerianisation' of the country's educational system, the structure of the school organisation was changed, and a single unified system adopted.

*New Africa, published in London, remarked editorially in its issue of August-September 1965 that Boumedienne should show his strength by employing leniency towards the imprisoned Ben Bella, 'thus escaping the mistake of creating another Lumumba-type martyr'. Both the UAR and the communist press in France and Italy tried (vainly) to make of Ben Bella 'another Lumumba'. (See chapter 10.)

Children were now taught through the medium of Arabic, which was no longer treated as a 'foreign' language, to be learned along with English and Spanish. Of course, the main obstacle here was the lack of adequate teachers, for instructors sent by the UAR were not a success. During the academic year 1962-63, in primary schools 7½ hours a week were devoted to Arabic; this was increased to 10 hours in 1963-64. But in the higher grades of secondary schools, because of the acute shortage of teachers, Arabic was taught for only 4 hours a week. There was a serious shortage of technically trained people; to meet the need, new educational institutions were created to train technicians. For the primary levels of education, a target was set which envisaged by 1970 the provision of 58,000 more classes and the training of 35,000 more teachers. For the secondary levels, the target set was 2,500 more classes and 3,800 more teachers by 1970. (To meet these targets, Algeria in 1965 sought 4,000 more teachers from France; see chapter 9.)

This effort in the field of education explains in part why the few who protested against Ben Bella's overthrow were nearly all students. Of the 4,402 muslim Algerian students at Algiers University, 2,205 had government scholarships.

Simultaneously with this educational drive, there was undertaken 'opération cireurs': Operation Shoeshine Boys. This sought to take off the streets the thousands of wartime orphans who were begging for a living, and accommodate them in houses left empty by departed French families so as to look after them intelligently. It was a positive social measure, certainly, but nowhere nearly so strikingly original and 'revolutionary' as supporters of the regime made out. However, in the absence of any other concrete achievements, Ben Bella found it convenient to use 'opération cireurs' as a propaganda boost for the regime, vaunting it out of all proportion to the actual scope of the scheme. And, in fact, by 1965 the economic situation had deteriorated so fast that child-beggars were again to be seen on the streets: a consequence of the same economic crisis which was leading to serious unemployment among the adult population.

Even when giving the fullest possible credit to Ben Bella for his efforts in the educational field, and taking 'opération cireurs' at his own valuation, one has to conclude that his regime made a deplorably poor showing in tackling the grave social and economic problems of the country. The Tunisians, who were closely interested observers, had few illusions about Ben Bella, and already by the end of 1962 were expressing their doubts about him in private. C. Hourani, Bourguiba's political adviser, told me categorically: 'Ben Bella is an adventurer.'

The reader may wonder to what extent Ben Bella, who grew so quickly to a world-wide fame, was a 'fake'. It is important to realise that even his closest supporters never regarded him as a leader. Generally speaking—and in particular the army—they regarded him as a convenient figurehead, nothing more. This was made abundantly clear to me at the time of the FLN Congress of 1964. I asked Mohammed Harbi, then Ben Bella's chief adviser on socialism, whether it was true that Ben Bella was succumbing to army pressure and letting him down. Harbi replied: 'The problem, as you should know, is not what Ben Bella thinks. The problem is whether this congress will be swayed by the army or by us [meaning Harbi's marxist group]. Ben Bella will then rally to the winning side and be used as a symbol by it.' This view was shared by many of Ben Bella's civilian 'supporters'.

When Ben Bella read out the Charter of Algiers at the same congress, he was seeing much of the text for the first time, including Chapter II ("The Economic Tasks Facing the Socialist Edifice"), which had been written by Harbi and his friends and handed to Ben Bella at the last minute—just in time for him to read with great spirit and conviction! This incident goes a long way to prove the validity of Harbi's first point, for the Charter speech was not the type of address which politicians would normally leave to their aides for drafting. It concerned a 'charter': the document that was to set out the 'philosophy of a new country'. The incident also underlines the fact that there could have been no debates during such meetings, for how could Ben Bella defend a charter of which he did not know the contents? The procedure was that Ben Bella made parrot-like statements; these delivered, the machinery for approval went into action.

The criminal waste of talent was one of Ben Bella's first great mistakes. Apart from the obvious objection that this is no way to run a country, it stands condemned as making Algeria even more dependent on outside (particularly French) technical help than it need otherwise have been. We have the paradox of Ben Bella, so sharp in his censure of neocolonialism, making Algeria once more into a French preserve. Even more serious, his inconstancy and empty manoeuvrings exacerbated the social and economic difficulties of the mass of the people. There is a grim irony in this, for of all Algeria's nationalist leaders he was, by origin, perhaps closer to the mass of the people than the middle-class intelligentsia who furnished most of the prominent figures in the independence movement. There is here both a personal and a national tragedy. Able by his background to appreciate and sympathise with the needs and aspirations of the Algerian peasantry, his government proved to be a lamentable example of 'rhetorical' taking precedence over 'social' revolutionism.

Ben Bella was born on December 25, 1916 at Marnia, a frontier village near the Moroccan border, south of Tlemcen. His family were *fellahin*, owning a small plot of land on which his mother and sisters still lived in a simple way after independence. He had four brothers, none of whom survived to adult life. He finished primary school at Tlemcen at the age of thirteen and went to a secondary school until eighteen. He then joined the French army (it is not clear whether he was conscripted or was a volunteer), and became an adjutant of the 14th RTA; he was mentioned four times in despatches and decorated for bravery during the Italian campaign. Returning to Algeria as a civilian in 1945, he joined Messali Hadj's Parti Populaire Algérien, and in 1947 was elected a municipal councillor for Marnia. In 1948 his name figured among the candidates put up for the Algerian Assembly by the Mouvement pour le Triomphe des Libertés Démocratique (MTLD), but French rigging of the election secured his defeat along with that of the other nationalists. A year later, in 1949, Ben Bella became part of the Organisation Spéciale. He was arrested the following year and two years later, in 1952, condemned in absentia by the French authorities for his participation, on April 14, 1949, in a successful OS raid on the Oran Post Office, from which the raiders rifled some 3 million (old) French francs. The condemnation was in absentia because, after having been gaoled in Blida, he succeeded in escaping from the prison there. It was at this stage that he first established close contacts with the Egyptians and the *Muhabarat*. French intelligence, as reported by rightwing French writers, identified one

'Fayek'—well known all over Africa—as one of the *Muhabarat*
agents in permanent contact with Ben Bella. From Cairo and under
various disguises, Ben Bella travelled extensively, particularly to
buy and ship arms, in Switzerland, Italy and Libya. There on
December 12, 1955 a member of La Main Rouge, a French fascist
organisation, almost succeeded in murdering him in his hotel. Ten
months later Ben Bella became famous throughout the world. In
October 1956, he was kidnapped with Khider, Boudiaf and Hocine
Ait Ahmed in an act of French air piracy. The four Algerian
leaders were on board an aircraft of Air Atlas (a Franco-Moroccan
company) on their way from Morocco to a Maghribine conference
in Tunis. Invested by French fighter planes, the pilot was forced to
land in Algiers. From then until the Evian Agreement in 1962, Ben
Bella and his three colleagues, together with Rabah Bitat, were to
remain in French captivity, forming the group that was to become
known as the 'five historic leaders'.

The 'five historic leaders' had the good fortune of disproving the
maxim 'les absents ont tort'. Locked up in French prisons, they
could not be held responsible for the mistakes of their colleagues in
Algeria during the war, and were able to argue that, if they had been
free, things would have gone differently. Ben Bella was the luckiest
of the five in that enemies and friends abroad singled him out as the
most likely leader. He was regarded as the Algerian leader par
excellence both by de Gaulle and by the anti-gaullist, non-communist left which wanted to outmanoeuvre the general. He was so
regarded by King Hassan of Morocco and by President Nasser,
though the latter rated Khider as a better politician. All these people
were attracted as much by Ben Bella's malleability as by his merits.
He made convenient promises to all of them, implicit and explicit.

The Algerians have been bright enough to leave intact many of
the propaganda posters put up by the French army bearing in
huge painted letters such slogans as 'Armée Française = Victoire,
Démocratie'. On the other hand, the French psychological services
were far more successful in their methods when dealing with their
five prisoners than with the Algerian population. They accentuated
their differences and gained goodwill by making each feel separately
that he was in a privileged position. They were not treated as
ordinary prisoners, but were given VIP treatment in comfortable
châteaux where they had television and could even receive female

visitors. The French chose wisely when they decided to back Ben Bella. From their point of view he was an excellent choice for, underneath his 'Arabism' and violent nationalism, Ben Bella shared the feeling of inferiority many of his countrymen evince in the presence of the French. Indeed, so deferential was his attitude to de Gaulle that this formed one of Boumedienne's secret grievances against him. De Gaulle was perhaps the one man who was not taken in by Ben Bella. Was this because the Algerian leader unconsciously reverted to the role of corporal and to exhibiting his real personality in his relations with the general? The answer would seem to be, yes; for at bottom Ben Bella was a simple soul. In a series of interviews to a French writer preparing his biography—the last of which was granted only a few days before his dramatic overthrow in June 1965—he expressed a touching nostalgia when recalling his life as a French corporal. Of this period spent as a colonial in the coloniser's army, the man posing as a leading, if not *the* leading, 'revolutionary' figure of the Third World, said: 'J'étais heureux, je crois.'[3]

On learning that de Gaulle's choice had fallen on Ben Bella, the non-communist left in France, especially the group gathered under the banner of *L'Express*, lost no time in building up his image as a leftwing leader, all in an attempt (vain, like the others) to out-manoeuvre the general. In the press and on the radio, since it was not practical to mention the names of all the imprisoned Algerian leaders, it proved convenient to speak of 'Ben Bella and his companions'. Among supporters of Algerian nationalism, the name itself 'sounded well', especially when punctuated by car-horn blasts or by rhythmic clanks on saucepan lids—as Algerians had learned to do from the OAS settlers. The OAS had used horns and saucepans to rap out three short and two long strokes for 'Algérie française'. The nationalists reversed the rhythm, producing two long and three short strokes for 'Yāhyā Běn Bèllȧ'.

The Algerian revolution has produced no great orators. Ben Bella, a man of simple appearance and Mediterranean warmth, was the only one of the nationalist leaders who knew how to address a crowd. Algeria was too divided for any leader to attain popularity on a nation-wide basis, but Ben Bella at least succeeded in becoming the most widely known Algerian leader. His regime became established because, thanks to the backing of the ALN, it was the only one strong enough to impose itself. The Algerian people craved for order and security, while the foreign powers, whether in Moscow or Washington, were anxious to see a stable government in Algeria. I met the 'five historic leaders' only after they had been freed from prison and had reached Morocco. The man who introduced me to them was Abderrahman Yusufi, now editor of the Moroccan leftwing paper, *At Tahrir*, and during the independence struggle the lawyer of the gaoled leaders, acting also as a secret courier for them. With the authority of close personal knowledge of them, he summed up the 'historic leaders' thus: 'Boudiaf and Ait Ahmed are the men of action; they are the intellectuals, the thinkers. Khider is the old political wolf, a fiery man of action, but no great thinker. As for Ben Bella: as you already know, he is the starlet of the group.' (Bitat was not mentioned.) Ben Bella owed his success to Khider as well as to the ALN, for without Khider's audacity he would not have climbed to power so quickly. It was Khider, in fact, who induced him to leave his Tlemcen sanctuary for Algiers, arguing with him over the telephone that 'if you do not come at once, it will be too late'. On several occasions Ben Bella asserted: 'There will never be any misunderstanding between Khider and myself.' But these were only words. The clash between the two men came at the time of the creation of the party. Khider was willing for Ben Bella to have all the positions with resounding titles, but he wanted for himself the key post of secretary-general of the FLN—yet to be formed into a properly organised party, although it was supposed to have been in existence for years. Khider wanted it to be a 'party of the people', while Ben Bella wanted it to be restricted to a policy-making elite. Such was the issue in the great debate—in theory! In actual fact, each of them was interested only in getting control of the party—a point they had in common with Boumedienne. Khider had always been suspicious of the army; this was known and it brought about a tactical alliance against him of Ben Bella and Boumedienne.

The differences between them became clear at a conference of the cadres of the FLN which met in a conspiratorial atmosphere at El Riath, a suburb of Algiers, in April 1963. 'Ill-intentioned people are saying that there are differences between Khider and myself', Ben Bella complained to the conference. 'But I tell you that there will never be any difference between brother Khider and myself.' This could have deceived few present, for it had become clear that

Khider was demanding, not only a 'people's party', but 'the preponderance of the party over the state'. Against this Ben Bella was firmly attached to his formula of an 'avant-garde' party, refusing to submit the state (which he had well in hand) to the FLN (over which he did not yet have real control). Khider was also pressing for the summoning of the full congress of the FLN, fixed for 1962 by the last CNRA meeting. He felt confident he could fill the congress with his supporters. Ben Bella, not so sure of his own support, argued for a further postponement. Khider was outvoted on this and Ben Bella won the day. Khider's resignation was delayed for a few days because of the attack on the life (April 11) of Khemisti, the foreign minister. But, as Khemisti lay dying and preparations were being made for Nasser's first state visit, Khider announced his resignation 'because of fundamental differences . . . concerning the holding of the National Congress of the FLN before the expiration of the mandate of the present Assembly'. Ben Bella, who had been campaigning against Khider in Constantine, returned to Algiers, where he was nominated secretary-general of the Political Bureau and of the FLN by two faithful lieutenants: Benalla Hadj and Mohammedi Said. (The latter was later to prove somewhat less faithful.) It was quite a family affair. From now on, Ben Bella was well in the saddle as premier and as secretary-general of the party. Boumedienne remained a potential danger to him, but the general opinion at the time was that the army leader was not ambitious enough to seek to replace Ben Bella. Moreover, it seemed obvious that the two men needed each other.

The Political Bureau was a notable example of the way in which the Algerian politicians adopted the language of advanced political science without applying its conclusions. For the Algerian Political Bureau—an impressive name—functioned like a petty municipal attorney's office. Political and police orders were shouted day and night, but the deep thought that should go with such an office was never there.

The question of whether or not underdeveloped countries can afford a multiparty system is outside the scope of this book. So is the question of whether the Algerians—who are not underdeveloped when compared with so many countries in Africa, Asia or Latin America, particularly in regard to their intellectual and educational standards—can or cannot afford a multiparty system. Observers in

Algeria said that the disorders of midsummer 1962 had 'caused the train of the revolution to run off the rails'. At best, it would have been no easy task to reroute it, but the totalitarian methods of enforcing haphazard ideas adopted by Ben Bella's regime threw everything out of gear. The patriotic fervour of those who had struggled in the resistance during the war subsided into disgust as they saw careerism and opportunism become the order of the day for anyone wanting to succeed. In fact, many of the young Algerians who had faced the post-independence tasks with drive and enthusiasm now became apathetic and tried to find posts abroad. Who could blame them? The regime was one of grotesque contradictions and there seemed no hope of preventing the moral collapse of the nation.

First of all, there was the exaggerated emphasis on the party. Ben Bella insisted that the party should come before everything, including parliament and individual conscience. In fact this unimpressive party was equated with the state. An analysis of Algeria's Constitution (the first one) will show that it revolves around three institutions: parliament, presidency of the republic, and the party— the first two being, in effect, subordinated to the third. Presenting this Constitution to the National Assembly, a deputy said that it was 'neither presidential, nor parliamentary, but a constitutional regime of government by the party. . . . The party is everything.' According to the Constitution it was the duty of the party to designate the man whom public suffrage would afterwards elect to the presidency of the republic, and also to appoint candidates for parliament, and to dissolve it. The party, in fact, had unlimited power since, according to the preamble of the Constitution, it had to 'secure the harmonious functioning of the institutions set out in the Constitution . . . decide the policy of the nation . . . inspire the action of the state . . . control the action of parliament and the government . . . realise the objectives of the democratic and popular revolution and build up socialism in Algeria'.

To most people the party was an insubstantial thing, but everyone knew that its secretary-general was Ben Bella, who was scheming to become president of the republic and commander-in-chief of the armed forces as well. There was a glaring contradiction between the fiction of 'national sovereignty' of the people and the supremacy of the party, controlled in fact by a small group headed by Ben

Bella. But Ben Bella had a ready 'resolution' of the contradiction: 'The people are the party and the party is the people.' A member of parliament, basically in agreement with Ben Bella's proposals, nevertheless wanted to make an amendment to the effect 'that the party admits within itself a free exchange of opinions and tendencies'. But even this timid opening for discussion was rejected. The party admitted no 'tendencies', so monolithic was it. Ben Bella knew what he wanted: a strong, very strong regime. Events, however, were to prove that he did not know how to achieve his aims. The party existed in name only. The first serious attempt at establishing it was made at the FLN Congress in April 1964. It had no central committee or any other body to direct it. The politicians went on paying lip-service to it in their struggle for power, but the bulk of the people regarded it with huge indifference. The 'Revolution' consisted of political splinter-groups quarrelling amongst themselves 'in the name of the people'; the people themselves had nothing to do with it. The Algerian people, more mature than their politicians, had prevented the civil war from spreading in the summer of 1962, but they were now reduced to the role of spectators. The patriotic and revolutionary spirit of the politicians was expressed by frantic gestures, banging on conference tables and shouting in front of the microphone. Their utter disregard of public opinion was consistent with attitudes exhibited during the war, but then there had at least been a certain esprit de corps and some sense of collective responsibility at the headquarters of the GPRA and the ALN. During the war, the leadership did not explain: it just issued orders. Now, for all that the country's leaders were preaching the best revolutionary doctrines (they were familiar with French leftwing writing and some of them had read their Sartre), they were in fact behaving in a thoroughly undemocratic and high-handed way. Many of those claiming to be dedicated revolutionaries displayed the worst qualities of the petty-bourgeois mentality. One of the most deplorable aspects of the legacy of colonialism was the French 'esprit de guichet'. Onto this the Algerians had superimposed the new regime's additional refinements in bureaucratic tyranny.

In the early days of Ben Bella's regime, there appeared on walls in Algiers slogans like 'il n'y a pas d'historique, mais le peuple est le seul historique'. This was a reaction against the overbearing arrogance of the 'historic leaders'. But opposition to the Ben Bella-Boumedienne combination did not take firm root; the regime's opponents were disorganised and sharply divided among themselves. Indeed, the regime survived as long as it did not because of its own merits but because of the weakness of the opposition to it. Ben Bella showed himself very adept at playing off one group against another. For example, many Kabyles, though in sympathy with the Kabilya opposition group led by Hocine Ait Ahmed, declined to give it active support because of their fear that this would permanently impair national unity; while refusing to be dominated by the Arabs, they did not want to go so far as to create an autonomous Kabilya. The only effective centre of opposition to Ben Bella was the army under Boumedienne. Even when they were in alliance at the time when they both needed each other, well-informed observers were saying privately that the two leaders would eventually fall out. Boumedienne's attack on Ben Bella had long been expected. What came as a surprise to all, as we shall see in chapter 10, was the timing of Boumedienne's coup.

One consequence of Ben Bella's totalitarian methods is the deplorable fact that, at the time of writing, there is not a single newspaper worthy of the name in a country which is by no means devoid of intellectuals with the gift of sophisticated, critical judgement. Today, the press of independent Algeria is unintelligent and servile. It is not even effective as an efficient mouthpiece for the regime. When it was decided to cease publication of *Le Peuple*, this, the official daily, was selling only three or four thousand copies a day. Such a poor performance was certainly not due to technical difficulties, for the Algerian newspapers inherited efficient presses, offices and equipment from the French. The case of the Algerian press is interesting because it shows that it is not so easy to rouse enthusiasm with empty revolutionary or anti-colonialist slogans in countries where the ordinary man has reached a certain level of maturity. The constant harping on the anticolonialist theme proved the reverse of stimulating for the paper's circulation: the only effect was to deflect popular interest from the conduct of political affairs and to increase the circulation of French newspapers, which Algerians have come to appreciate even more since independence than they did before. *Révolution Africaine* in its issue of August 22, 1964, published a survey entitled "What do Algerians read?", which concluded that readership of French papers had increased since independence. Serious readers followed *Le Monde* religiously, which sells no less than 85,000 copies in North Africa, most of them in Algeria. The general public were devotees of *France-Soir*, the Parisian mass-circulation daily, because they found it 'entertaining'. Revolutionary Algeria was becoming more interested in Princess Paola and Sophia Loren than in national politics. But the Algerians liked best of all the highly specialised 'presse du coeur'. Few of them read the rightwing *Figaro*—not surprisingly in view of its attitude during the war; but, equally, few read the communist papers. Eventually *France-Soir* had to cease publication of its special North African edition because of repeated seizures in Algiers. The government also took measures against Hachette, the French publishing and distribution house which had established a monopoly in colonial times. In November 1964 an official publishing and distribution agency was established: *Editions Nationales Algériennes* (ENA).

The press and radio were heavily censored, sometimes to the point of absurdity. The world learned of the assassination of Khemisti a few minutes after the attack on him outside the Algerian parliament, but the Algerian press and news services never mentioned it at all. They preserved a similar silence when one of the two frigates given by the UAR suddenly sank in Algiers harbour just before Nasser's arrival. The situation has not improved under Boumedienne. Neither press nor radio mentioned the fire that broke out on August 17, 1965, at the site in Le Parc des Pins of the abortive Second Afro-Asian Conference, even though the flames were visible in Algiers. In matters great and small, information is suppressed or distorted under Boumedienne as it was under Ben Bella. (See Appendix IV for details of the Algerian press.)

The governments since independence have made a mockery of justice. Judges are regarded merely as tools of the state, to be ordered about unceremoniously. As the years go by, Algeria is likely to pay heavily for having let her leaders make such a parody of justice. Even in the affair of the assassination of Khemisti, it took more than a year for the state to prepare an official case for this crime. The suspect, eventually declared insane, threw himself off a balcony. Rumours that Khemisti's was a political assassination are still current today.

Judges and journalists are not the only ones whom Ben Bella brought to their knees. The trade unions were also forced to give way. The only labour leader who had the courage to resist was Ali Yahia Abdennour, wartime secretary-general of the Union Générale des Travailleurs Algériens (UGTA) in Tunis and later a member of the General Assembly. He had to take refuge for a time with Hocine Ait Ahmed in his native Kabilya. (After the coup in 1965, he became a member of Boumedienne's government.) The UGTA, which had played a courageous part in the war, wanted to retain a certain working-class autonomy 'within the framework of the government's policies'. But Ben Bella and Khider had other ideas; they were particularly determined not to allow the UGTA to retain the right to strike. Ben Bella maintained that, as colonial rule was over, strikes 'no longer made sense'. At their congress on January 17, 1963, UGTA members stoutly insisted on their right to strike. It happened that Khider was in the Middle East at the time and it was not until his return on January 20 that any action was planned by the government: an indication of how much Ben Bella relied at this period on his colleague's intelligence and aggressiveness. That night the trade union leaders were invited to dinner with Ben Bella and Khider. As they sat at table, the house was surrounded by police. Ben Bella delivered a warning. He said that it mattered little to him that among the UGTA leaders there were men who had collaborated with the French. (This may or may not have been true: it was certainly blackmail.) Only one thing mattered: 'I want men who obey!' The point was hammered home again the next morning when delegates and observers attending the congress were astonished to see bands of toughs arriving in lorries and invading the hall. They had been sent by Khider to remind the trade unionists of what had been said the night before. After that, the UGTA gave no more trouble.

It was not only national organisations but entire regions of the country which were required to submit. And most did bow in resignation. As might have been expected, however, the Kabilya region—the land of the *Amazigh*, with its proud Berber traditions— did not kiss the rod. The Kabyles resisted and then broke out in open revolt. By the second half of the summer of 1962, Algeria found itself once more on the brink of civil war. It was a bitter and tragic situation, for Kabilya, which had been the first region to revolt against the French and throughout fought the colonialist forces with the greatest spirit, was now invested by Algerian troops. These latter were, in the main, ANP units composed of men drawn from the more Arab provinces of the country, and in many cases they acted as ruthlessly as the 'paras'. Independence had arrived, but Kabilya was again under a repressive army of occupation.

It is true that Ben Bella for a time resisted Boumedienne's pressure for a 'military and energetic' solution of the Kabyle problem. But, as with the case of Wilaya IV in mid-1962, he hesitated only to agree in the end to a military solution. As it turned out, both Ben Bella and Boumedienne sought to avoid public responsibility for armed action, each putting the onus on the other in the course of a widespread whispering campaign. Two years later, on June 20, 1965, in the course of conversation with Mohammed Hassanein Heykal (cited by the latter in an article in *Al Ahram* on October 8, 1965), Boumedienne declared that Ben Bella had ordered Hocine Ait Ahmed, leader of the Kabyle revolt, to be arrested and 'killed like a mad dog'. Charging that Ben Bella wanted him and his ANP general staff to appear as the villains of the piece, the colonel added: 'We arrested Ait Ahmed and turned him over to Ben Bella, saying, "Do with this man what you want". He pardoned him. Ben Bella was ordering us to hit while reserving to himself the right of pardon. We had to shed blood while he was making peace. He wanted us to appear as bloodthirsty men.' This was certainly not far from the truth.

Because of the policy of discrimination against Berbers pursued by Ben Bella's government, the Kabyles had been forced to take action—though not with the aim of creating an independent Kabilya, as official propaganda would have it believed. Ben Bella was anti-Kabyle mainly because he was so emotionally pro-Arab, and the Kabyles were the greatest sufferers politically, and especially economically, from his assertive Arabism. The discrimination against them in government and administration helps to explain why a man of no great calibre like Mohammedi Said rose to such heights in the cabinet. Said was a Kabyle, but a stooge Kabyle through whom Ben Bella tried to show that even the highest posts in the state could be attained by a man from Kabilya. But Said was one of those Kabyles—and they have been few—who gave unquestioning obedience to Ben Bella. Algerians referred to him as 'le Kabyle de service'. It was on economic grounds, however, that Ben Bella's policy of discrimination hit Kabilya most cruelly. Though this was the region which had suffered most from the war, it was badly neglected by the Algiers government. Discrimination was practised even to the extent of distributing war pensions with a parsimonious hand to Kabyle claimants—and this despite the fact that at one time Mohammedi Said was the minister responsible for the *mujahidin*. Oran—certainly more prosperous as a region than Kabilya, and less seriously disrupted by the war—benefited more in the way of state economic assistance. Kabyles asserted that this was not only because Oran was more Arab than Kabilya but because it was also Ben Bella's own region. Between Arabs and Kabyles there has existed mutual suspicion for centuries. Through his policy of blatant discrimination, Ben Bella intensified the bad relationships between the two main racial groups in Algeria.

In view of all this, it was not surprising that elections in independent Algeria proved to be no more representative than those held in colonial times. The situation was well summed up by *Alger Républicain* (before the communists who dominated it decided to support Ben Bella) when it complained of the single list of candidates for the elections of September 1962 for the Legislative Assembly. 'Voters are offered the one ticket and told to take it whether they like it or not.' In fact, Ben Bella, Boumedienne and their aides drew up the Constitution without ever offering it for approval to the Assembly which was convened on September 20, 1962, for that very purpose. Ben Bella decreed simultaneously that the parliamentary mandate be prolonged by six months and that the Constituent Assembly register his Constitution. After this he no longer felt it necessary to submit his actions to the scrutiny of parliament.

At first, the Algerian parliament appeared to have a fairly promising future. There was some hope that it would serve as an outlet for the voice of opposition. But this hope was short-lived, and by early 1963 those members who did not sit in silent resignation or simply cease to attend had joined resistance movements. One of these was Hocine Ait Ahmed who had tried in vain to introduce a measure of genuine debate into the sessions. He had been ridiculed by his opponents for his habit of quoting Shakespeare in English and buying his clothes in London, but he soon showed his mettle by establishing a resistance movement in his native Kabilya. Another dissident was Ferhat Abbas, the president of the Assembly, who resigned on the issue of the Constitution. 'A Constitution cannot be prostituted in a cinema', he declared, alluding to the meeting held in a cinema hall where supporters of Ben Bella and Boumedienne 'voted' for the Constitution. But Ferhat Abbas's protest was of no avail, for he lost a good deal of his prestige when he joined Ben Bella at Tlemcen in resentment against the GPRA'S making Ben Khedda president of the republic instead of himself. A liberal bourgeois, Ferhat Abbas had hoped Ben Bella would be content to be prime minister, and went into alliance with him in the belief he could influence the course of Ben Bella's policy. The extent of his self-deception was soon revealed.

When the Constitution, after its cinema-endorsement, was put before the Assembly in the summer of 1963, there were between sixty and seventy members of parliament of the total of 195 who were prepared to vote against it. But cajoling, blackmail and intimidation diminished the opposition, and the Constitution establishing a presidential regime in favour of Ben Bella was adopted by 139 votes to 23. A week later a referendum was held confirming the Constitution, and the week after that Ben Bella was elected to the presidency.* He now held all the positions that mattered: presidency of the republic, secretary-generalship of the party, and supreme command of the armed forces.

---

* The results of the various votings in independent Algeria are as follows: September 20, 1962, elections for the National Constituent Assembly (single list): *registered* 6,504,033, *voted* 5,303,661, *blanks or invalid votes* 19,647, *valid votes* 5,284,014, *ayes* 5,265,377, *noes* 18,637. September 8, 1963, approval of Constitution: *registered* 6,391,818, *voted* 5,287,229, *blanks or invalid votes* 16,173, *valid votes* 5,271,036, *ayes* 5,166,195, *noes* 104,841. September 15, 1963, election of President of Republic: *registered* 6,531,340, *voted* 5,827,618, *blanks or invalid votes* 22,515, *Ben Bella* 5,805,103.

6

WHAT SOCIALISM?

BEN BELLA was not the only national leader in the Third World to try to rule by public statement and to make the microphone a vital instrument of government. But he lacked the ability, for example, of Sukarno, who in his heyday was the supreme exponent of 'ruling by statement'. The Indonesian leader proved a real master at stirring up vast audiences. But in Algeria, where general apathy soon replaced revolutionary enthusiasm, Ben Bella's meetings were attended only by a small and regular clique of followers. His 'rule from the tribune and the microphone' has been scathingly illustrated by Jean Lacouture:

> Brothers! Scouting is a noble activity which prepares citizens for the service of the state. (Cries of *Yahya Ben Bella! Yahya Ben Bella!*)
>
> I am convinced that if scouting were made compulsory, it would render the greatest service to Algeria. (*Yahya Ben Bella! Yahya Ben Bella!*)
>
> Brothers! With your approval, I proclaim that henceforward scouting is compulsory for Algerians.[1]

(Algerian nationalism was always boy-scout-minded. Ben Bella sought to give it a more militant character, renaming the movement 'Les Scouts Mussulmans Algériens'.)

Ben Bella (and his successor, Boumedienne, is one with him in this) firmly believed that Islam represented an advanced form of socialism, and 'socialism' as a term was scarcely ever off his lips. Yet of all peoples it is probably the Algerians—and not merely the leaders—whose disputations about socialism have been the most pointless. 'In this respect', notes Gérard Chalian, 'Algeria provides a striking example of the gulf between words and deeds.'[2] The whole country, and particularly Algiers itself, was smothered with socialist slogans: on the walls, in the press, over the radio and from the mouths of innumerable speakers. Since these had very much the same ring as the slogans of the communist world, the West gained the impression that Algeria was a 'socialist state'—indeed, was 'going communist'. Visitors were very impressed by all these signs of Algeria's socialism. But to anyone who knew the country well it was not difficult to scratch the surface and see all this talk of socialism for what it was: empty words.

Michel Leuleu, senior correspondent on Algeria for Agence France Presse, turned down the directorship of AFP's Algiers office on the grounds (as he explained to me) that: 'This country will unfortunately—I can feel it—be one of empty, tiring slogans. I just won't be able to stand it.' How right he was! On one occasion an Algerian friend asked me, all agog with excitement, what I thought of the current 'Keep Algeria Clean' and 'Socialism is Cleanliness' campaign? We were in the 'Gouvernement', the main administrative building in Algiers, on the very floor where Ben Bella's office was. The floors were covered with cigarette ends and dirt. Former maquisards turned ushers were standing idly around. At this time the Algerians were fond of comparing themselves with the Chinese. I could not forebear to reply: 'One difference with China is that if you people were there, you would now be too busy cleaning these floors to have time to ask me what I think of the campaign.' Boumedienne was later to object, with good reason, to this 'verbal socialism', but even his closest lieutenants cannot be exonerated from the charge of having indulged in it. Ahmed Kaid (Cdr Slimane), for one, spent a good deal of time and money as minister of Tourism under Ben Bella in an attempt to create this 'national and popular' Algeria which was proclaimed on posters at home and abroad. But his greatest achievement in office was to organise two wild boar hunts, exclusively for diplomatists stationed in Algiers!

In fact, Ben Bella was no socialist, and neither were his ministers. The only one of his ministerial team with any marxist training was Amar Ouzegane, who had been a communist. However, Ben Bella and his colleagues were quick enough to grasp the usefulness of the myth of 'socialist Algeria'. At home their regime cashed in on the desire of the 'have-nots' for a better life; abroad its profession of socialism was aimed at serving Algeria's economic and diplomatic interests—as we shall see in chapter 8. In the amosphere of quick and superficial judgements which is the bane of modern journalism, it was easy to foster the grotesque fallacy of 'socialist Algeria'. A long, hard look at the only serious effort made to apply socialist principles—in the vital matter of land reform—is enough to show what a fiasco the so-called 'Algerian socialism' has been.

The more lucid and courageous among Algerians themselves were the first to point out the cardinal error of failing to distinguish between 'socialism' and 'circumstances in which socialism may be established'. On July 13 1963 Khelifa, editor-in-chief of *Révolution Africaine*, wrote (in a reader's letter, be it noted; he did not dare voice his opinion in an editorial):

> Through some strange reasoning and in spite of the half-failure which resulted—due to lack of intensive preparation and political understanding—some people have believed and still believe that a few opportune decrees and the immense thirst for justice among the mass of the people are enough to give life to and launch the socialist experiment. They are confusing socialism and the conditions favourable for its establishment. They are losing sight of the fact that the socialist revolution aims not only at a re-distribution of wealth but also at a total transformation in depth of the nature of our society. This is the most difficult transformation and the one which needs the most devotion, patience and intelligence.

Mostefa Lacheraf observes: 'Some people have thought that in the Algerian peasant, with his misery, his backwardness, and his social disabilities, so well nurtured until our own day [i.e. by colonialism], they had discovered an authentic revolutionary spirit founded on an ideology, which he did not and cannot have, given his economic and cultural background. To draw analogies with other revolutions which have stemmed from an uprising of the peasant is entirely superficial.'[3] By 'other (peasant) revolutions' Lacheraf refers to the Chinese experience.

Algerian politicians and commentators have always referred to their insurgence as a 'peasant revolution'—hence the references to the 'agrarian revolution' and to the 'Chinese analogy'. It is perfectly true to say that the burden of the war fell very largely on the peasant class under the guidance of the bourgeois intellectuals, but this is far from saying that it was 'a socialist revolution' as far as the peasant was concerned. The *fellah* fought for nothing more than his land, his means of livelihood. Certainly in all this there were elements of insurrection against the foreign usurper, but in essence the *fellah*'s aims were capitalistic: he wanted to own his own land. Socialists have for long seen this urge as something that can be turned to their own ends, and have declared that land should belong to those who work on it.

In the midsummer of 1962—when, in spite of the efforts of the Provisional Executive to guarantee the rights of Frenchmen who wanted to remain in Algeria, other influences caused the European minority to flee—vast tracts of land, farms, small factories, villas, houses and flats, not to mention cars, yachts and furniture, were found suddenly to have no owner. These were to be the 'biens vacants': a phrase which will continue to obsess Algeria for a long time. Within a few days, the 'have-nots' and the petty bourgeois saw their dreams come true. They took over all this rich booty, and so created a quite impossible social and economic situation. Because it lacks the proper machinery to deal with the problem, no Algerian government so far has been able to establish the fate and actual legal position of the hundreds of thousands of flats and houses left as 'biens vacants'. In the Département of Algiers alone, there were 200,000 housing units left empty by departing Frenchmen. French authorities estimated, three years after independence, that losses from non-payment of rents, gas and electricity bills cost Algeria some 14 billion francs a year. (In 1965, only 150,000 out of a total of 300,000 users in Algiers were paying their gas bills.) This does not take into account the great depreciation in value and serviceability of these premises from lack of proper maintenance. (It is reckoned that deterioration of premises leads each year to the loss of housing accommodation for 30,000 persons.) The problem of regularising this situation is indeed formidable, especially as the granting of choice flats and villas once owned by the French was a favourite bribe of the Ben Bella regime. As for the private cars appropriated in the same way: the situation here is so complicated that it is unlikely that any Algerian government will ever manage to clear it up.

How much of this 'Algerianisation' was truly 'a socialist experiment', and how much sheer looting? Is there not a differentiation between the just redress through revolution of past wrongs, and plain pillage? The men who had fought and made such great sacrifices were now advancing down the road to socialism from plush villas in private cars with built-in bars and record players. The biggest slice of the revolutionary cake went to the most astute. The transformation was so abrupt as to seem comic—until one thought of the brave words about transforming Algerian society on socialist lines, and then it was tragic. What little revolutionary integrity had survived until then took yet another blow. In the orgy of looting, the authorities tried to maintain order, but their own practice reflected nothing of their preaching to the pillagers. Though Ben Bella himself continued to lead a simple and quiet private life and seems not to have exploited the situation for purely personal ends, he and his colleagues made lavish use of 'socialistically appropriated' property as political bait to catch more adherents.

The most pressing problem when the new regime took over was the survival of agricultural production. Peasants and agricultural workers were moving in to occupy the farms left vacant by the French. There was a revolutionary element in this, certainly, but it was much more a natural and spontaneous operation essential to survival, not only on the part of the agrarian workers but also of the government. The first organisation to try to regularise the take-over of French agricultural assets was the UGTA, which formed a special commission for the purpose. Later, however, it came into conflict with the government and with the party as to how the 'biens vacants' were to be run and who should do the running. Unnoticed by many, including foreign observers, the army was dealing with the problem in its own way. In some cases assurances were given to French farmers that they would remain unmolested, and they were in fact protected from squatters by soldiers. This went on until the harvest was in—and then out went the French. They were no longer needed.

On the part of the government or of the party—the two were so inextricably mixed up that it is difficult to say which was which—there were at first various ad hoc measures taken to make 'socialist' sense of the confusion. On October 22, 1962, a decree was promulgated demanding that in each French farm with over ten agricultural workers a management committee of at least three members be elected. Elections were to be made by 'all the workers generally working in the establishment'. A month later, on November 23, a second decree obliged French owners still in Algeria to co-operate with the 'workers' management unit'. On the last day of the year came a further decree, creating a body of controllers for self-managed estates. But these measures still left unsettled the fundamental problem of the ownership of appropriated land. The first attempts to create a 'socialist' order out of the uprising came in spring 1963, when the now famous decrees of March 15, 22 and 28 were promulgated. These decrees of the proclaimed 'month of self-management' ratified the spontaneous action of the peasants and sought to control them by stipulating that all 'biens vacants' were to be placed under the administrative guardianship of Ben Bella's office.* The first decree (March 15) nationalised 728,312 hectares of French land which had not yet been occupied by the peasants. The second (March 22) legalised and formalised the management by Algerians of property hitherto French. In theory, each unit of management had the following hierarchy: General Assembly of Workers, Workers Council, Management Committee, President, Director. The third decree (March 28) established a scale of remuneration, on the basis of productivity, for the various operators in a self-managed unit. More decrees were to follow, but at this point it is instructive to examine closely the events of March 1963: 'the month of self-management'.

At the heart of the Algerian socialist experiment—and acting as far more than mere advisers to Ben Bella—was a small group of men under the leadership of Mohammed Harbi, Soliman Lutfullah and Michaelis Raptis. It is yet another indication of the lack of potential leaders among Algerians that, of these three, only Mohammed Harbi is an Algerian. Lutfullah is a Copt, a political refugee from the United Arab Republic who has several times been in Nasser's notorious desert concentration camps because of his

* In the first rush of appropriations immediately on the obtaining of independence, the Provisional Executive had, in its ordinance No. 62 of August 1962, tried to regularise the property-grab by stopping it. Article 3 of the ordinance declared that 'any person will be expelled who illegally occupies premises of residential, industrial, agricultural, artisanal or commercial character'. This was intended to reassure Frenchmen and prevent their exodus, but it failed before the nation-wide movement simply to occupy the 'biens vacants'.

leftwing activities. Lutfullah and his wife, a Jewess from Cairo, were only too well known to foreign press correspondents in Cairo. The *Muhabarat* knew all about his activities and, as if deliberately inviting their attention, he would make progressive speeches at the top of his voice, endangering not only himself but his visiting friends as well! Raptis is a refugee from Greece who had served the GPRA in many capacities, particularly in Holland. Mohammed Harbi, whatever his failings, remains to this day one of the most lucid brains in Algeria. He is as brave as he is clever. In Paris, during the war of independence, he managed to avoid arrest by parading in a French military uniform. Still a young man when independence came, he showed himself to be a man who suited his action to his word. When, in the early days, Ben Bella tried to get rid of him (as he succeeded in doing with others) because of his affiliations with the GPRA (he had been secretary-general of its department of foreign affairs), Harbi was the only one not to bow to the dictator. Rather than accept being 'kicked upstairs' as ambassador to the Lebanon, he handed in his resignation. 'My place is here, not in diplomacy abroad', he told me.

All three are marxists with leanings towards trotskyism—especially Raptis who, as Michel Pablo, is well-known to the French section of the Fourth International. The extraordinary power at times exercised by this trio can be attributed to the fact that they were the only civilians at the heart of things who really knew what they wanted to make out of the Algerian chaos. Their influence can also be explained by Ben Bella's need of them as suppliers of the aura of socialism desired for his regime. In the event, however, Lutfullah and Raptis were to be suppliers of the pretext for the xenophobia which developed, especially in the army and in religious circles, against 'foreign experts', and in particular against the 'pieds rouges'.* It incensed Algerians to see foreigners

---

* This term, the corollary of 'pieds noirs'—rightwing French settlers—was applied to leftwing Frenchmen in Algeria, and then by extension to foreign leftwingers in general. Many 'pieds rouges' (who were mostly non-communist leftwingers but included a fair number of trotskyists) served wartime Algeria with fervour and efficiency. But it is true that they afterwards tried to run Algeria pretty much as if it were their own show. The strength of the animosity against them can be judged by the ease with which Ben Bella's successor has so far disposed of them. On August 20, 1965, Harbi was arrested by Boumedienne's police on charges of subversive activities.

playing so vital a role in the affairs of their country. It incensed them still further when it became apparent that the men who were using Ben Bella—who, after all, was the leader of the Algerian people—were not the best men for the job. Their brilliance was admitted, but the Algerians found grounds for levelling serious criticism against them. Lutfullah was said to be unbalanced—perhaps as a result of his experiences in Nasser's concentration camps. As for Raptis, the expert mentioned on page 89 above as the first man to prepare a scheme for agrarian reform in Algeria: the view held of him was that he had been well rewarded for his services during the war, but now that he had been paid off he no longer had any right to concern himself with 'our affairs'.

But until the FLN Congress in April 1964, when Ben Bella yielded under pressure and started dropping his socialist advisers, the trio played a dominating role in shaping events in Algeria. Everything seemed to be going as they planned. Confident of the prevalence of their influence, Harbi told a meeting in Paris: 'In spite of the fact that our national revolution is not complete and that self-management in our country is heavily mortgaged, the choice is not between capitalism and socialism but between different forms of socialism and different forms of democratic self-management.'[4] The March decrees of 1963 were very much their work. Within Ben Bella's office, they formed the Bureau National d'Administration du Secteur Socialiste (BNASS). Their group took this title after the March decrees. Before then it had had the more bourgeois name of Bureau National de Protection et de Gestion des Biens Vacants. To formalise the work of the revolution they established other institutions, such as the Office National de la Réforme Agraire (ONRA), the Office National Algérien des Coopérations Ouvrières (ONACO), the Société Nationale Algérienne des Transports Communs (SNATC), and the Office National du Commerce (ONC).

It must be said in their favour that they set out to establish the necessary economic administrative arrangements for a genuinely revolutionary Algeria, doing so with a truly revolutionary opportunism. It can now be disclosed that Lutfullah, in order to free Algeria's foreign trade from French monopolies, resorted to a well-devised stratagem. He got the 'socialist sector' to export fruit to Marseilles in crates bearing the names of former French producers. This created a scandal among the numerous pieds noirs in Marseilles. The fruit was left to rot, awaiting the decision of a French commercial tribunal as to whether or not it could be considered as Algerian property. Lutfullah then made his prepared move: the ONACO was set up 'to prevent our exports from rotting in colonialist hands'.

A bigger and still more audacious venture was the action of the BNASS in provoking the second spate of decrees on the confiscation and control of the remaining French lands. On March 30, 1963, Ben Bella declared at a public meeting arranged with the UGTA: 'All Algerians have been awaiting the delivery of a child: socialism! . . . We have now seized 160 cinemas throughout Algeria. . . . We shall continue. . . .' But the climax of the day was the seizure of the La Trappe estate, which to Algerian leftwingers meant what the conversion of Buckingham Palace to a hostel for party members would mean to British communists. The owner of this huge domain was a M. Bourgeaud, archetype of the great French landowners in Algeria. He had thought he could stick to his remaining 2,000 hectares, and in fact some Algerian officials had intimated to him that this would indeed be the case. But at night ANP troops with two tanks suddenly invested his domain and Bourgeaud was bundled off without even being given time to pack. There were strong protests in the French press, but Bourgeaud—for so long a symbol of the French colonial profiteer—did not really deserve them. Like most of the rich Frenchmen in Algeria, he had already removed most of his fortune from the country. As is always the case, it was the little man—here the small French settler—who bore the brunt of the upheaval, not Bourgeaud and his kind. The Algerian leaders, acting on the suggestion of a French pied rouge adviser of Ben Bella's, had based their action on a wartime French law of March 17, 1956, which granted the governor-general special powers to secure public order. They alleged that workers on the La Trappe estate were being unfairly treated and that disorders might follow— and so the ANP moved in lest worse befall.

All these events were not unrelated to the explosion of the French atomic bomb on March 18, 1963, at Ein-Ekker in the Sahara. Foreign press correspondents had known of the forthcoming explosion a month beforehand. Ben Bella, however, had hoped the rumour would prove false and that de Gaulle would not give him so blatant a slap in the face. But the slap came—with a loud bang!

Ben Bella was all the more furious since the date chosen for the explosion coincided exactly with the anniversary of the Evian Agreement: an implication which escaped nobody. The socialist trio, needless to say, took the point and worked on Ben Bella to demonstrate his wrath in a useful and 'revolutionary' way. The second spate of decrees seizing Algerian land was the result.

An earlier batch of decrees, in January and February 1963, was concerned primarily with the accounting of self-managed agrarian units. During the year 230 francs were to be distributed to each worker of a self-managed unit that had been successful, and only 110 francs each to workers on those that had failed to reach their targets. In all, only 70,000 workers benefited from this unprecedented premium which, however small, was an uneconomic action aimed, politically, at boosting the morale of the self-managed sector.

The techniques of socialist self-management were first fully developed in Yugoslavia in 1950 following that country's departure from the Soviet political and economic ambit. Indeed it was Yugoslavia which played the biggest role among foreign countries in Algerian self-management; this was to cost her a severe loss of prestige in Algeria on Ben Bella's fall. But there were fundamental differences between the two countries. Not only was Yugoslavia controlled by a well-managed marxist party, but the self-management techniques were applied more in the industrial than in the agrarian sector. Algeria, by contrast, was committed to the agrarian sector, which was much more difficult to manage; and she also lacked all the other advantages: an organised party, a political theory, a government, and even the minimum number of experienced cadres to watch over the economic and social conditions of the peasants who were involved in this difficult experience.

The establishment of self-management meant that the rich and modern agricultural sector previously managed by the French had now become 'socialised'. By autumn 1963, practically all this land had been seized, following the decree of October 7 when Ben Bella, clearly as a political move during the Moroccan-Algerian 'little war' and the Kabilya crisis, ordered the nationalisation of the remaining 1,000,000 hectares of former French land. The classification of the lands of the 'socialist sector' according to their cultivation in October 1963 is as follows:

118

Produce	Area in hectares
Summer cereals	5,920
Winter cereals	763,020
Dry vegetables	23,240
Industrial plants	44,380
Fodder	11,010
Market-gardening	28,730
Other	2,690
Land lying fallow	856,640
Grasslands	15,560
Scrub	413,160
Vineyards	64,800
Unproductive agricultural lands	325,460
Orchards	94,800
	2,649,410

According to official Algerian statistics, by 1964 slightly more than 2·7 million hectares of the best Algerian land had been incorporated into the 'socialist sector', divided into some 3,000 self-managed units which, though varying widely in size, averaged about 1,000 hectares each. These units employed about 150,000 agricultural workers, or roughly one tenth of the total rural population. Most of the rural population were continuing their struggles in the 'traditionalist' poor sector. Until the implementation of the remainder of the agrarian reforms—and today this still remains to be done—the socialist sector was bound to be a privileged group benefiting from the lands, buildings and equipment left by the French. But this was only part of the anomaly. Self-managed units consisted of 'permanent' and 'seasonal' workers. Only the former had any right to bonuses. And against the privileged workers of the socialist sector, who with their families totalled 1 million people, there remained 6 million Algerians who derived no benefit at all from the agrarian revolution.

Although the units of the socialist sector were still living on the riches left behind by the French, most of them were already 'in the red', and, as we have seen, the bonuses that were distributed—on the only occasion so far that bonuses have been paid—were

E*

dictated by political considerations rather than by strict principles of accounting. It was easy enough to plant an Algerian flag over a farmstead; the real difficulty arose in connection with a man whose calling is neither glorious nor revolutionary: the book-keeper. He just was not there, neither was there any yardstick of economic viability. Moreover, the director of the self-managed units, theoretically responsible to the Assembly of Workers, was usually an official appointed by the state, with no knowledge of his task. Representatives of the party or the army, with conflicting interests, sought to insinuate their own protégés into the privileged 'socialist' sector. And at the same time, ironically enough, there developed a capitalist group-mentality among the self-managed units themselves. The individual or the unit had no sense of loyalty; the main preoccupation was petty thieving. Hence, even when the units were still able to draw on the legacy of efficiency inherited from their former French owners, the official Algerian statistics had to admit to a drop in the vital wine and cereals output in the first full year after independence(1963–64).

AGRICULTURAL PRODUCTION 1960-64
(in 000s)

	1960	1961	1962	1963	1964
Wine (hl.)	18,600·0	15,650·0	13,000·0	12,750·0	n.a.
Citrus fruit (qls.)	3,980·0	3,680·0	3,780·0	4,000·0	n.a.

	1960–61	1961–62	1962–63	1963–64
Cereals (qls.)	8,472·0	22,263·5	24,446·0	19,207·0
hard wheat	4,804·0	11,757·0	14,618·0	12,416·0
soft wheat	1,475·0	3,301·5	3,360·0	2,730·0
barley	2,008·0	6,900·0	6,150·0	3,714·0
oats	185·0	305·0	318·0	347·0

Two comments need to be made on these figures. First, the harvest of 1962–63 was an exceptionally good one; second, statistics cannot take account of the drop in the quality of products, notably of wine, early vegetables, citrus fruits and dates. Exports of these products in the years 1961–62 and 1963–64, respectively, were (in tons): citrus fruits, 297,000: 237,000; early vegetables, 1,800,000: 608,000; dates, 30,000: nil. (See also Appendix III, Table 5.)

It would be naïve to think that socialism thrives under deteriorating conditions, and it is clear that this experiment was bound to lead to a setback. Mohammed Harbi repeatedly warned Ben Bella against a facile socialist optimism, not only privately but in a series of remarkable articles. In June 1963, in *Révolution Africaine*, he issued a warning that 'time is getting short', and that 'we must close the gap between what we profess and what we achieve'. But it was to no avail. Ben Bella wanted to stay in power, and if that meant bowing to army pressure and getting rid of Harbi, he would do it. There were strong opponents of Harbi within the political secretariat of Ben Bella. One such was Ali Mahsas, whose views on agrarian reform were more conservative. He was well placed to counterbalance Harbi's influence since he was an old and close friend of Ben Bella's. (This did not prevent him from turning against his friend and chief, and becoming minister of Agriculture under Boumedienne.) Another of Ben Bella's ministers of Agriculture was Amar Ouzegane, whose confused ideas created havoc in his department; he was removed from it to take over *Révolution Africaine* when Harbi was ousted from the paper. (Ouzegane also changed sides after the coup in June 1965, but only to be ousted in his turn from the editorship of the magazine.)

At one stage, Ben Bella strongly criticised the members of UGTA, saying that he could not afford a privileged class of workers (with an average monthly salary of 400 francs) while the *fellah* was getting no more than 120 francs in a whole year. Yet not only did he establish a privileged class amongst the peasants themselves: he created a far greater one in the huge administrative edifice which he set up. In January 1964, the Algerian administration included no less than 134,550 posts of which 93,123 were then filled. As in her other colonies, France had paid officials in Algeria far more highly than their counterparts in France. The Algerian government reduced these salaries only by one third—corresponding exactly to the differential between home and overseas salaries in the French service. In spite of this reduction some of the salaries remained enormous: up to 2,000 francs per month for ministers. (Significantly enough, a policeman received as much as 700 francs per month.)

Something should be said about the application of the principles of self-management to the industrial sector in Algeria, for though of relatively small economic significance, its progress involves even more radical defections from the principles of socialism. The situation can be stated succinctly. The Algerian government did not dare to take drastically socialist measures for fear of scaring off foreign capital (in which Ben Bella was secretly placing his hopes) by nationalising the banks, foreign trade and the heavy mining industry. Yet unless banks and foreign trade are nationalised, industrial units, whether or not they are put under socialist self-management, are bound to remain the offshoots of private enterprise. And so industrial socialism petered out in half-measures.

Where it did not matter—in scores of minor enterprises like small hotels, coffee houses and cinemas—nationalisation was effected under the umbrella of 'industrial socialisation'. These were precisely the kind of enterprises which Yugoslavia, learning from her own mistakes, had previously restored to private hands, and in Algeria the only effect of their nationalisation was to stifle industrial initiative. Yugoslavs in Algiers tore their hair when they saw Ben Bella nationalising small hotels which had survived by economising on laundry costs and by not providing guests with soap. What the Yugoslavs did not know was that most of these enterprises were owned by Kabyles—and so were taken over by the anti-Kabyle Ben Bella. The leader of the nation would make fine speeches on the great occasion of the nationalisation of a small café in Algiers. But shortly after the spate of nationalisation, new decrees appeared discreetly announcing that 'enterprises nationalised in error . . . are being returned to their former proprietors'.

In what may properly be described as the industrial sector, 450 enterprises employing some 10,000 workers all told had, by mid-1964, been put under self-management, only to find themselves facing the competition of a better equipped private sector. Even among the 450, only some 5 per cent could be considered truly 'industrial'; of the remainder about 45 per cent were partly manual —such as the building industry—and the rest concerned with the processing of food. The figures (see Table opposite) relate to January 1964.

Industrial self-management began in January 1964. But a scandal soon broke out when it was discovered that at the largest industrial enterprise to be nationalised, the ACIOR steelworks, the managerial staff were busily feathering their own nests. The chaos prevailing in the heavy industrial sector was reflected in a marked drop in pro-

SELF-MANAGED ENTERPRISES: INDUSTRIAL SECTOR

	Algérois		Oranie		Constantinois		Totals	
	Units	Workers	Units	Workers	Units	Workers	Units	Workers
Construction	61	2,051	21	506	32	216	114	2,773
Timber	14	445	12	196	11	117	37	758
Metal and electrical goods	43	468	5	410	1	8	49	886
Food	28	1,102	41	655	16	502	85	2,259
Textiles	4	200	4	327	—	—	8	527
Chemicals	8	551	9	595	—	—	17	1,146
Others	10	416	13	362	12	394	35	1,172
Totals	168	5,233	105	3,051	72	1,237	345	9,521

duction. With the exception of oil production (entirely in French hands) where there was an increase of 16 per cent, production in 1963 was lower in practically all fields when compared with pre-independence figures. Public works and building dropped by 55 per cent, the number of people employed in construction falling from 200,000 in 1962 to 30,000 in 1963. Production of cement dropped from 1,300,000 tons in 1962 to 600,000 tons in the following year. Mineral extraction and exports (iron, phosphates, zinc, lead and iron pyrites) showed a decrease of between 10 and 20 per cent. Statistics issued by the Algerian government revealed a considerable decline in the production of steel and iron and of the mechanical and electrical industries. (The production of private cars, however, notably increased.)

	1960	1961	1962	1963
Steel ingots (tons)	31,034	30,535	5,507	9,480
Steel sheets (tons)	40,446	31,113	7,474	7,465
Steel castings (tons)	883	786	402	406
Cast iron (tons)	7,438	6,395	4,000	3,462
Hydraulic pumps (unit)	1,311	1,080	492	583
Railway wagons (unit)	355	362	236	189
Agricultural equipment (tons)	1,999	1,394	553	802
Small agricultural engines (unit)	—	355	173	126
Service vehicles (unit)	—	1,233	1,174	1,647
Private cars (unit)	—	2,087	2,056	3,198

It was officially reported in September 1965 that the production of non-ferrous minerals had improved in 1964; production of lead had increased, compared with 1963, by 15 per cent to reach 13,602 tons; that of zinc by 11 per cent to reach 64,274 tons. Copper production was 3,900 tons as against 3,745 tons in 1963. But that private cars should be on the increase while agricultural equipment was on the decrease in a country where agrarian reform was paramount—this speaks for itself. So does the drop in cement production in a country which needed building materials so desperately for reconstruction.

The future of the nationalised industries, taken over with such pomp and ceremony, and so many speeches against 'colonialism and capitalism' began to look very bleak. There was clearly no room for bonuses for the workers, even symbolic ones. The prescient Harbi in a remarkable lecture warned Algeria:

> With the coming of the revolution, hundreds have found themselves thrown into positions of [revolutionary] responsibility while they remain, subjectively speaking, bourgeois. . . . The kind of regulations and the acts necessary for wartime and for underground action discourage the free confrontation of ideas. . . . Slogans become a substitute for explanations. . . . By trying to concentrate the complete machinery of production within itself by any means at its disposal, the state disassociates itself from society and tends to become a deified entity superior to it. . . . This leads to the creation of a bureaucracy which is a very serious blemish on the edifice of socialism. . . . The centralised machine is responsible for all decisions, and, if it has not come to a decision, you must wait for it. The masses are exhorted to be creative and to be constructive, but no sense of initiative is left to them.[5]

The attentive faces of hundreds of young Algerian intellectuals at Harbi's lecture was indeed a hopeful augury for the country's future. But Harbi, in expressing his views with such clarity, was only digging his own grave. His idea did not appeal to the army's authoritarian cast of mind, and Ben Bella either could not or would not grasp what Harbi wanted to put across.

This lack of any truly contemporary revolutionary spirit in Ben Bella—who was being heralded throughout the world as a 'brilliant revolutionary leader'—was further evidenced when, in 1964, the

Cuban 'Che' Guevera suddenly left the International Trade Conference at Geneva to visit Algiers. Few found out what he said to Ben Bella, but Harbi was very happy to learn that, after having listened to Ben Bella's fears as to what Boumedienne's forces might do to take over the country, Guevera said: 'Don't be afraid—arm the people; never be afraid of arming the people.' Ben Bella was frightened by such a prospect; not so Harbi who, a true revolutionary, started campaigning in summer 1964 for the establishment of what came to be known as the 'milices populaires'.[6] Boumedienne opposed the idea categorically and told Ben Bella: 'Anyone who carries arms in this country will take his orders from me.' A wretched compromise resulted by which the popular militia would be directed by 'the party' but trained by the army. Captain Mahmoud Guennèz, a member of Boumedienne's staff at his wartime GHQ at Ghardimau, was put in charge of this body. It was no surprise, therefore, when at the critical point he sided with Boumedienne. Ben Bella depended throughout on crafty political gambits and petty manoeuvres for his support, rather than gaining really solid support from the people.*

It was no light matter for Harbi and his colleagues to write as they did in *Révolution Africaine*, for nobody knew what would happen next. So they resorted to the tactics, previously used in *Alger Républicain*, of persuading others to express their opinions. In *Révolution Africaine* of December 28, 1963, there appeared the following significant 'reader's letter':

> I live in Khenchela. I am writing to express my surprise and indignation. Some of the people of Algiers are living in fantastic luxury which is an insult to the workers in general and to the peasants in the poorer regions in particular. Everything is to be found in Algiers, everything is expensive, yet in spite of this a lot is being bought. The price of a cinema seat is higher than the daily wage of an agricultural worker in our region. The cafés are

---

* It is not without interest to note that Fidel Castro—who after the overthrow of Ben Bella attacked the Boumedienne regime as 'fascist'—ordered that all weapons still in the hands of civilian Cubans should be handed over to the government just at the time when the Algerian colonel, now become premier, ordered the disbanding of the 'milices populaires'. Of course, the situations in the two countries were different; nevertheless the coincidence is significant, especially as 'Che' Guevera, known to be in conflict with Fidel Castro, at that time disappeared so mysteriously from the scene.

full of idlers—not to speak of the unemployed—and charge ludicrous prices. I should like to ask whether socialism is being reserved for the interior?

A. AMRANT, Khenchela

The situation in Algiers indeed gave grounds for alarming comparisons. Against the ever-present background of the misery and squalor of the *fellah*, there was in the city a horde of well-paid, well-fed bureaucrats living beyond their means and squandering the nation's resources. This new bourgeoisie lived in 'bien-vacant' flats, paying neither for accommodation nor services and running their own luxurious cars. There were, it is true, a few conscientious and overworked men in the administration, but otherwise Algiers had degenerated into uninspired idleness. History and the misfortunes of post-independence days have made Algiers the saddest capital of the Arab world—Damascus included.

Contrast this with the situation in the poorer rural areas. The UN estimate of the average income of a 'typical' *fellah* family, cited in chapter 5, would appear to refer to a 'typically well-to-do' peasant family, for there are great tracts of Algeria where poverty is much more profound. A sociological survey made of these regions showed that there meat was considered 'a great luxury' and that 230 francs as an estimate of monthly income (based, it seems, on industrial workers) was too high for rural workers as a whole. Families were living in one-roomed dwellings with scarcely the barest necessities of life.[7] While the slogans, part hectoring, part smug, and the parallels with the Chinese revolution were being churned out, Ben Bella's regime did virtually nothing to improve the prosperity of the country, either on a socialist or on a capitalist basis. Even according to official statistics, of the 8,000 *meshta* destroyed in the war, only 60 were reconstructed—and this in spite of much large talk and fine writing about 'voluntary workers', 'youth brigades' and so on.

Harbi warned Ben Bella that true socialism could never stem from such a confused hotchpotch. France, he pointed out, still had a strong economic hold on the country through the army of cheap Algerian labour that emigrated to France. Although this meant that some 50 billion francs were sent every year from France to families in Algeria, it also opened the door towards the French capitalist system. If it were to prove necessary, Harbi argued, all emigration to France should be forbidden and all available Algerian hands put to work for Algeria. This, again, was too much for Ben Bella, although it did not prevent him from continuing to point out the supposed parallel between 'the two agrarian revolutions of Algeria and China'. He even had the effrontery to maintain (in an interview granted on the very day before his fall) that 'self-management was more successful in Algeria than in Yugoslavia'.[8]

While the interminable talk went on, Algeria was sinking deeper and deeper into economic chaos. Conservative estimates indicated that by 1964 some 3½ million people—no less than 84 per cent of the total active population—were unemployed or severely under-employed, and that 68 per cent of the total man-years which were in principle available were not utilised. (See Appendix III, Table 3.)

In what remains the best marxist analysis of post-war Algeria, Gérard Chaliān arrived at the obvious conclusion: at the very best, Algerian 'socialism' would end up as state capitalism—and a very poor version of state capitalism at that. As for the people: their feelings were well summed up in a statement attributed to a *fellah* and published in *Révolution Africaine*. 'Socialism is four-fifths for Number One, and one-fifth for the other chap!'

7

LOST MAGHRIBINE
OPPORTUNITIES

THE HISTORY of the emergent nations of post-war Africa has demonstrated that unity of purpose and action is essential to a newly born nation, if it is to rid itself of the contradictions and divisions arising from its former colonial rule. African leaders have so far achieved no more than vigorous speeches on the subject of unity, but this in no way detracts from the principle of unity; it is rather a measure of the difficulty of achieving it. The long list of Britain's failures in her attempts to establish federal government in Africa and Asia as the base for launching new nations into complete independence, is yet another illustration of the fact that the Third World still has much to learn before it can grow out of narrow concepts of nationalism.

In the Maghrib, there are strong historical and geographical reasons which make unity a perfectly feasible proposition. Yet projects, statements and conferences have been immediately contradicted by the actions which followed them. This is not to say that Maghribine unity is not to be striven for: it simply shows that the path towards it is difficult.

Recently, however, there have been some signs of change: a new generation of technocrats has been succeeding to responsible posts in North Africa. Such men understand that the key to future prosperity lies not in speeches but in economic development. They fully realise that the production statistics of an entire country count for very little when they are hardly more than the output of a single major city in Western Europe. To continue the traditional pattern of exporting a few well-established commodities is no way to economic expansion. Only the fullest co-ordination of industrial development on a regional or subregional basis can overcome the difficulties of increasing production, and concerted efforts are needed to establish markets common to the economies of all the new nations of Africa, and so reduce the disparity between them and the highly industrialised communities of both Eastern and Western worlds.[1] This is well enough understood by the younger technologists, but their elders—the nationalist leaders who founded the new countries—are inevitably preoccupied with narrower problems of national or even personal interest. Any observer of North Africa will accept that the vital and quite practicable goal of Maghribine unity may well suffer further setbacks as a result of the deep-rooted national and personal differences between the present leaders of Libya, Tunisia, Morocco and Algeria. Plans for uniting nations always take a long time to come to fruition, and the task of working towards this goal falls to future generations.

Nevertheless, the Algerian war has shown clearly that in times of crisis there is a solidarity among the Maghribine peoples that can play a decisive part in affairs. In this the Maghrib differs markedly from some other parts of Africa. For example, one is struck when visiting the African countries which border Portugal's colonies and South Africa by the fact that none of them, words apart, seems willing to assist anti-Salazarist or anti-Verwoerdian nationalist movements to anything like the extent that Tunisia and Morocco aided Algeria. It is difficult to envisage how the Algerians could have survived from 1954 without bases in Tunisia and Morocco, let alone how they could have won the war unaided.

Yet, when the war was over, Algeria proved to have a very short memory and did not even acknowledge the help of her neighbours. History will record that Ben Bella and Boumedienne (who certainly should have known better since he was based on Ghardimau in Tunisia) lacked even the smallest courtesy and gratitude in their dealings with Tunisia and Morocco. The Algerian government also failed to acknowledge the invaluable help given by Libya. During the war Libya had acted as a transit centre and depot both for civilians and armed forces, and great sums of money were donated by the family of King Idris. But Algeria found it convenient not to remember all this until 1964 when a Libyan delegation was invited to Algiers as part of an unsuccessful attempt to scare both the

Libyans and the French over oil. Of course, it must have been intensely irritating to many Algerians to find after their victory so many countries, whose support at the crucial time had been more in words than deeds, boasting of the help they had given during the war. When Ben Bella visited Moscow, Khrushchev introduced him to a Soviet worker with the words: 'Here is the man whose hands furnished the arms with which you won your victory.' Ben Bella enthusiastically agreed. But everyone knew that even if Russia had, of necessity, provided the largest number of arms to the revolutionaries, such help came rather late in the day—well after China, and certainly well after the Arab countries had made their contribution. (It was, incidentally, one of the charges levied later against Ben Bella by Boumedienne that he was oversusceptible to the 'red carpet' treatment.)

The cold attitude of the Ben Bella regime to Morocco and Tunisia is partly explicable by its anxiety to keep in with Nasser. Both from a political and an emotional point of view, it found it expedient to hail the UAR as the saviour of Algeria. Moreover, Ben Bella and Boumedienne held the neighbouring regimes in contempt and fully expected them to be swept away by the eddies from the Algerian revolution. While it is true that UAR, being richer than Tunisia, was able to provide more weapons and financial aid, Tunisia stands out as the first country to make the symbolic gesture of giving arms to the Algerian revolutionaries. Like Morocco, Tunisia made use of her advantageous geographical position to give them all the help she could, at considerable risk to herself. Algeria's ingratitude is a reflection of the extreme complexity of the North African political scene.

Tunisia's assistance took the form of 'co-belligerence'.[2] She gave every possible kind of military and political aid, short of actually openly declaring war on France. When Tunisia decides to release the details of her recent history, the extent of this aid will amaze many. But disclosure of its extent and character may not be made for a long time; the Tunisians not only need to be careful of what they say about their most powerful neighbour: they also feel that it is not for them to give the first account of events which primarily concern Algeria. When I tried to get further information in the summer of 1965, registered letters and cables failed to produce even an acknowledgement from the authorities in Morocco and

Algeria. In Tunisia—where things are rather more efficient—an interview was granted by Caid-el-Sebsi, the minister of the Interior, and some facts and figures made available; but the authorities there were not yet ready to give full details since, as the minister said, 'it will take some time to get all the papers together from different archives in different ministries'. Much of the information given below about Tunisian and Moroccan relations with the independence movement in Algeria during the war, especially in connection with the ALN organisation in Morocco, was provided by the former Algerian minister, Abdelhafid Boussouf. Needless to say, all the views and interpretations about these relationships are my own.

From 1954 onwards, Algerians began to flood into Tunisia: refugees with their families and guerrillas looking for arms and a base for training and preparation for activities in Algeria. By the end of the war there were 170,000 Algerian refugees in Tunisia—70,000 in Souk el Arba, 60,000 in Kéf, 25,000 in Kasserine, 13,000 in Gafsa and a similar number in Tunis and its suburbs. In the words of Dr Lundt, the UN's 'High Commissioner for Refugees', the problem was 'not to leave those human beings to rot in idleness'. So, quite apart from sheltering and feeding the refugees (in which the Red Crescent and many other international organisations helped), the Tunisians had to guarantee law and security and provide work for the refugees. In 1965 the state of Tunisia paid a last bill of some 2½ million dinars (now roughly on parity with the French franc) solely for transporting the refugees.

These purely civilian and refugee problems were complex enough, but the military aid which Tunisia gave Algeria posed even more difficult and dangerous problems. At the time Tunisia herself was disarming her guerrillas in view of the independence that she was shortly to gain. The Tunisian authorities gave Algeria 4,000 rifles, revolvers and machine-guns, while at the same time, unknown to them, the Tunisian *fellagha* were selling arms privately to the Algerians. The country, which had still not completely attained independence, was full of Algerians coming and going and engaging in all kinds of trafficking in arms. The situation became so chaotic and dangerous that President Bourguiba was compelled to make strenuous appeals for order 'so that the war can be more effectively waged'. Finally an agreement was reached with the Algerian authorities. Some kind of order was certainly necessary for, due to the closing of the barrages in late 1957, by the end of the war there were 30,000 ALN men stationed in Tunisia. The GHQ of the ALN, which also included the headquarters of COM-EST was at Ghardimau. This meant that the part of Tunisia along the Algerian border from Babouche south of the port of Tabarka, to Kasserine south-west of Sbeitla (where the Sahara begins) was entirely in the hands of the Algerian army. The width of this stretch of land varied between 20 and 40 kms. The main ammunition depots of the ALN were at Kairouan, some distance from the border, and in Tunis itself. But there were also some depots nearer the border, in the Kéf region. It was impossible to keep an exact count of what went in and out of Tunisia, for the Algerians tried to maintain strict secrecy, not only for war-security but because they were anxious not to alarm the Tunisians. Even so, the Tunisian authorities recorded that 130,000,000 items 'from hand grenades and shells to machine guns and pieces of artillery' entered the country from 1954 to 1962.

The war activities of Algeria along the border inevitably involved Tunisia in military matters. France's war against Algeria began to escalate towards Tunisia. French troops fighting FLN units on Tunisian soil could hardly be expected to differentiate Tunisians from Algerians. On several occasions the French accused the Tunisians, with good reason, of conducting military operations. This led France to claim, like General MacArthur in North Korea, the 'right of pursuit', and resulted in many operations by the French on Tunisian soil. The most grave was the attack on the village of Sakiet Sidi Youssef on February 18, 1958, which had wide international repercussions and led to the severing of diplomatic relations between France and Tunisia. After several times giving warning, the French had begun attacks on Tunisian territory on September 1, 1957; on October 4, Tunisia recalled her ambassador from Paris following a French announcement that bombers would also be used against Tunisia. Arms from America and Britain were sent to the poorly equipped Tunisians, which provoked the French to walk out in protest from a NATO parliamentarians' meeting on November 14. Meanwhile, on October 7, the Tunisian UN representative, Bahi Ladgham, had proposed that the French, Algerians, Tunisians and Moroccans should meet round a conference table. The late King Mohammed V and President Bourguiba both proposed peace talks to Paris, but in vain. This intensified world-wide concern with the events in North Africa, and on December 28, 1958, the International Red Cross launched an appeal for the refugees in Tunisia and Morocco. But the war continued and world opinion received a severe shock when the French bombed Sakiet Sidi Youssef.

According to private information from Tunisian officials, the losses sustained by Tunisia as a result of the Algerian war and of the violation of her territory by the French army were of the following order: 1,550 established cases of violation of Tunisian airspace by French aircraft; 272 incursions of French troops into Tunisia intent on their 'right of pursuit'; 960 cases of bombardment of national territory by French artillery; 80 cases of reprisals against border villages suspected of collaborating with the Algerians; 35 clashes (from 1954 to 1957, when such actions ceased) between the French army and the Tunisian Garde Nationale. The human cost to Tunisia of these operations has been officially put at 600 dead and 800 wounded (civilian and military); another 220 are reported as still missing to this day, most of them kidnapped by the French to get information. The dead included K. Hedgeri, secretary of state for External Affairs, and among the wounded was Caid-el-Sebsi, the present minister of the Interior. During these operations, 1,100 *meshta* and 5,000 head of cattle were destroyed, and an appreciable part of Tunisia's best agricultural land was rendered useless.

Figures alone, however, cannot convey what 'co-belligerence' meant to the Tunisians in terms of human, economic and sociological factors—and in particular the internal and external political implications. One must remember that, in 1954, Tunisia had only just attained internal autonomy, and that French troops were still on her soil. They were not due to begin to evacuate the country before 1958, following the agreement of June 17, 1954 which called for 'progressive' withdrawal; and they were not due to evacuate the base of Bizerta until 1962–63. This meant that, until 1962, there were three armies on Tunisian soil: the Algerian insurgents, French forces and the Tunisian army, which was by far the weakest of the three. There were two governments in the country: the Tunisian and the Algerian revolutionary directorate, which set up its own administration, its own civilian and military police, and its own ministries, including those of Internal and External Affairs— all of them conducted from Tunisia. When the insurgent leaders began to organise the ALN and the civilians (for, apart from the 170,000 refugees and the 30,000 members of the ALN, there was also a permanent colony of 20,000 Algerians, to which were added another 10,000 brought by the GPRA), the Tunisians were presented with a fearsome problem of internal security. The extremist Tunisian nationalist group, known as the 'Youssefites' after their leader, Salah Ben Youssef, wanted to align their country completely with Algeria in 'spreading the revolution to the entire Maghrib' and rejecting the idea of gradual independence for Tunisia.

In the world of diplomacy, the government in Tunis did all it possibly could to help the Algerians. Bourguiba even went so far as to incorporate the problem of the French enclave at the Bizerta base into the broader question of the Algerian problem. But the French took no interest until de Gaulle had decided exactly what kind of settlement he wanted in Algeria, and Bourguiba had to embark on what became known as the 'battle of Bizerta' (in which it is said nearly 5,000 Tunisian lives were lost) to rid the country of the remaining French forces. Things were not made any easier by the closeness of the alliance between the Algerians and the UAR; there must be few leaders who detest each other more heartily than Bourguiba and Nasser. (Indeed, in October 1958 their governments were to break off diplomatic relations.)

In some ways Morocco had less of a burden to bear than Tunisia, not only because she is a much stronger country but because the war was concentrated in eastern Algeria, where the revolution first broke out. Consequently there were far fewer ALN troops in Morocco. Whereas in Tunisia a modern state was being established, so that it was possible to negotiate with the GPRA on rational lines and to arrive at sensible compromise solutions to problems, it was quite different in Morocco. Here the Algerians could co-operate with the royal family and practically nobody else for, especially during the reign of Mohammed V—a sovereign who won universal respect—the king's word was law. The most wholehearted of the help given Algeria seems to have come from Mohammed V, his son Hassan and his sister Princess Lalla Aycha (who became Morocco's ambassador to Britain in 1965). Relations with the political party then in power—the Istiqlal—were to turn sour;

according to the Algerians, Istiqlal elements even attempted to curtail supplies of arms to the FLN which they regarded as a dangerous 'revolutionary rival'. Algeria maintained better relations with the leftwing opposition, the Union Nationale des Forces Populaires (UNFP), but since it was not in power it could do little more than provide journalistic aid. 'The Royal family apart, it would certainly not be wrong to say that it was not the politicians, but the people of Morocco who came to our aid', Abdelhafid Boussouf told me, adding that during the war 'thousands upon thousands of Moroccans living near the border volunteered for the ALN'. The Moroccans were the only non-Algerian volunteers that the ALN accepted, save for a few Youssefites who joined from Tunisia. The ALN hoped to have many more Algerian volunteers from Morocco, where the only mobilisation order issued by the GPRA during the war was proclaimed. The limited response showed that the sizeable Algerian community there—mostly employees in the Moroccan administration and members of the liberal professions—had little enthusiasm for the ALN.

Even so, despite the poor response from the permanent colony of Algerians—most of whom elected to stay where they were after Algerian independence—there was much nationalist activity in Morocco. First of all there were the refugees: 130,000 of them. The ALN also was active, secretly operating small-arms and ammunition factories and trafficking in arms. The Algerian police caused many disturbances by raids, which went as far as Casablanca on the coast, to capture deserters and political opponents. And of course, as in Tunisia, there were the ALN troops facing the French barrages —some 10,000 of them—with all the problems their presence meant to the local population. In 1958 COM-OUEST established its bases in exactly the same strategic positions as had been occupied before Moroccan independence by the French 32nd Infantry Division: Martimprey, Berkane, Oujda (ALN headquarters), Berguent and Figuig. The last-named was especially important as it dominated one of the few natural crossroads linking North Africa with the Sahara. During the occupation, the French had found it practically impossible to defend, and the Algerians used it as a main line of communication.

For all the help given them, the Algerian nationalist leaders lost little time once the war was over in showing hostility to their former benefactors by word and deed, and indeed it became evident that they wanted to overthrow the regimes of Bourguiba and Hassan. In failing to take advantage of the goodwill engendered during the war, the Algerian leaders may well have lost their first big opportunity of giving Maghribine unity practical encouragement. Their aim may have been to spread the revolution to their two neighbours, but they only created confusion both at home and abroad. The very people whom the Algerians wanted to attract, the common people of Tunisia and Morocco, were in fact those who were most alarmed by the policy of the new regime. The Tunisians and Moroccans were soon able to judge for themselves the sincerity of the Algerian slogans and they suspected that they would have to contend not so much with the spread of 'revolution' as with the unleashing of chaos.

Of course, the different characters of the three regimes— monarchical, revolutionary and republican—presented an obstacle to further collaboration. If the decisions taken at Tangiers, on April 30, 1958, by the three political parties—Neo-Destour of Tunisia, FLN of Algeria, and Istiqlal of Morocco—to create a federation among the three countries* were to be applied, how was the problem of the incompatibility of the three regimes to be resolved? The Algerians had a simple reply to the question, one which dated back to the days when they complained that their troops in Tunisia and Morocco were not being helped as they should be ('this was not Maghribine fraternity as it should be'), and said that after independence their revolution would brush aside the regimes of Bourguiba and Hassan. But as we have seen, things turned out very differently. As the domestic situation in Algeria deteriorated, more and more Algerians began to regard their neighbours with envy rather than contempt, seeing Morocco and Tunisia, particularly the latter, as havens of peace. A great number of Algerians went as tourists to Tunisia and Morocco in the summers of 1963, 1964 and 1965 to breathe the fresh air of peace and tranquillity. The failures in Algerian domestic policy were not without their repercussions on those in the two neighbouring states who were banking on the

---

* The decision was taken in a moment of nationalistic euphoria and has since been completely a dead letter. On June 20 in the same year, these three political parties made another decision which was to remain a dead letter: to establish a Constituent Assembly of the Maghrib.

Algerian revolution to overthrow the regimes there. They were discouraged and disappointed, and public opinion in the two countries gradually came to the conclusion that, whatever the defects of their own governments, the situation in Algeria showed that things could be very much worse.

This was especially the case in regard to Tunisia which, out of all Africa, has the only smoothly running modern administration and certainly the best-organised political party, the Neo-Destour, whose machinery is said to be as well-oiled as that of any communist party. This is not only due to Bourguiba, the founder of modern Tunisia, but also to the fact that Tunisia has, for its size, the greatest number of highly trained people in the whole of Africa. These cadres exist because, while France suppressed native education in Algeria, she did not worry greatly about Tunisia, which had few economic attractions. So the Tunisian bourgeoisie, who were mostly of Turkish origin, not only had the means to educate their sons, but found that the opportunities to do so remained open to them. The rich country of Morocco also has a large number of highly trained people, but there the royalist regime has not instilled a spirit of vigour into the youth of the country, and the cadres are deeply divided between the extremely pro-Western and those who have retained more of the traditional spirit of Islam. This is not the case in Tunisia where a more contemporary attitude is widespread, doubtless due to Bourguiba.[3]

In the summer of 1962, in the early weeks of Ben Bella's Political Bureau, I was told by Khider and Benalla Hadj (who was later to become president of the National Assembly and to be arrested with Ben Bella, whose closest lieutenant he was) that the Algerians kept a 'secret dossier of the Bourguiba regime to which additions were made every day'. This was being done with the help of a few Tunisian Youssefites who had transferred their allegiance from Cairo to Algiers, and with direct assistance from the Egyptian *Muhabarat*. A certain Abderrahmane Cherif, a Tunisian-born Algerian who had been condemned to death in absentia in Tunisia, was particularly active in this matter. The GPRA kept him under restraint in the Tripoli office but he returned to Algeria as head of the Bureau of Arab Affairs and was later made a minister of high rank in Ben Bella's government. The plan was that Tunisia and Libya should be squeezed out of existence between the Algeria of

Ben Bella and the Egypt of Nasser. In this way, both Egypt and Algeria intended to make Bourguiba pay for his 'great treason'.

Bourguiba's 'treason' was committed when, before Tunisia and Morocco had achieved independence, the leaders of the Neo-Destour and the Istiqlal refused to accept the Algerian idea that they should refuse the French terms for independence and join the struggle of the FLN-ALN, and then proceed together to create a free and united Maghrib. In this Algeria was supported by the Youssefites and by some of the Moroccan Army of National Liberation. Certainly the concept looked very revolutionary and idealistic. But Bourguiba tenaciously maintained that the whole idea was far too nebulous, and that it would not lead to freedom for anyone in practice—on the contrary, it might well lead to their being crushed by the French once and for all. The Algerian nationalist leaders, with the Youssefites and the supporters of the ALN in Morocco, maintained quite the reverse, contending that granting independence to Morocco and Tunisia and not to Algeria was a colonial trick of the French intended to keep Algeria in subjugation for ever. In this they were quite right: such was indeed the French idea; but their grandiose scheme was not the way to overcome it. Bourguiba maintained that a formal, declared attack would only play into the hands of the French and that it would be much better for Tunisia to lend practical assistance by giving all the help she could as an independent country.

Bourguiba may have his faults and may have made his mistakes*

---

* In 1964, Tunisia proceeded to nationalise all the lands that remained in foreign hands. These were very largely French, but there was also some in Italian and British hands—including those of Baron d'Erlanger who was in fact doing far more good to Tunisia than to the Exchequer of the United Kingdom, which in the end refused to allow the baron to transfer sterling to Tunisia. But this action, which de Gaulle has not yet forgiven and which led to the French refusal to trade with the vital wine-growing industry of Tunisia, was caused by Bourguiba's anxiety to demonstrate to his people, and to the world at large, that the promise of decolonisation in his country was ahead of the revolutionary Algeria. The verdict of history may be that Bourguiba's most serious mistake is the strong streak of political paternalism in both himself and the power groups which have inevitably gathered round him, which may well largely destroy the spirit of initiative and enthusiasm in forthcoming generations. In a speech on January 18, 1963, he said that 'total liberty, such as the one enjoyed by the British, could only be granted to Tunisians the day their level nears that of the British'—which may take some time!

but—anti-communist though he is—he has applied Lenin's maxim of 'one step backward, two steps forward' far better than many a marxist. The results of his subtle combination of moderation and aggressiveness speak for themselves. Tunisia is not only the most modern country in Africa, but also the only one to become so completely decolonised that there are now very few traces of ex-colonial complexes among Tunisian intellectuals. Events were to prove that Bourguiba's tactics were right and his opponents' wrong, however full of glory and emotion they may have been. The French would undoubtedly have crushed a general Maghribine insurrection, whatever encouragement it might have received from Cairo's 'Voice of the Arabs'. As it was, with the help that independent Tunisia and Morocco were able to provide, the Algerian revolutionaries were able to succeed. But it is the nature of men, and particularly of politicians, to be guided by sentiment and emotion, and not by hard facts, and the Algerian leaders of today still believe in Bourguiba's 'great treason'. When the ALN entered Algeria in 1962 and a public demonstration was organised in the capital, Ben Bella openly accused Bourguiba (and also some foreign press correspondents) of being 'agents of Zionism'.

To this day, Bourguiba has not visited independent Algeria. When he met Ben Bella in Cairo in 1964, he told him that he could not visit Algeria until the question of the border between the two countries at 'Borne 233' (see Map 1, pp. xiv–xv) had been resolved. This was a 'matter of principle'. Algerian officials say very forcibly that it is of 'minute importance and should not be allowed to stand in the way of better relations between us'. Ben Bella assured the Tunisian president that the matter would certainly be settled, and even that it 'could already be considered as settled'. But when Mokkadem, the former foreign minister of Tunisia, stated on an election tour that 'the matter of Borne 233 is settled', there was a loud outcry in Algeria. The Algerian leader was accused of 'giving away the land of [the] country on [his] own authority'. Ben Bella retorted that he had never made any such promise, and that Bourguiba was well known to take an inch and claim that he had gained a mile. Nevertheless, the matter of Borne 233 was to find its way into another 'secret dossier'—that maintained by Boumedienne and his colleagues as a compendium of Ben Bella's crimes. The issue is still unresolved, with the consequence that the Tunisians are now spending money on building up their tiny army, previously neglected by them not only because they could not afford one but also because Bourguiba had an instinctive dislike of 'the colonel type'.

But perhaps the most striking example of bad blood between neighbours came in 1964 when Tunisia, a country with poor natural resources, struck oil at last. It was found near the Algerian border at El Borma by the Italian state-sponsored company, Ente Nazionale Idrocarburi (ENI) which had set up the Société Italo-Tunisienne d'Exploitation Pétrolière (SITEP) in association with the Tunisian government. Here, at last, was the big economic break-through of which the Tunisians had dreamed, and which they hoped would enable their country to supply the refinery at Bizerta (also built by ENI) with its own supplies of oil. It did not take long for the Algerians to show their teeth. The border, they claimed, was an artificial creation of French troops during the war and was incorrect; moreover, the oil found in Tunisia was coming from a source which was really in Algerian territory. If the find in Tunisia were only a small one, then Bourguiba might keep it; but if it were important, then Algeria would step in and claim it for herself. It was characteristic of Bourguiba's energy that he at once ordered ENI, which was asking itself in bewilderment whether or not it ought to consider its installations as being in Algeria or in Tunisia, to go ahead and 'drill right on top of the border'. Algerian appetites, however, had been whetted by the operations of United States and French companies on their own side of the border at El Borma. The matter is still unresolved.

Between the incidents of Borne 233 and El Borma, much befell to worsen relations. Officials of Tunis and teachers were gaoled by Algerians on charges of espionage. Animosity reached a high pitch when, in December 1962, a plot to kill Bourguiba was uncovered. Tunisia maintained that Algerians were concerned in the plot. Ben Bella asserted that, on the contrary, the exiled Boudiaf, with the assistance of some Tunisians, was plotting against his own regime. Insults and threats were exchanged and diplomatic relations broken off. The crisis was temporarily mitigated as a result of Moroccan mediation in February 1963. That the relations between Tunisia and Algeria did not deteriorate still further was very largely due to the patient labours of Mestiri, the Tunisian ambassador to Algeria, who, profoundly convinced of the future feasibility of Maghribine unity, believed that all these disturbances were ephemeral.

Much more serious border disputes were to arise between Morocco and Algeria, and were to lead to armed clashes. As Jean Lacouture has said,[4] it is easy enough to deride these border disputes between the Maghribine countries, but Europe has only to look at its own history, even now marred by stupid territorial disputes. What of the disputes between Britain and Spain; Italy and Austria? What of the menacing frontier conflicts in Asia: China and India; India and Pakistan; Pakistan and Afghanistan; China and the Soviet Union? It is trite to say that North Africa inherited its frontier problems from the days of colonial rule. Certainly, the French were ruling North Africa through different administrations, and the French occupiers of Algeria defended 'their' territory from the French of Tunisia and Morocco; then came the Algerian war and the establishment of many a no-man's land. But this gets us nowhere. The real criticism that can be directed at the new countries of North Africa is that, while maintaining that they were 'new countries of the future', they could do no better than the old countries of Europe in settling their disputes.

Morocco has always insisted, following Mohammed V—in whom even the Algerian revolutionaries can find little to criticise—that parts of the so-called 'Algerian' territory in the Tindouf and Colomb-Béchar regions (see Map 1, pp. xiv–xv) are, in fact, Moroccan. There was no point in emphasising this during the war; nevertheless, as came to light later, an agreement was made in January 1960 between the late king and the GPRA, establishing a 'principle of negotiation' in this matter to be followed after Algeria gained independence. But like so many agreements entered into by the GPRA, this was regarded as null and void by the new Algerian regime. This was neither the first nor the last of the efforts made by Morocco to settle the issue by negotiation. In his book, *Où va l'Algérie?*, Boudiaf comments on the armed clashes of 1963:

It is hard to believe that . . . war with Morocco has become a reality. There was nothing to indicate such tragic events between two peoples whose nearness and common aspirations are surely worth far more than a few dunes and rocks, even if these contain fabulous mineral wealth. . . . The reasons which have been put

forward by both sides seem to me to be very unconvincing.
. . . During the spring of 1956, at the time of the Spanish visit of
the late king of Morocco, Mohammed V, the question of the
Algero-Moroccan frontiers was raised by the Algerian delegation,
then consisting of Dr Lamine Debaghine and Ben Bella. The
same year, when I was in Morocco, at each interview I had with
the king my attention was drawn to the importance of the problem. The different GPRAs have had to debate this question, as the
agreement signed by Ferhat Abbas demonstrates, and the
Moroccan government has never failed to point this out to the
Algerians responsible. After the liberation and the great celebrations in Rabat, this problem was at the very heart of the
discussions at two meetings with members of the Sherifian
government.

At the second of these meetings, King Hassan, according to Boudiaf
said that, while determined to guard Morocco's national heritage,
he was willing to propose the setting up of a committee of enquiry
to seek the best means for a just solution, 'either by discussions
leading to territorial adjustments, or through an economic agreement which would be wide enough to cover these problems'.

The GPRA's reply was made in the presence of ten of its members
through Ben Khedda, who declared: 'While Algeria has still to
gain independence and has no definitive government, it is better
to leave the question in abeyance.' At the beginning of July 1962,
before leaving Tunis, the GPRA received the Moroccan minister,
Alaoui, bearing a note from Hassan II on this same subject.
Since Algeria has had its definitive government, how often have
the Moroccans reopened this question? Six times, according to
the Moroccans.[5]

For all their willingness to negotiate, however, the Moroccans were
determined not to let their interests go by default. A few days after
Algeria formally became independent, their auxiliary forces, the
maghzan (but not, be it noted, the royal army), moved in to take
possession of the land around Tindouf. Algeria reacted strongly.
Rabat tried to play down the incident by saying that the posts
occupied by Moroccan forces had been established by agreement
with the French as being no-man's land territory during the war so

as to avoid the involvement of Moroccan troops in clashes. A few months later, however, a pro-Moroccan demonstration was staged in Tindouf. The Armée Nationale Populaire (the ALN in its post-independence guise) suppressed it vigorously and many of the local Moroccan population were killed.

From the time of this incident and throughout the summer of 1963 the situation deteriorated still further. Algeria drove many Moroccan nationals from her territory, and Morocco did the same to many Algerians living in hers. About October 8 small clashes occurred which built up by the end of the month to a minor war. Internal factors on both sides contributed to this. Boudiaf says that the Moroccan affair was used by Ben Bella to crush domestic opposition, and that it was also made to take on the appearance of a struggle for national survival and a crusade in the cause of socialism. Boudiaf's first allegation is perfectly true, but his second needs certain qualifications.

Ben Bella was, in principle at least, opposed to the Moroccan monarchy, but he was realistic enough to appreciate that King Hassan would be a tough nut to crack. Moreover, the domestic situation in Algeria was disastrous both politically and economically. The Kabyles under Hocine Ait Ahmed and Mohand ou El-Hadj were in open rebellion, and already the deteriorating economic situation was leading to isolated episodes of agitation and revolt in the country. With Kabilya under strict occupation by the ANP, rumours that arms from abroad were being brought in for the Kabyle insurgents gave credence to fears that the internal conflict might be internationalised. Official circles in Algiers said that Salazar was sending weapons to Hocine Ait Ahmed. It was not possible to ascertain the truth or falsity of this charge, but it certainly was aimed at discrediting the Kabyle leader. It may not have been as wild a charge as might appear. Forces opposed to Ben Bella's 'socialist revolution' were not likely to be indifferent to the possibility of the Kabilya affair's bringing down his regime.

But if, from the point of view of domestic politics, the Moroccan struggle was a dangerous venture, it also offered a useful scapegoat for the country's difficulties. Harbi was pressing Ben Bella to exploit the situation 'in a revolutionary manner'. Thus, as the Moroccan crisis intensified, Ben Bella proclaimed 'the birth of the child for which every Algerian has been waiting': the seizure of all

French-owned land. Mehdi Ben Barka, the leader of the Moroccan opposition exiled in Algiers, proclaimed in *Révolution Africaine* (October 26, 1963) that the struggle with Morocco was 'anti-imperialist' and 'pro-socialist'. He also said, this time in his capacity as leader of the Cairo-based Afro-Asian Peoples' Solidarity Committee (AAPSC) that this fight would be for a 'greater Maghrib' which would be the 'extension of an Arab Union'—this reflecting Nasser's interest in the matter.*

The AAPSC takes its tune from Moscow, and the Russian attitude towards the Algero-Moroccan conflict was indicated by a statement in *Pravda* on October 16, 1963, to the effect that 'the duty of all peaceful nations is to assist the Algerian people to consolidate its revolutionary conquests'. Moscow's pro-Algerian line in this affair had its embarrassments as the Moroccan army partly owed its superiority to some fifty heavy Soviet tanks purchased from the USSR during the Algerian war. The French communists, following the line from Moscow, at once lined up with Algeria against Morocco, *Humanité* asserting that 'French democratic public opinion is solidly for the Algerian people engaged in a just cause'. At the same time Cuba also expressed her full support 'for the heroic people of Algeria in their struggle against the manoeuvres of imperialism, colonialism and neocolonialism'. In a surprise move, Castro sent badly needed tanks (and military instructors) in a ship which docked at Oran and which the Algerians themselves believed to be carrying a cargo of sugar. *Borba*, the official organ of the Yugoslav government, took a more balanced view and requested Morocco 'to withdraw her troops, to return to the status quo and not to compromise herself in the eyes of Afro-Asia and of the entire world'.

In Cairo, *Al Gumhuriya* declared that 'the Moroccan aggression is a flagrant contradiction of law, both international and simply human. It makes nonsense of everything that the leaders of Morocco have said since the accession of the country to independence.' The

* Mehdi Ben Barka was condemned to death in his absence by the Moroccan authorities, and even the Moroccan opposition disliked his close affinities with Cairo. Though given the chance in 1965 of returning to Morocco under a general amnesty, he elected to remain in exile. At the end of 1965, he was kidnapped in Paris by French secret agents, apparently working in concert with their Moroccan counterparts, and subsequently murdered. The Ben Barka Affair has become the gravest political scandal of post-war France.

Egyptians gave more than merely verbal support to Algeria. They immediately established an airlift (which flew over Tunisian territory without authority) carrying troops and equipment. As it turned out, however, this token of solidarity was to prove something of a Greek gift for Algeria, and was to have unexpected consequences for relations between herself and the UAR. Boumedienne, who was staking his entire past reputation and political future against the Royal Moroccan Army, had sought this aid from the UAR. Ben Bella, although strongly pro-Nasser, objected to this move since it had been made behind his back. A major quarrel broke out between the two, which the UAR ambassador in Algiers, Kachaba, tried to moderate. Shortly after this affair, Ben Bella suddenly promoted Colonel Tahar Zbiri to be chief of the General Staff, without the knowledge of Boumedienne, the minister of Defence, who at the time was in Moscow seeking arms. This was destined ultimately to backfire against Ben Bella. Ironically enough, as we shall see later, it was over the question of the vital military aid which the UAR was giving to Algeria that Boumedienne fell out with Nasser.

But Ben Bella once again proved incapable of following a truly revolutionary line. Harbi told me at the time: 'It is over. Ben Bella has missed the boat once more. He will now play at war with Morocco, in the traditional nationalist manner, under the influence of Boumedienne.' In traditional war, the Moroccans proved the stronger and inflicted a serious defeat on the Algerians, not only because they had the larger and better equipped army, but also because the spirit of nationalism in Morocco was far stronger. Moroccan forces occupied Tindjoub and Hassi Beida, and inflicted losses on the Algerians which have been estimated at between 3,000 and 6,000, including many prisoners. An episode which became well-known was the capture by Moroccans of a UAR military helicopter carrying five Egyptian officers and the Algerian, Abderrahmane Cherif. The latter was released some months later, after having been brutally treated by the Moroccans. The Egyptian officers were released in 1964 as a royal gesture when, before an Arab summit meeting in Cairo, Rabat wanted to re-establish good relations with the UAR.

The ALN had not yet been thoroughly transformed into the ANP and it was sadly lacking in vital equipment. This was not guerrilla warfare, but a full-blooded traditional war in which the Moroccan army proved by far the stronger. Ben Bella, who, as we have seen, had on Harbi's advice shown enough nationalist spirit to appropriate all the French-owned land in Algeria, now refrained from extending his revolutionary principles to the conduct of the war. Harbi had recommended a 'general mobilisation on revolutionary lines' to accelerate the progress of the revolution, but Ben Bella, though ordering mobilisation, fought the campaign on more classic grounds. One of the consequences was that Boumedienne's army was inundated with a mass of ill-equipped maquisards whom he could not even provide with adequate food and shelter. The regime seemed to seek compensation for the ineffectiveness of its forces in symbolic militant gestures. The military tunic became regulation dress for all government officials from the head of state downward, and Ben Bella swore in parliament that he would never take off his uniform 'until the socialist revolution is achieved'.

The Moroccan crisis did, however, enable Ben Bella to split the Kabyle opposition against him. Colonel Mohand ou El-Hadj went over from Ait Ahmed to the Colomb-Béchar headquarters of Boumedienne 'to save his country'. The famous Colonel Chaabani also came across 'to serve his country'; but his own headquarters and troops remained at some distance from Boumedienne's: officially they were to constitute the 'reserve'. Meanwhile, the order for general mobilisation was creating chaos. The workers were leaving their jobs, and the unemployed were joining up by the ten thousand in the hope of at least getting regular food and wages. Things had to be put straight; accordingly Ben Bella issued an order that all Algerians who had been mobilised should stay put. The situation was even more critical at the front where at one time French troops secretly fed Boumedienne's men for two days. The French also gave assistance to the ANP when its transmitters broke down. The Algerians succeeded in taking and holding the mountains overlooking the oasis at Figuig, but elsewhere the Moroccans carried the day and it seems as if only bad management on their own part prevented them from inflicting a still greater defeat on the Algerians.

Some foreign correspondents, with insufficient experience of the Maghrib, got the shock of their lives after they had joined a visit to the front organised by the ANP. An account was later given in *Time* magazine of how they had been loaded into a lorry on the top of a lot of wooden crates, with nothing but canned sardines for food, inadequate supplies of water, and no blankets to protect them from the freezing night of the Sahara, in the charge of a lone driver who did not know the country. After many vicissitudes they found themselves under fire—from Algerian troops. At the same time, it dawned on them that they were sitting on crates of ammunition!

Harbi was heartbroken to see the country's leaders wasting such an opportunity to mobilise the people of Algeria, but he could do nothing about it. Ben Bella must have feared not only the Moroccan army, but also the possibilities of domestic disorders, for he left the Villa Joly for the Ministry of Defence where he could have better protection. In the end, Haile Selassie of Ethiopia arranged a cease-fire at a meeting in Bamako (Mali) which the Organisation of African Unity subsequently tried to improve on. While in Bamako, however, President Modibo Keita, whose sympathies were squarely on the side of revolutionary Algeria, made it plain to Ben Bella that he did not welcome 'interference in the internal affairs of others'—the great fear of all newly independent Black African countries.

After the cease-fire, Radio Algiers put an end to the violent attacks that it had been making on the royal regime of Morocco. All the same, it would seem as though the Algerian government has not stopped training anti-royalist Moroccan groups in its special camps around Tindouf for, as late as August 17, 1965, Radio Rabat broadcast an official announcement that anti-royalist Moroccan elements trained and armed in Algeria had been captured entering Morocco 'before they were able to endanger the security of the state'. This happened after Ben Bella's downfall and shortly before detailed preparations were due to be made for a Maghrib summit meeting. In consequence, not only was the scheduled summit meeting indefinitely postponed, but any real prospect of Maghrib unity was again set back indefinitely.

Should Libya be included among the Maghribine countries? In principle she should, but because of her peculiar position she is not considered as a true partner by the other three Maghrib countries. For a time, certainly, Libya seemed to be moving in the 'right circles' and during the Algerian war was officially regarded as a member of the extreme revolutionary Casablanca pact which grouped Ghana, Guinea, Mali, Morocco, the GPRA and Libya. This was the group of the African 'revolutionaries' to which Bourguiba's

Tunisia would not adhere. Royalist Morocco was part of it, however, as a tactical necessity: to appear 'revolutionary'. But in fact Libya was never a full member of this group, for her delegate signed the pact 'subject to the ratification of his action by His Majesty King Idris'—a ratification that had still not come about when the Casablanca pact was disbanded with the formation of the Organisation of African Unity. Few realised this, however, and Libya was generally accepted as a 'full member'.

We have already seen that Libya provided extensive aid to Algeria during the war. But after the war, the Algerian leaders looked on Libya—as on Morocco and Tunis—as a country where things would have to change. They also were not unmindful of the fact that Libya is Algeria's largest rival in the production of oil and natural gas. In 1963, officials of the French embassy in Tripoli disclosed privately to me that 'a secret plan' was in existence between Nasser and Ben Bella by which Libya would have pressure exerted on her from both sides in a pincer movement. Nasser, who was known to have inundated Libya with army officers and agents disguised as teachers, had his eye on the former Italian farmlands which would do very nicely for the surplus population from the Egyptian delta. The Frenchmen supported their arguments by pointing out that, of the two roads then under construction in independent Algeria, one would establish a direct link with Libya running from In Amenas to Ghadames, and was being built, they said, with 'military objectives in mind'. (The second road, also of strategic importance, was being built from Colomb-Béchar to Tindouf, along the territory claimed by Morocco.)

These political manoeuvres on Algeria's part were not the only obstacles to the attainment of unity in the Maghrib. There were also economic considerations, in which Algeria was particularly closely involved, for she inevitably sets the economic pace in North Africa.

The first economic obstacle to unity was concerned with oil and natural gas. Ben Bella, purely on ideological grounds, brushed aside any scheme by which gas should be piped to Italy through Tunisia or to France through Morocco, even though these routes were obviously the most economic. (See chapter 9.) One cannot entirely disregard the subtleties of the policies of the great international oil interests, but even so it seems strange that the Tunisian refinery at

Bizerta should receive its supplies of crude oil from Iraq, and not from neighbouring Algeria. In fact, Ben Bella showed more eagerness to co-operate on oil and gas matters with Franco's Spain. All this is in sharp contrast with the statements of Ben Bella to the effect that the Algerian resources of oil and natural gas were at the service of the Maghrib.

A comparable situation arose in connection with the iron ore of the Gara Djebilet. These deposits, which are the largest known reserves of iron ore in the world (estimated at 3 billion tons and with an iron content of 58 per cent), are in the territory which is claimed by Morocco. (See Map 2, page xvi.) The latter has often proposed 'a joint exploitation, in keeping with the concept of Maghribine co-operation', making it clear that she would be prepared to forgo any territorial claims in order to achieve this end. But Algeria has still not come to any decision to collaborate, even though all the international survey teams sponsored by the Algerian government itself have stressed that any attempt to export the Gara Djebilet ore other than via Morocco's Atlantic coast would be 'not recommended' because wildly uneconomic. Ben Bella insisted, however, that evacuation of the ore should take place through the Algerian port of Nemours.

Finally, the Algerian government's procrastination, and its confusion of economic issues with so-called concepts of 'anti-neocolonialism', resulted in each of the Maghrib countries considering the vitally important issue of the EEC independently, instead of acting in concert. What has so far inhibited any unified approach to the vitally important question of trade is the declaration by Algeria—much encouraged by the communists—that the Common Market was a 'neocolonialist' exercise. Not that this prevented Ben Bella, soon after the revolution, from asking the EEC, in an official letter dated December 24, 1962, for time so that Algeria might think over her position. This was in fact intended to give Algeria the chance to make the most of a uniquely privileged position, for, in spite of having become independent, she remained, under article 277 of the Treaty of Rome, a full member of the EEC in the guise of a 'French territory'. So when independence came, in spite of the fact that her leaders were denouncing the EEC as being inimical to her policy of non-alignment, Algeria nevertheless did her best to preserve the status, as far as the EEC was concerned, of a

'French territory'. It was not until February 1964 that Algeria finally established formal relations with the EEC. But although this privileged position suited Algeria very well—and France too—it was an irritation to other members of the EEC, all of whom (except Western Germany) cancelled the favoured treatment that they had previously extended to Algerian products.

Between 1958 and 1963, the value of EEC imports from Algeria increased from $473 to $666 million, while the value of EEC exports to Algeria fell from $1,012 to $585 million. During the same period imports from other North African countries rose from $524 to $807 million, exports to them increasing from $576 to $691 million.[6] The over-riding importance of the EEC in North African trade is indicated by the fact that the Common Market countries account for about 85 per cent of Algerian, 60 per cent of Tunisian and 58 per cent of Moroccan exports. The trade statistics also explain why it suited France for Algeria to continue to have preferential treatment in the EEC since France also benefited thereby. But, having already opposed Britain's entry into the EEC on the grounds that it was contrary to Common Market principles for a country to have all the benefits of membership while remaining 'un adhérent sans titre', France could not justify indefinitely the privileged position of Algeria. While Algeria had yet to clarify her position, Tunisia and Morocco—quite independently of each other—established their own positions vis-à-vis the EEC. On June 14, 1965, the Community's Council of Ministers agreed to discuss with Tunis and Rabat an economic association based on the principles of a free trade area. All the Maghribine countries had at any rate one thing in common: none of them wished, for political reasons, to become fully integrated, like Greece. Yet this is a very modest degree of accord between countries which should have maintained a common Maghribine front on such an issue.

In the face of the political and ideological obstacles to unity in the Maghrib, the younger generation of technocrats, which is becoming increasingly influential in Maghribine affairs, has been trying to establish at least a modest measure of technical collaboration between the North African countries in matters like communications and postal services. This is a sensible and realistic approach to the problem, and Philippe Herreman, a shrewd observer of North African affairs, was able to say in January 1965: 'Notwithstanding the serious obstacles in the way, the present prospects of an entente between Maghribine countries seem more promising.'[7] He was referring to the frequent conferences among Maghribine countries which were initiated towards the end of 1964, with the intention of seeing what could be done towards economic collaboration in spite of the political problems. It had become clear that, divided as it was, North Africa could hardly command its destiny economically in the face of the economic might of Western Europe. In fact, the kind of technical and administrative collaboration which the Maghribine countries are only now beginning to set up has long been established between the Eastern and Western blocs.

It is certain that the aims of the younger technocrats of the Maghrib are on the right lines, however modest their achievements may have been. Nevertheless, full economic integration is more than a logical exercise, for it will require a radical change in the way of thinking of the North African countries. While it is true that since Algerian independence some forty agreements, mostly of a technical nature, have been reached between the Maghribine countries, observers have noted that these are all bilateral agreements. The Maghribine countries have yet to reach a common accord on any question. In relations between Algeria, Morocco and Tunisia, it was always two against one—not yet 'three together'. It is the absence of any such change of heart that stands in the way of Maghribine unity.

8

PROJECTS AND BOOMERANGS

IF YOU WANT to put a telephone call in Dar-es-Salaam—at least at the time of writing—through to Cairo, it is routed via London. It is the same for a call from Nairobi and Khartoum. The situation was similar in the Maghrib countries. Colonial administration being what it is, a call from or to Rabat, Algiers and Tunis went through Paris. When independence came, these countries very soon set about shaking off the link with Paris and establishing direct lines with each other. At the same time Ben Bella declared that he would have direct lines between Algiers and Cairo, Algiers and Havana, Algiers and Moscow, Algiers and Bamako (Mali). This is not to say that these links, particularly the one with Cairo, were not necessary. They are mentioned here as symbolising the ambitions of Algeria in the world of international politics.

Ben Bella's aspirations in this sphere—and those of many of his countrymen—grew so incredibly quickly that, within eighteen months of gaining power, he was seeing himself as the champion of the 'exploited southern hemisphere'. His own country could hardly stand on its own feet and was only keeping its head above water with the aid of capitalist money from France. No matter! Half the world was waiting for his inspiration and leadership. And in this attitude he received much hypocritical and demagogic support from overseas. It is not difficult to detect again a parallel with the case of Lumumba, who, having failed to organise his own party effectively, let alone his country, unfolded—to the umpteenth press conference held on a day just before his fall in his villa of refuge protected by Ghanaian troops—his great new scheme . . . to liberate Southern Africa!

The sincerity of Ben Bella's intentions to complete the liberation of Africa, to bring economic freedom to South America, and to raise the standard of living in Asia, is not questioned. But the whole concept was ill-conceived and naïve to a degree. Every time Ben Bella offered to send Algerian forces to liberate this country or that, Boumedienne—the man who really knew what was involved in that kind of undertaking—sat tight-lipped and silent. Ben Bella was certainly not the first statesman to attempt to direct attention from domestic difficulties by seeking scapegoats in foreign countries, though the extent to which he employed this ancient political gambit was perhaps rather excessive. But it was possible to interpret these wild ideas for the extension of the political regime of Algeria in terms of an inadequate assimilation of the revolutionary theories of communism. In foreign affairs, Ben Bella turned to concepts of communism, but, like so many in the Third World, he failed to learn the lesson so well understood by Stalin: that you first consolidate your domestic front and then, and only then, expand to foreign countries. The marxists who wielded the greatest influence in Algeria were trotskyites, and the regime's enthusiasm for the exporting of revolution as quickly as possible was certainly not unrelated to their influence. Ben Bella's policies were so wild that even the collaboration with the UAR—which was quite logical and desirable—was to prove a spectacular boomerang to its projectors.

The Axis with Nasser

The United Arab Republic includes Arab, muslim and 'progressive' elements in its make-up. Moreover it provided considerable help to Algerian nationalism during the war of independence. So it was entirely logical that Algeria and the UAR should establish a close working entente. The reason why the collaboration between them failed so ignominiously was because Ben Bella fell in too readily with Nasser's pan-Arabic ambitions. Cairo was, in fact, trying to penetrate into Africa under the cover of association with Algeria. Ben Bella, moreover, allowed Nasser to meddle far too much in the internal affairs of Algeria. This led to great resentment among the Algerians.

Of course, every example of international assistance entails its quid pro quo, in varying degrees, either overt or indirect. The characteristic of assistance from the UAR is the rigid obligation which it imposes on the recipient to accord with the demands of the donor. This is so much a characteristic of the UAR that even the African freedom fighters in South Africa and Portugal's colonies, whose demands in all conscience are modest enough—a bit of money, a few arms, and the chance of rudimentary military training—have started complaining of it. Like many—including the present writer —whose first direct experience of Algeria was after her independence, UAR officials entertained preconceived notions about the country. But, while it is not difficult for an individual to modify his views and to set to and do his homework, it is not so easy for an entire administration to reorient itself—particularly the UAR, which had well-established plans for Algeria based on pre-existing concepts. Of course, by now the officials of the UAR, and certainly Nasser (who, whatever one may think of his policies, certainly has the flair of a world statesman), have come to learn that their Algerian brothers are not the Arabs that they took them to be. This was quite soon made clear to UAR journalists, but they could hardly write articles in opposition to the official line.

Another characteristic of the UAR—particularly irritating to the Algerians, who, perhaps more than any other people in the world, hate to be ordered about—was the tendency of Egyptian officials, both civilian and military, to act the 'big brothers'. This caused a violent reaction in all walks of Algerian life even when Ben Bella was still in power. The Algerians, on the whole, had little real knowledge of the UAR, apart from what a few of them learned when they were training during the war. So when Ben Bella and Nasser embarked on their intimate collaboration, they were alone at the top. All the way down the line they lacked support, and their peoples had little idea of the implications of their actions. Nasser himself saw this very plainly. In an interview with *Révolution Africaine* he said:

In mutual sympathy, relations between our two countries are good. But this could hardly suffice. These relations must be developed on both governmental and popular levels, to put an end to prejudices arising from the absence of contacts. Therefore, we never miss an occasion to send strong delegations to Algiers whenever there is an occasion. We did it for the congress of doctors, for the students of Algerian military schools. There is nothing better than direct contact. But, in parallel, we must quickly reinforce our economic relations. By so doing, each of us will have accentuated his disengagement from imperialism and worked towards reciprocal advantages.[1]

This interview was all the more interesting since it had been conducted by Mohammed Harbi, who was critical of the UAR's Arab Socialist Union. Men like Harbi and the leaders of the Moroccan Union Nationale des Forces Populaires (UNFP) consider that the UAR revolution is a failure because the masses have not played an integral part in it, being no more than puppets dancing to the tunes called by officialdom. (Many people, not all of them marxists, subscribe to this viewpoint. In considering what the consequences might be of the renewed widespread outburst of the *Ikhwan al Muslimun*—the Muslim Brotherhood—*Jeune Afrique* of September 7, 1965, said that the 'Muslim Brothers' could always count on achieving an appeal to the emotions of Egyptians as long as Nasser's Arab Socialist Union remained 'official'.) The question which Harbi put to Nasser—'How do you think, Mr President, we should set about providing a solid foundation for the relations between our countries, both in Egypt and in Algeria?'—is in itself a repudiation of the official line that a firmly cemented relationship had already been established between the two countries.

Many Algerians believed that Nasser's *Muhabarat* was actively operating in Algeria, giving instructions on policy to Ben Bella's Bureau of Arab Affairs (headed by Abderrahmane Cherif) and, what is more, pointing out which Algerians Cairo wanted to be removed from the scene. With Ben Bella taking an increasing interest in foreign policy, the Bureau of Arab Affairs was becoming more and more Algeria's Foreign Office for all practical purposes—very much to the dislike, as we shall see, of Bouteflika, the minister of Foreign Affairs, who belonged to the ANP. Abderrahmane Cherif was to become unexpectedly important (and hence his Egyptian masters were to achieve greater influence) when Ben Bella reshuffled his cabinet and made him a minister delegated to the office of the prime minister, which made him very much the Number Three man of the cabinet. This was to have great consequences later.

In Mauretania in early 1965 one heard bitter complaints of the technical assistance the Mauretanians were getting from Egypt. 'We all know that they are spying for Nasser, but they are not even any use as teachers or technologists.' What the Mauretanians were complaining of was a repetition of what had already happened in Algeria on a much larger scale. In Algeria there was, to start with, a serious language barrier between the two forms of spoken Arabic, and the Algerian students in the towns soon began ridiculing their Egyptian instructors (the Algerian student, like his Parisian counterpart, has a bit of the 'gamin' about him). The Egyptian technicians were termed 'a lousy crew'. Much worse was said of the doctors; they were accused not only of incompetence, but of being out for all they could get from Algeria. ('They even use ambulances to go and get their hair cut.') In Algeria and Mauretania, people had been accustomed to the standards set by the French.

In his interview with Mohammed Harbi, Nasser referred to the need for economic exchanges between the countries. This is readily understandable, for Egypt had set up her own industries, and now needed to seek out overseas markets for them. Algeria, too, had an interest in developing economic relations with Egypt, anxious as she was to develop her trading interests and so break the monopoly held by France. Hence it was sensible enough for Egypt and Algeria to agree that they should get together. But economic exchange broke down quickly in practice. The Algerians took one look at shoes imported from Egypt and remarked: 'How much better are the shoes we can get from France!' What made this all the more ironic is that, with the Algerian shops no longer as fully stocked as they were in the days before independence, it was the visiting Egyptians who rushed to buy what consumer goods remained to be had. The French press commented (not without considerable satisfaction) that every time a UAR warship or merchantman put in at Algiers, Egyptian sailors were to be seen returning on board loaded with transistors, tape-recorders, household gadgets—and French-made shoes. Clearly it needed better products than anything Egypt had to offer to break the French trading monopoly in Algeria.

When Nasser on May 2, 1963, visited Algeria for the first time, there were wild scenes of real enthusiasm—far more riotous and disorderly than the well-regulated demonstrations to which he is accustomed in Cairo. But it would be a mistake to read into them any real acceptance on the Algerians' part of the UAR's intended role of 'big brother'. Nasser's visit was for them a symbol of their country's status: even the great Nasser felt he had to visit them! (For similar reasons, the king of Morocco also was given a very warm welcome when he visited Algeria.) It soon became known, however, that Nasser had expressed his reservations on Ben Bella's headlong rush of activity, and particularly on the 'hectic' character of his interferences in world affairs, from Cuba to Vietnam. To say that Nasser did not want Ben Bella to steal too much of his thunder as leader of the Third World is only to tell part of the truth. More important was the fact that Nasser, a much maturer statesman, had a far shrewder idea than Ben Bella of when you should shout your head off and when you should remain discreetly temperate. But the gravest disappointment to the Egyptians in Algeria, from Nasser himself down to the least *muhabathin* (agent of the *Muhabarat*), was the realisation that, in spite of all that had happened, the Algerians still had much closer affinities with France than with the Arabs of the Middle East. However fervent in principle might be the emotional agreements between Nasser and Ben Bella for the creation of Arab unity from the Mashrik to the Maghrib, the defective 'Arabism' of the Algerians became only too clear when the Egyptians got down to brass tacks with them. It was obvious to most outside observers of the situation that Nasser's plan was to make the Maghrib a mere extension of the 'socialist'-dominated (i.e. pro-Nasser) Middle East. But Bourguiba and his Neo-Destour party were proving a tough nut to crack, and were not to be easily shaken by Nasser and his plans. 'Socialism' now being the order of the day, Tunisia's party had, of course, become the 'socialist Neo-Destour party', but this did not mean, far from it, that the Tunisians accepted Nasser's definition of socialism. Egypt and Algeria decided that, as with Libya, they would do well to defer tackling Tunisia until later.

Cairo and Algeria fully agreed that the Moroccan monarchy was a more likely immediate target. The enthusiasm with which Nasser leaped on his royal prey is clearly shown by the help that he gave to Algeria during the short war with Morocco, and by the efforts of the Egyptians to take over control of the conduct of the war. But what seemed a splendid opportunity for the Egyptians proved to be a complete fiasco. Not only was the Moroccan army far superior in the field, but the ineptitude of the Algerian approach to Egypt for military aid, and of the Egyptians in granting it, created a serious breach in the relations between the two countries.

When Boumedienne asked for extensive Egyptian military aid on his own initiative, without reference to Ben Bella, he found himself in a tight corner. As we have seen, Ben Bella took the move very badly. Although he was pro-Egyptian, he was still enough of an Algerian to find very distasteful the prospect of large Egyptian forces in his country. Later on Boumedienne was to show that he felt this way too, even more strongly than did Ben Bella; but at the time he was faced with the bald alternative either of getting Egypt to help him or of being completely annihilated by the Moroccans. The quarrel between Ben Bella and Boumedienne over this matter, and the former's appointment of a new chief of staff behind the latter's back, has already been described (chapter 7, page 145). But the major rupture in relations between Egypt and Algeria came when Boumedienne almost literally threw out of his headquarters some UAR army officers who were playing at being general staff officers there. 'You may have better equipment than ours, but when it comes to fighting, let's get this straight: we know our job better than you can tell us', Boumedienne is reported to have told them. Other members of the ANP were even less diplomatic: 'Why not go and fight your own war in the Yemen properly?'* Boumedienne quite clearly could not stomach the behaviour of the Egyptians who had been sent to his aid. It was to be his own police force which later ousted from Algeria scores of Egyptian teachers, doctors and technologists on account of their inefficiency, and because they were meddling with the internal affairs of Algeria. Antagonism of this kind, though unreported in the international press, was steadily developing even while Ben Bella was still in power.

A Plunge into Black Africa

It was not only over the Moroccan war that relations between Egypt and Algeria turned sour. Events south of the Sahara were also to lead to conflict between the two countries.

* The military fiasco of the Yemen was to have profound repercussions throughout Africa. Many African statesmen, and particularly African fighters for freedom, were to ask observers with experience of Egypt, 'How is it, with all their formidable arms and equipment, that the Egyptians are doing so badly in the Yemen?'

In Algerian activities in the continent of Africa there is a clear-cut distinction between intention and performance. There is no doubt that Ben Bella and the Algerians generally were perfectly honest and sincere in their desire to liberate the whole of Africa, to extinguish the racialist regime of South Africa and the Salazarist colonialism in Portugal's possessions. I cannot think of one instance where the fighters for freedom in African territories still under European rule have not acknowledged (in private, of course) that the general help provided from Algeria was the best that they had received from anywhere, communist or not. (Though when it comes to guerrilla-type help, they unanimously give the palm to China.) Certainly Algeria did not attach the same kind of strings to her aid as did Egypt; here again the nationalist leaders complained bitterly that they only got help from Egypt if they were prepared to follow the Nasser line. But in the execution of these principles, things went sadly astray, chiefly because the Algerians were without any real understanding of the problems of Black Africa—an understanding that they are only now beginning to acquire—and the more they attempted in Africa, the bigger their downfalls.

The history of independent Africa is being made from day to day, and, to paint a picture of it, it is necessary to fall back on personal experience. What follows may be hard to believe, but it is true. Both East and West were soon to learn that the handling of Algeria's grandiose and belligerent African policy was based on planning about as skilful and durable as that of a child building sandcastles.

Shortly after Algerian independence, L.B. (who was later to become an ambassador) and Commander S. asked me, as the only person they knew who had any knowledge of the Congo, to brief them about the country. They were about to visit it on a mission to give help to Holden Roberto's Front of Angolan National Liberation (FLNA). The only definite and indisputable information I could give was that the best-looking women were to be found in and around Coquihatville; after two years' absence from the Congo, there was little useful I could tell them about day-to-day political happenings, without actually going with them to size up the quickly-changing situation on the spot. However, I did at least try to disabuse them of some of their wilder ideas about raising battalions to march on Luanda—though not with much success. As it turned out, both of them fell over each other in their haste to get out of the

Congo to give as adverse a report as they could concoct of what they had seen and learned.

This was the only report on the Congo that Ben Bella was to receive from his own agents up to the time, in May 1963, when all the African heads of state met to sign the charter establishing the Organisation of African Unity at Addis Ababa. There were some discussions at this meeting on how frequently the heads of state should meet. Ben Bella wanted a meeting every six months, but Bourguiba considered that once a year was enough. Not only was it an expensive business for them all to get together, he said, but not much was likely to accumulate over six months for them to talk about. At this, Ben Bella banged the table with his fist and shouted: 'It must be every six months—and in six months' time I shall invite you to hold the second summit meeting in Algeria, where you shall witness the victory parade of the battalions of Angola!' How could any responsible man in Africa—let alone a head of state—utter such nonsense? It was only too obvious that Ben Bella had not the slightest idea of what he was talking about; and that is a dangerous state of mind for a head of state with ambitions to be the leader of the new Africa. The Algerian press and radio were also given to making similar statements about the future liberation of all Africa, and about the part that Algeria was playing in this.

The following episode would be completely ridiculous if it did not provide an illustration of the almost incredibly silly tragedy that lay beneath the pretensions of Algerian policy. On travelling by air from Tunis to Algiers, I sent a cable announcing my flight arrival to a friend whom we will call X, holder of a key position in conducting African affairs. At Algiers airport I was met by a group of X's colleagues who were under the impression that he was on board the plane. It seems they had misread the cable and took it to mean that its sender, for some obscure reason, was advising them of X's intended arrival. Finding this was not the case, they asked me: 'But where then on earth is X? Since he left four months ago, all we have heard from him is a postcard message from Dar-es-Salaam saying that he preferred French women after all.' This may appear a trivial incident, but there is a serious moral behind it. For four whole months Algeria had been telling the world of what she intended for Africa, and X himself had been making frequent statements from wherever he happened to be. Yet during all this time there had been no direct communication between the Algerian government and its only representative in Black Africa. (There were as yet no Algerian embassies.) No instructions; no reports; no exchanges of information—just one postcard to say that cavorting in bed with black women was not all it was cracked up to be. It is small wonder that Ben Bella's African policy was a miserable failure when this was the extent of the advice he received from his emissary.

Whenever things went wrong for Ben Bella or for Nasser in Africa, they attributed it to the influence of 'imperialist manoeuvres'. Certainly the imperialists were not indifferent, but for most of the time all they had to do was to sit back and watch. In fact, Ben Bella was personally responsible for delaying still further what prospects there were for achieving unity between the rival nationalist movements of Angola. While Algeria's war with the French was still waging, the ALN was already training men of Holden Roberto's FLNA in one of its Tunisian camps at Wadi Melleg. Through their unit serving with the United Nations force in the Congo, the Tunisians were the first of the Maghrib to see something of Central Africa and to get a realistic grasp of the Angolan problem. This determined them to support the FLNA—support which they have continued to give to this day—thus providing the first incentive for Algiers to take an interest in Angola. The late Frantz Fanon, whose theories of revolution for a time were held in great respect in Algeria, also advised Algiers to make Angola its concern. But Ben Bella decided to support the rival nationalist movement in Angola, establishing very good relations with its leader, the poet Mario de Andrade. Now, it could have been strongly argued that this was probably the better choice, for the People's Movement for Angolan Liberation (MPLA) seemed more progressive in its attitude, and its leader less preoccupied with striking poses as 'a head of state in exile' than the leader of the FLNA. However, all this proved to count for very little. At a congress of the Union Générale des Travailleurs Algériens on January 17, 1963, Ben Bella—partly as a gambit to distract the delegates from the real issues at stake—suddenly announced that he was transferring his support to the FLNA. This was very much against the advice of men like Harbi. It was certainly an extraordinary move. A Soviet correspondent sitting behind me when Ben Bella made his announcement remarked: 'Well, if you want to divide and weaken the movement for national liberation in

Africa, this is the right way to set about it'—and he was right.* The Angolan movements have become even more divided among themselves, and Salazar seems to have been relieved of a good deal of the pressure which had been building up against him over the Angolan problem. (Since then, the MPLA—which operates within the Kabinda enclave—has been receiving support from Russia. China, though managing to get a foothold in the door in nearby Brazzaville, has so far been unable to attract the MPLA.)

However, much more serious as an impediment to African unity than Ben Bella's rash switches of support was the axis between him and Nasser. Whether Egypt should concentrate attention on Africa or the Near East is a problem often debated in Cairo. Critics of Nasser have been saying for a long time that all his aspirations towards the East have led to nothing and that Egypt's real destiny lies in Africa—not, of course, to the exclusion of the Arab world east of Egypt, but as a necessary and vital factor in Egyptian policy.

Certainly Cairo tried its best in the situation created by the actual and impending granting of independence to so many states. Nasser made vigorous endeavours in the Congo, and if he burnt his fingers there—well, who did not? While Egypt's lamentable experiences in the Congo are well known, what is not so well appreciated is her failure to exert influence on the regions of Eastern Africa south of the plains of the Nile: regions where strong Islamic influence and the presence of substantial Arab minorities could have made her path an easy one. Egypt's attempts to infiltrate in this area were clearly at the expense of Algeria, with Cairo taking every advantage of the prestige that Algeria had gained there to use the cover of such organisations as the 'Committee of Liberation' (or 'Committee of Nine') of the Organisation of African Unity.

In fact, until the first Algerian diplomatist arrived in Dar-es-Salaam, the UAR officials there were living in partial seclusion in their embassy, following an incident which took place when the first UAR ambassador presented his credentials to President Nyerere. The ceremony had got away to a bad start with the Tanganyikan band playing a favourite march of King Farouk by mistake instead

---

* In fairness to the Algerians, it should be mentioned that the two most workmanlike liberation movements in Africa—the PAIGC in Portuguese Guinea and the ANC of South Africa—continue to benefit from and make good use of assistance from Algeria which has come to them without interruption.

of the national anthem of the United Arab Republic. And then Nyerere reacted very strongly when, after presenting his credentials, the UAR ambassador made his first request: that Tanganyika should forthwith expel all Israeli technologists and other experts. According to eye-witnesses of the scene, Nyerere became very angry and retorted: 'We are an independent nation, and it is our business what friends and what enemies we choose. Enemies of our friends are not necessarily our enemies too.' After that, no more was heard or seen of the UAR contingent in Dar-es-Salaam until the Algerian representative arrived. Then the Egyptians woke up, and used the Algerians as a means for putting forward all their schemes—especially the matter of the Israelis in Tanganyika—with the final upshot that the Algerian ambassador was declared persona non grata by Nyerere. The revolutionaries of Zanzibar, too, had a grudge against the Egyptians, accusing them of having given shelter to elements of the Arab bourgeoisie who fled after the victory of the more strongly Africa-oriented Afro-Shirazi party. The new regime in Zanzibar was also not particularly impressed by the achievements of the Algerian revolutionaries after independence. The Algerian ambassador in Dar-es-Salaam, who had been a political commissar of the ALN at Oujda and was one of the few Algerians who spoke English, was a key member of the 'Committee of Nine'. Using him as a front, Cairo tried very hard to get UAR (and also Algerian) officers appointed as instructors at the centre for the various freedom fighters based in Tanzania. The Black African members of the committee, and particularly Kambona, the foreign minister of Tanzania, were not in favour of this suggestion. There has always been a deep distrust of the Arabs in Black Africa, and Nasser (and Ben Bella, who was acting on his advice) somehow managed to revive these old antagonisms.

Indeed, the UAR and Algeria between them did more to stir up dissent between the Arab and the Black African worlds than even the most reactionary colonialist diehard could have dared to hope for. This was due to their insistence that, at every level, it was the Arabs who were to be the leaders of the New Africa: an idea quite inimical to Black Africa. Ben Bella, with his usual facility for glib oversimplification, stated that 'there is no black or white' in Africa—just like that, and the Algerian press and radio followed suit, denouncing as 'imperialist' anyone referring to 'Black Africans'. But decrees are one thing, personal reactions quite another. The Algerians have yet to come to terms with their own dark-skinned minority of the Sahara, and in Black Africa they felt very much the same about the black man as the French colons felt about the Algerian. In spite of all his talk and super theories, Ben Bella in fact saw nothing of Black Africa until he visited Dakar and Accra in 1963-64. Like a good many other people, he came back with the feeling that 'there is nothing you can do with these blacks'. His visit to Black Africa was all the more disappointing because of a sharp rebuff that he received at a meeting of the OAU in Dakar. This was a routine meeting of foreign ministers to which Ben Bella was not invited, but he announced that he would attend. Senghor, the president of Senegal, felt that he could hardly forbid a head of state to visit his country, but discreetly went on holiday to the French Riviera, putting his palace at Ben Bella's disposal. Ben Bella took the rather belated advice of his aides and crept away on tiptoe from the OAU meeting—but not before he had committed another serious gaffe by receiving Senghor's political opponents in the president's own palace.*

The more sophisticated Egyptians hold the Black African in great contempt. Tshombe, who is the most astute of politicians, saw this very clearly, and in return very skilfully introduced an 'anti-Arab' theme into African politics. In presuming that they were essentially superior to the blacks and were the natural leaders of Africa, Nasser and Ben Bella neglected two important factors: first, that Black Africa had certainly not thrown off the yoke of one set of masters merely to acquire new ones; and secondly, that the Arabs are no more than a minority in a continent where all have equally the right to shape their own destiny as they please. It is true that the spirit of revolution was stronger in Algeria than anywhere else in Africa. Indeed, as has been stressed at the beginning of this book, the Algerians are the only people in Africa to have fought a real war for

* In Algiers, after this OAU meeting, Mohammed Harbi asked me to disclose the truth of what had happened at Dakar, as it was essential that public opinion in Africa and Algeria should not be misled by the false claims that it had made real progress towards African unity. Indeed, largely due to the pushing actions of Ben Bella, African unity was receding rather than advancing. As a result, an anonymous article appeared in *Révolution Africaine* entitled "Dakar, Recul ou Progrès?". Ben Bella disliked the article intensely, but Mohammed Harbi, who is a man of principle, accepted responsibility for it as editor of the review.

their independence. But both the Algerians themselves, and many European observers, fell into the cardinal error of thinking that, having thus blazed the trail of liberation in Africa, the Algerians were thereby qualified to act as the leaders of the new Africa. The mistake in this assessment probably lies in its ascribing similar reactions about the Algerian war to the Africans as were entertained by de Gaulle (and by the British as well, though they were in advance of the French in granting independence to their African colonies). As a result of colonial rule, Africa was far too divided and kept in seclusion for the Algerian war to have the kind of repercussions that it would have had in a more highly developed society. Lack of communications, censorship imposed by the colonial powers, and racial and geographical barriers, all combined to dissipate the impact of the revolution. Only Guinea and Mali, with a high proportion of intellectuals in their population, took any serious interest in events in Algeria, and then only at a late stage. Neither of them, nor Senegal, did anything to help the Algerians, not even by exerting influence on the thousands of their nationals serving in the French army in Algeria. The Algerian revolution, in fact, meant much more to the Western and the Arab worlds than to Black Africa.

The events in Ghana and in the Belgian Congo were to have a much more profound influence on African thought. Indeed, the example of the Congo was probably a greater influence than that of Algeria in accelerating France's liberation of her remaining African colonies. Even today Paris is obsessed by the repercussions that the French-speaking nationalist colossus of the Congo might have on their own little 'républiquettes'. Black Africa takes a similar view of the influence of events in Africa. A notable Black African political theorist, Seydou Badian—Mali's minister responsible for economic development and a marxist with, for the time being at least, marked leanings towards Peking—after commenting on how the war in Vietnam led to the French defeat at Dien-Bien-Phu, how the Mau-Mau insurrections proved a grave economic embarrassment to the British, and how the Algerian war developed in a way that was beyond all expectations and which surprised and frightened the diehard colonialists, goes on to say:

These great events were to influence the destiny of Black Africa. An essential for independence, the awareness of the foreign powers that weighty events were taking place, was secured, with the result that they moved towards wise solutions based on the realisation that a friendly route to independence was preferable to a ruinous war. . . . Finally, for Black Africa, internal considerations were to become important with the vigorous political action of Dr Nkrumah which led to Ghanaian independence in 1957. The historic role which Nkrumah played in the destiny of Africa will only appear in perspective in the future. . . . His action aroused great enthusiasm among African intellectuals . . . and indicated to the people of Africa the course that their future history was to follow.

The most important external influence determining the fate of French Black Africa was General de Gaulle, who released French colonial policy from the rut into which it had been thrust by the chauvinistic and narrow views of the powerful colonial interests. As a result France, whose colonial policy was the most determined and the most integrationalist, decided to grant independence to thirteen Black African states.[2]

There were, indeed, vast tracts of Africa which remained unaffected by the Algerian war and knew very little about it. In former British East Africa, the Mau Mau were to many a more immediate example of revolution than Algeria. At a reception given for the conference of the Afro-Asian Solidarity Committee held in Dar-es-Salaam in 1963, on being introduced to President Nyerere as the very first representative of the Algerian press to visit Tanganyika, I asked him 'to be so kind as to say a few words to Algeria—nothing very tremendous, Mr President; just a few formal words'. Nyerere gave one of his well-known shrewd looks, and said: 'I have nothing to say, Brother, because there is nothing that I expect from North Africa. Please keep your revolutions and your Casablanca pact to yourselves. Here in Tanganyika we mean to do things in an orderly fashion.' It is true that only some six months later, when visiting Oran, Nyerere was loud in his praises of the Algerian revolution. Yet the fact that he came to alter his attitude so completely cannot change the fact of his earlier point of view: a view which was essentially a consequence of the unawareness of many parts of Africa about each other's affairs. Such considerations, ignored by many Western observers, even those sitting behind official desks in

London or Washington, further explain why Black Africa rejected Algerian leadership so promptly, and the more firmly when they detected Nasser's hand behind Ben Bella.

The Algerians themselves were the first to detect the antipathy of the Black Africans towards them, but instead of trying to analyse the reasons for it objectively, they found it easier simply to label the Black African leaders as 'petty bourgeois' or 'ignorant' and to decide that they could impose their leadership by 'greater revolutionary action'. Sékou Touré, at one time *the* leader of Black Africa, was quickly dropped by the Algerians who labelled him as 'pretentious and unreliable' because of his many changes of front. As for the Ghanaians: the Algerians would not hear mention of them. There remained only one 'truly revolutionary' Black African for Ben Bella: Modibo Keita of Mali. The Algerians were impressed by the way he had been able to create the structures of his political party. But his turn to be dethroned soon came after he agreed to hold discussions with Tshombe in an attempt to resolve the dilemma of the Congo. Ironically enough, it was the impossible Tshombe who later was to be the indirect cause of one of the major charges which Boumedienne levelled against Ben Bella—that of having trusted de Gaulle too much. The Algerian leader persisted with his pseudo-revolutionary actions with the encouragement of Cairo, which was anxious to push the *Muhabarat* into the vanguard of Algeria's advance in Africa. He was also, needless to say, encouraged by China—with Russia, who had by now learned from experience, somewhat reluctantly playing second fiddle to Peking. The Soviets had rushed into the Congo with fists flailing, but very soon had to get out as quickly as they could; they were, understandably enough, most reluctant to repeat their Congo setbacks elsewhere in Africa.

It was inevitable that Ben Bella should get his biggest buffeting in the Congo, for there were two factors there which most seriously thwarted his ambitions in Africa. First: it very soon became clear how mistaken was the idea that all that was needed was to send arms and instructors from Algeria. To begin with, Algeria lacked the resources to carry out such an operation, and the so-called 'Algerian assistance' in fact took the form of Soviet arms, ferried to the Sudan by Soviet planes manned by Soviet airmen, with perhaps an occasional Algerian co-pilot. (Moscow eventually claimed this as its aid to the Congo, in reply to Chinese accusations that the Soviet Union was giving no help to revolutionaries in Africa.) But what happened to these resources when they arrived? Algeria treated with disdain any suggestion that the rebels had no idea how to handle modern arms and that therefore it was useless to send military equipment to them. Yet, in fact, if the arms were not sold by the Congolese rebels themselves to rebels from Southern Sudan, they were falling directly into the hands of Tshombe. At a victory parade in 1965 to mark the anniversary of the Congo, Tshombe was able to make a display of weapons originating from communist countries. Anti-aircraft guns of Chinese origin, previously sent from Algeria to the Congo, ended up heaven knows where in the jungle— certainly not at Stanleyville where the Belgian parachutists were dropped. As for the Algerian instructors: they could do little, not because they were incompetent but because they did not know the terrain; nor did they know when arriving how unreliable were the men they were supposed to train in crash programmes.

African politics were shaken by a major scandal when Nkrumah's ideological weekly, *The Spark*, denounced as 'amateurish' the work of the Committee of National Liberation of the OAU. It disclosed the contents of the main confidential report of this committee, which had been prepared by Algerians. This purported to establish rules of conduct for the freedom fighters of Africa, down to the number of cartridges that each man should carry, and how he should carry them. *The Spark* censured this as nothing but paper work, and bad paper work at that. Algeria retorted that Ghana was only saying this out of pique at not being part of the Committee of Liberation. This may well be partly true, but the fact remains that the Algerians were trying to apply their own guerrilla experiences in the terrain of North Africa to the vastly different circumstances of the jungles of Black Africa. Applied to the Congo, their principles indeed looked amateurish.

The second factor, closely related to the first, not only shook Ben Bella's African policies but, even more, undermined his over-all judgement. This was the fact that Tshombe—the man whom he was reviling, and whom he would dearly have liked to have eliminated— was received early in 1965 by no less a person than de Gaulle. Ben Bella in Algeria was not the only one to be taken by surprise by this action of de Gaulle's, but the writing on the wall had been there for some time. Most of the leaders of Africa were becoming impatient, and even scared, of the 'Arab leadership' policies of Ben Bella particularly as they implied the replacement of the established governments of many of the newly independent states by 'more revolutionary' administrations. Leading officials of the OAU in Addis Ababa were saying that if the UAR, Algeria and Ghana persisted with these 'revolutionary' tactics, all the effort and compromise that had gone into establishing a modicum of African unity would be in vain, and that the OAU would face the prospect of being dissolved.

By 1965, it was clear, from private conversation with them at the OAU meeting in Kenya in that year, that senior Algerian officials were beginning to understand the real changes which were occurring in Africa. The attitudes of the earlier 'sixties were fading and giving place to a more mature Africa. Pseudo-revolutionary ideas were being superseded by a more objective realisation that constructive changes can occur only by a process of evolution. Nkrumah's ideal of a closely-knit African unity forged by the fiats of heads of state was now a subject of open ridicule, and its place was being taken by plans for a more practical collaboration among African states, first between subregions and then between regions. But how were these ideas to be got across to the Algerian leaders? When Bouteflika, visiting Nairobi privately, discussed the situation with me, he was surprised to learn that Algeria and her allies were in a minority over Congo. (Between sixteen and eighteen members of the OAU were ready to support the more moderate concept of 'recognising the legal government in Leopoldville', whoever might be at its head.) This was not the kind of information which percolated to Algiers. But soon afterwards he came to see the situation for what it was, and—a pleasant and unpretentious man—told me: 'So now we are going to drown the goldfish in the pond', meaning that Algeria would be attempting a hopeless task if she continued to support the policy of overthrowing Tshombe by force.

The lead in rejecting the ideas of Nasser, Ben Bella and Nkrumah was taken by the French-speaking Africans. The Union Africaine et Malgache (UAM), which had previously been left in a state of suspended animation while its members waited to see what the OAU would come up with, was transformed into the Organisation de Coopération Africaine et Malgache (OCAM). 'We cannot waste our

time on the little games that OAU get up to; we have got to live', said
the leaders of French-speaking Africa. OCAM is not the creature of
France that some consider it to be, though certainly it had the
sympathy and support of the French. (Both the French and the
British have been aware for some time now that the day is over when
they could set up or dominate political institutions in Africa.)
France had already shown similar sentiments of sympathy to
Leopoldville, where she was providing extremely valuable technological assistance. When Tshombe was received a second time by
de Gaulle, in May 1965, the prime minister of the Congo had just
been elected a full member of OCAM. And while an enraged and
dumbfounded Ben Bella was still waiting in Algiers for the French
head of state to be graciously pleased to tell him when he would be
officially invited to Paris (a meeting that Ben Bella badly wanted as
he regarded it as the best card he could play at the projected second
conference of the Afro-Asian countries), Tshombe, smiling broadly
and acting with greater assurance than ever, was holding a conference in the Place de la Concorde.

Communist Miscalculations

Algeria is a part of a continent where communism has so far almost
completely failed, both as an internal force and as an influence
from outside. The only exceptions to this are: the Sudan, where
the local communist party has shown great resourcefulness—yet
its successes have, up to the present, always been temporary; the
United Arab Republic, where the USSR has achieved a privileged
position—though less firmly entrenched than many believe; and
the tiny island of Zanzibar, where both local and external communist
forces are still dominant. On July 23, 1965 the United States State
Department issued a survey according to which there was a total of
12,500 card-carrying communists in Africa at the beginning of
1965. The distribution of the bigger communist groupings was:
Algeria 5,500; the Sudan 2,500; Morocco 2,000; United Arab
Republic and Tunisia, about 1,000 each; South Africa 800. Nigeria,
the 'colossus of Africa', had only about 100. An article in *The Times*
noted, in this connection:

> The less ideologically rigid attitude of the Soviet Government
> in recent months has been demonstrated in particular of late by

the much less doctrinaire stance of the African Institute of the Soviet Academy of Sciences. When the Academy was first set up some 10 years ago, under the directorship of Professor I. I. Potekhin, Soviet hopes were high that the emergent African states would within the next decade embrace Soviet communism, and Professor Potekhin himself was a leading exponent of the denigration of African socialism. He produced many historical and political books about Africa, written mainly from the Marxist and Leninist viewpoint.

When, however, Professor Potekhin died in September 1965, he was replaced by a new director, Mr V. C. Solodovnikov, an economist who was formerly deputy director of the Soviet Institute of World Economics and International Relations. In an article in *Pravda* last December, Mr Solodovnikov claimed that many African countries had chosen 'the path of non-capitalist development', and another article on June 4 made clear that the prospects of 'scientific socialism' in developing countries were not bright. It took the view that there was 'no insuperable barrier' between socialism on the Soviet model and other socialist trends in developing countries. This was less than six months after the final article of Professor Potekhin, published posthumously in *Kommunist*, denied that any valid form of socialism could exist with roots in traditional African society and with a unique African character.

None of this means, however, that the Soviet Government will in any way relax its efforts to win over African opinion. The drive to influence young Africans is steadily increasing, and in December 1964, according to recent American researches, the number of African students studying in Russia and east Europe rose to a record of 8,700—an increase of about one quarter over the figure of 6,700 estimated in December 1963. The total number of foreign students studying in communist countries at the end of 1964 was estimated at 18,500 against 14,600 a year before.

Those figures put into perspective the scale of the Russian effort in Africa when set against the comparable Chinese effort. The Chinese took only 200 African students for training in 1964, and 165 in 1963. There is an increased tendency among the African students who go to the Soviet Union to concentrate on technical rather than ideological or academic training. This applies in particular to students from Algeria, Ghana, Somalia and Kenya.[3]

The figures quoted for the communist party membership in Africa are not very big, yet to many who know Africa well they may seem an overestimate. It is a poor total, in any case, in view of the fact that there are in Africa some fifty countries and territories of which thirty-six have recently emerged from colonial rule, and that the population of the continent is over 200 million. Why so great a failure in a field which, according to communist theory, should have been so fertile? The case of Algeria may provide an answer to this question.

To Algerian nationalists, both civilian and military, the communists of Algeria have come to be regarded as 'traitors', not only because they failed to understand the patriotic feeling which culminated in the insurrection of November 1954, but also—and this is bitterly remembered—they actively opposed the Algerian revolution in the beginning. This opposition sprang from their obedience to political instructions from Moscow routed via Paris, and from their utter inability to gauge the nationalist pulse in Algeria. As in almost all the Arab countries of the Mediterranean, it was the more radical elements among the Jewish minority which formed the hard core of Algerian communism. When banned by the French in 1955, the Algerian Communist Party (PCA) established a clandestine organisation under Dr Saddock Hadjarès, Henri Alleg, Jacques Sallot, Célestin Moreno and Lucette Manarancha. It was headed by Dr Hadjarès, an Algerian Jew, for Moscow had not been able to decide whether it should be led by a Frenchman or a muslim Algerian. In the list of leaders one looks in vain for a single Algerian name. Lucien Guerrab, one of the most active of the muslim-born Algerian communists and who had renounced French nationality, changed allegiance, joined the FLN and became an official in Algeria after independence. (It was he who helped me secretly to enter Algeria.) Larbi Bouali, another important muslim-born Algerian communist, was in Moscow throughout the war of independence and never showed his face in Algeria.

The predicament of the position of the Jewish leadership of the Algerian communist movement had a tragic quality, for many of them genuinely wished to be assimilated into the mass of the indigenous population, but were often misunderstood or simply rejected on grounds of race or religion. But even if these prejudices had not been operative, they would still have been incapable of converting the mass of Algerians to their standpoint. The communists of Algeria, like those in other Arab countries of the French empire, were labouring until recently under the grave disadvantage of being responsible to a foreign authority, the French Communist Party, which in turn was subject to yet another alien power: Moscow. Perhaps one day the sophisticated ideologists of the communist world will explain how they expected such an arrangement to work in countries where men derived the inspiration of their struggle for human rights and dignity from the force of nationalism and Islam. The masters in the Kremlin could not have been utterly blind to the situation, yet the first agents by which they tried to overcome the problem—the 'musulmans de service' from Tadjikistan or Uzbekistan—were so naïve that they produced only polite smiles in progressive muslim circles. (They did, however, give the muslim countries opportunities for extorting political blackmail from Western governments. Even so, it seems improbable that the USSR's later policy of pouring arms into the Arab countries will be any more successful than the former British policy of stocking the armouries of Middle East governments.)

Eventually, Moscow tried to correct its gross error by freeing the North African communist parties from the disastrous supervision of the PCF, and by asking the far more intelligent Italian Communist Party (PCI) to take a more detailed interest on Arab affairs—in particular those of Algeria and the United Arab Republic. But the Italian communists needed time and experience to gear themselves to this task, and the idiotic—it is the only word for it—conduct of the PCF in the past had created havoc past repairing. Moreover, by this time the communist world was in considerable intellectual and political disarray in consequence of the greater ability of capitalism to adjust its economic principles to changing circumstances.

In his book, *Le Meilleur Combat*, Amar Ouzegane—a former leader of the Algerian Communist Party—tells all that is to be known about the Algerian 'communist treason'. He continued his denunciations of the Algerian and French communists as editor of *Révolution Africaine*, before his ousting by Boumedienne for other reasons. Originally Algiers and its suburbs had been such a stronghold of the PCF that it acquired the same name as the working-class districts of Paris: 'La Ceinture Rouge'—the Red Belt. The trade unions which were grouped within the pro-communist union, Confédération Générale du Travail, were especially powerful and efficient. (Other French unions, such as Force Ouvrière and the Confédération Française des Travailleurs Chrétiens, had no influence in the Maghrib.) But overnight, when the separatist movement started, all the Frenchmen living in Algeria—many of them of Spanish origin, refugees from Franco—became true pieds noirs. The communists were no exception, exhibiting the most violent racialist feeling, even to the extent of joining the official French forces to help put down the revolution. The Algerian Communist Party worked with the French army and police at Guelma and Bougie during the massacres at Sétif in 1945. The links between the PCA and the French authorities were so notorious that it came as no surprise when books were published giving the names of French members of the party accused of practising the most savage tortures on muslim Algerian nationalists. No Algerian nationalist has ever been able to forgive the communists for this. Communist ministers of the post-war government in Paris authorised special powers for the colonial authorities; and it was the communist minister for Aviation, Charles Tillon, who sent the French planes which first machine-gunned nationalists in the Kerrata mountains in 1954, and collaborated with Hadj Abdelkader and Messali Hadj of L'Etoile Nord-Africaine in an attempt to crush the FLN and to make political capital out of the mass of Algerian workers in France.

A few days after the start of the revolution on November 1, 1954, the official PCF organ, *Humanité*, condemned it in the following terms: 'The Party could hardly approve resort to individual acts likely to play into the hands of the worst colonialists.'[4] Taieb Boulharouf, a well-known nationalist leader—formerly head of the Fédération de France, a negotiator of the Evian Agreements, and, since independence, Algerian ambassador in Rome and Belgrade—pointed out in an interview with Favrod that by the end of 1954 *Humanité* was saying of the Algerian revolution that it was composed of 'terrorist groups, who have no point of contact with the masses and who are heading for failure'.[5] Nine years earlier, on June 30,

1945, Caballero, the secretary general of the PCA, speaking at the Tenth Congress of the French Communist Party, said: 'Those who want the independence of Algeria are conscious or unconscious agents of imperialism. We [Algerian communists] do not want to change a one-eyed horse for one that is totally blind.' One could go further back and cite abundant material from Maurice Thorez and *Les Cahiers du Communisme* of the PCF to show how much French communists and their Algerian associates were against the country's independence.[6]

But whether the PCF and Moscow liked it or not, the revolution was a fact, and the communists soon saw that they had to make use of it to their own advantage. By mid-1955, *Liberté*, the secret mimeographed news sheet of the PCA, was paying fulsome lip-service to the ALN and exhorting communists to give it 'all possible support'. The Algerian communists several times approached the FLN with a view to forming a 'joint front', but the nationalists persevered to the end with their decision that communists could only join the FLN as individuals—and when they did so they were required to sign a renunciation of their communist principles. It was not until March 1956 that the PCA at last made the decision to participate in the revolution—but even so it still wanted to play a separate role in it. In April 1956, Lucien Guerrab, then a lieutenant in the French army, together with a French communist NCO called Maillot, tried to set up a 'maquis rouge' at Beni-Boudouane in the environs of Algiers, using arms which Maillot had stolen from the French army. The 'red maquis' soon came to be known as 'the ephemeral maquis', for it did not last long. It was an obscure business. The arms Maillot had stolen for the 'red maquis' were in fact turned over by the PCA to the FLN as a token of their co-operation, and while Guerrab made his escape, Maillot, left high and dry, was killed by French troops. This was the first and the last attempt by the communists to set up an armed resistance group in Algeria.

After this, many muslim Algerians abandoned the PCA to join the FLN, which at the same time was making the fullest use of the offers of aid which the communist party was making through those of its members who had remained loyal to it. The FLN used them in certain capacities—for instance to manufacture explosives in Algiers—but never let them attain any kind of position of responsibility. In 1960 the PCA again tried hard to join the Algerian national-

G

ist family. By then it was clear to everyone that the FLN was to be the future power in Algeria. Though the talks between France and Algeria at Melun on June 27, 1960, had come to failure, it was obvious that France was going to negotiate. The point was not lost on Moscow. On September 27 Ferhat Abbas, the president of the GPRA, and Lakhdari Bentobbal left Tunis on their visit to Moscow and to Peking (FLN representatives had first visited China and the USSR at the end of 1958). On November 10, the communist leaders of the world (the leaders of the PCA included) met at a conference in Moscow, and *Kommunist*, the official ideological organ of the communist party of the USSR, published in its November issue an appeal for co-operation to the FLN from the first secretary of the PCA. It was not a very able article, for apart from addressing 'ideological' criticisms to the FLN, it maintained that the PCA had been right in not dissolving itself, as requested, to become integrated with the FLN because, by remaining independent, it had been able to make a contribution to the nationalist struggle 'of an incomparably higher quality'.

Amar Ouzegane—who, as a former communist leader, ought to know—ridicules this assertion of the PCA by citing an old Maghribine proverbial anecdote: 'Father, let us disguise ourselves as *shorafa* (nobles).' 'My son, it is easy enough to confer on oneself a patent of nobility by faking the *shajara* (genealogy) of one's ancestors. But before you do it you must wait for everyone who knows you to pass away.' Ouzegane goes on to explain that the total of members of the PCA who, as such, joined the FLN after the party had ordered its members to join while secretly retaining their communist allegiance, was thirteen for the zone of Algiers and about two hundred for the whole of Algeria. He cuttingly observes that the PCA had been able, on the instructions of its French bosses, to raise no fewer than 2,000 Algerians to join the International Brigades to fight Franco.[7] He lays responsibility for the attitude of the PCA to the revolutionary movement on the shoulders of the Central Committee of the Communist Party of the Soviet Union.

However, the chaos that reigned after independence gave the PCA a chance to appear in the open again. Whatever their demerits, communists the world over still hold the palm for political organisation and agitation. This was shown by a mere handful of communists in Algeria who produced *Alger Républicain*, which remains to this day the best paper ever published in Algeria.

Removed from the electoral register and realising that they could not openly oppose Ben Bella, the communists resorted to the tactics of trying to infiltrate the FLN and thus influence Ben Bella indirectly. This was welcome enough to Ben Bella. Although not himself pro-communist, he wanted to make use of the communists both because his internal administration lacked men of ability, and also because their support would secure from abroad additional strength to his revolutionary platform. In this game of mutual exploitation, the two protagonists were both to resort to extremes of demagogy. Scarcely had Ben Bella solemnly declared, 'I will never resort to anti-communism'[8] than he was ordering the PCA to be suppressed. But even this volte-face was surpassed by the communists themselves. In a statement made at the Salle de la Mutualité in Paris during the week of the 'Pensée Marxiste' (March 13–20, 1963), Bachir Hadj Ali, a leading figure of the PCA, said 'Since Ben Bella's government was first set up, we have given support to every single positive measure that he has taken, even after he suppressed our party.'[9] Was this the most subtle of finesse or the genuine support of measures meant to alleviate poverty? For in fact Ben Bella's actions were governed by exactly the same tactics as Nasser has adopted in dealing with communists in his own country, where he is still either putting them in important propagandist positions where they can draw the most attention to themselves, or throwing them into prison and into his detention camps in the desert. The only difference is that Ben Bella did not imprison the communists of Algeria.

Alger Républicain received a big boost to its circulation after *La Dépêche d'Algérie* was banned, but this was not the only activity of the PCA. A confidential French report of 1963 drew attention to the following activities:

It is worth noting that the communist party, far from being discouraged, is carrying out a far longer-term policy in Algeria. There are important factors working in its favour stemming from several conditions: disorder, disillusionment of the population and its anti-military sentiments, great poverty and, finally, unemployment.

The Communist Party and the Working Classes. The communist party is taking a close interest in the only organisation which is truly representative of the workers of Algeria: the UGTA. In the first place, no unions of direct communist allegiance have been created. This would not have been possible in any case given the present political climate in Algeria, where the various trade unions, including the surviving elements of the CFTC, are being absorbed into one comprehensive union. Furthermore, the communist party is trying to infiltrate the different grades of the UGTA, placing its own people in responsible positions. This concerted effort is particularly successful as these . . . militants . . . are very acceptable from a purely trade union point of view. At a different level, the demonstrations organised by the trade union headquarters during the clash between Wilaya IV and the Political Bureau bore the mark of the PCA. The organisation of the march-pasts, the repeated slogans, the presence of certain leaders, were, in the opinion of some journalists, signs that the PCA were behind the disturbances. Moreover, the PCA made no effort to hide its official approval of certain movements apparently patronised by the UGTA.

The Communist Party and Youth. The communists are working very hard to win over the youth of the country to their ideas. With this in mind, they are already manoeuvring to establish control of the teaching profession. In the first place, militant communists have been exhorted to answer the appeals by the political authorities to fill the gaps before the beginning of the scholastic year. In the second place, these tactics are carried even further, and the French Communist Party has been brought into the matter. People returning from France say that the French Communist Party has started an important campaign to send out militant communists to teach in Algeria. It is said that communist primary and secondary school teachers are volunteering for Algeria in their hundreds.

It is in this way that the communist party is trying to establish a foothold in Algeria at present. Its noisy protests at being banned from the elections is more than compensated for by its patient work 'in depth'.[10]

'Work in depth' was certainly going smoothly enough for the communists. Ben Bella was allowing Algiers to become a major platform for worldwide communist activities and propaganda so that he would thereby receive publicity throughout the world. Even after the FLN decided to suppress all newspapers which did not belong to them, and ordered *Alger Républicain* to merge with *Le Peuple*, it seemed that the communists would not disappear completely from the press, but might even gain a stronger tactical position through their influence in *Moudjahid*, the strictly official daily paper of the FLN. It seemed that they would achieve this not only through their own resourcefulness, but also through the connivance of Ben Bella. But after the coup of June 19, 1965, it became clear that *Moudjahid* would have to appear without communist assistance. The PCA went still deeper underground, and there—for the present—it remains.

The extensive and well-publicised overtures that Ben Bella and the communist countries made to each other have deflected the attention of many foreign observers from the true relationship between Algeria and, on the one hand, Moscow and its associates, and, on the other, Peking. It was quite clear to Algerians that it was Moscow's decision which led the PCF to refuse them even a semblance of the assistance that it had given to the Viet-Minh—in spite of the more favourable geographical factors and of the fact that the large French minority would have made things far easier for the PCF than was the case in Indochina. Moscow took the view that, ideological principles apart, the interests of Russia required careful handling of de Gaulle's France. Moreover, unlike the Vietnamese nationalists, Algeria was not likely to turn communist. China was not involved in similar considerations and she gave direct assistance to Algeria, giving recognition to the GPRA at once, while the Moscow axis procrastinated. During the Algerian war France had announced that she would break off relations with any country (Arab states excepted) which aligned itself with the GPRA. This threat proved sufficient to deter Moscow from promptly recognising the GPRA. The Algerians took good note of this, and they saw fit to include mention of it, tactfully disguised in the formal language of political doctrine, in the Charter of Algiers:

> Because of diplomatic considerations, other socialist countries have not always clearly expressed their attitude to the Algerian revolution. At the birth of the GPRA, the socialist countries of Asia

gave Algeria unconditional support. The socialist countries of Europe only followed later, although they gave us constant help at the humanitarian level. Under the pretext of not antagonising the West, the directors of the revolution [for which read the GPRA] did not confront the socialist countries, for their own policies were based on Western illusions.

The authors of the Charter thus stood in judgement not only on the GPRA but also on Moscow, which they accused of having failed in its socialist duty towards the Algerian revolution. Moscow could scarcely be expected to take kindly to such instruction in doctrinal matters, especially as it smacked strongly of trotskyism. It was impossible for the Russians overtly to express their disapproval of a man like Mohammed Harbi, but in private it was quite a different matter. When, in May 1964, Ben Bella paid his first official visit to Moscow and other communist capitals, and was given the red carpet treatment by the Soviets, including the Order of Lenin, Harbi wrote in *Révolution Africaine* to praise the 'disinterested' support of Algeria by the socialist countries, which he contrasted with 'imperialist and neocolonialist manoeuvres to divide us'. But he also gave his views on the direction in which the socialist world was moving.

The socialist world has changed. The course adopted since the Twentieth Congress of the Communist Party of the USSR has, quite independently of its real motives and conclusions, made a giant breach in the citadel of taboos. The lifeless formulae are disappearing little by little under the pressure of contact with reality and a renewal of conscience. The marxists have understood that marxism applies to them also. With this starting point, science has regained its rights in the teeth of ideology.[11]

Is it possible that the men in the Kremlin could approve of thoughts of this kind ? Or of Harbi's assertion that:

In giving the delegation led by the secretary-general of the [Algerian] party, Ahmed Ben Bella, an enthusiastic welcome, the socialist countries have raised the barriers created by the idea that our country is one of national democracy, one in which the nature of society is not yet defined. The idea that the gradual emergence of a socialist regime is impossible if the revolution has not been directed by a communist party, must, in the present situation, be reviewed and modified.[12]

No more could the Chinese agree with Harbi, who demonstrated his independence of them in a way that almost amounted to insult. This incident, quite unknown outside the circles of *Révolution Africaine*, occurred when Chou En-lai was in Algiers in 1964 and had promised to grant that newspaper an interview. This was particularly interesting since *Révolution Africaine* had previously been directed by the pro-Chinese Mansour Vergès, whom Harbi had been largely instrumental in ousting from Algiers. As the time of going to press got nearer, and telephone calls to the Chinese embassy had produced no more than the polite but infuriating 'yes, of course, of course', Harbi wrote a terse letter to the embassy saying that if Chou-En-lai's text did not come at the arranged time 'as had been promised several times', the embassy could regard the interview as null and void. The issue of *Révolution Africaine* that week appeared with a front page headline INTERVIEW WITH CHOU EN-LAI, but under it appeared a picture of the Algiers representative of the Vietminh regime and, inside, the text of an interview with him—not with Chou.

Neither Moscow nor Peking took kindly to such independence of thought. Although aware that Harbi was encouraging Ben Bella to the widest and closest possible collaboration with the communist world, the Soviets and the Chinese knew very well what tricks he had up his sleeve while playing this game. They therefore turned their attention to collaboration with the more nationalist elements in Algeria, in the hope of influencing and using them for their own ends. But they found this an even more difficult problem than Harbi, who at least was prepared to go along a lot of the way with them. An official French report on this matter set out what many foreign correspondents had appreciated much earlier from talks with communist diplomatists and journalists: that they were very hostile to the Ben Bella regime—one Czech journalist even going so far as to say it was 'the worst possible regime'.

They [overseas communists] accuse the Political Bureau of suppressing the organisations which genuinely represent the people, such as the UGTA. (They show little concern for the UGEMA.) They also accuse it of singling out the wrong leaders, of eliminating the progressive elements, and of talking of agrarian reform without doing anything about it. Naturally, they find it difficult to forgive Ben Bella for suppressing the PCA, although they do not like to say so in so many words, and in fact avoid mentioning it at all. They seem almost on the point of accusing Ben Bella of neocolonialism. They were very struck by the way in which the Political Bureau exonerated the French army of responsibility in the incident of the Basse Casbah, after the accusations of Ben Khedda and Wilaya IV. (When pressed, however, they have to admit that the behaviour of the French army has been exemplary.) They are surprised at the semi-official support which the French appear to be giving the present regime and are rather hoping that some Algerians may resent it as interference, and that if another regime were to succeed the present one, it would share this outlook.[13]

Moscow continued, despite the great difficulties, to try to collaborate with the FLN. Nevertheless, it could hardly stand on one side and say nothing when the PCA was banned—even if only because of what the Chinese would say. (Peking, in fact, remained silent since the PCA was pro-Moscow.) But what could Moscow say or do without antagonising the FLN? The theoretical Soviet periodical, *Mirovaya Ekonomika i Mezhdunarodnzye Otnosheniya*, which was not likely to come to the attention of many Algerians, said: 'The unity of all patriotic forces is vitally important. Progressives throughout the world are therefore all the more bewildered and disturbed by the [Algerian] government's suppression of the Algerian Communist Party.'[14] This article again sounded the old PCA refrain when it pointed out that it had previously proposed to the FLN 'a union of all patriotic national organisations'. Naturally enough, the TASS news service to Algeria did not carry this article.

All these doctrinal controversies were beyond Ben Bella's intellectual scope. They were much more Harbi's kind of thing. It is now generally accepted that Ben Bella was drawn into them by his ambition to become the great leader, for by nature he tended towards pragmatism. When Boumedienne took over he struck first at Harbi and his adherents since they were the inspiration of the doctrinal speeches that Ben Bella had been making. Harbi was criticised for indulging in abstract intellectual exercises, albeit with total conviction, at the expense of the fate of an entire country. The communist world—Soviet or Chinese—failed in the eyes of Algerians not on matters of doctrine, but on very practical considerations: neither their material aid nor their advice had done much to resolve Algeria's problems. The mistake that Algeria made was in thinking that such external aid could alone solve all her problems. Harbi and his colleagues must be absolved from responsibility for this error since they fully realised that such help could only be useful as a complement to Algeria's own efforts towards socialism. Apart from the Yugoslavs, one wonders what other communist country had the courage and the honesty to try to prevent the Ben Bella regime from indulging in its daydreams.

In spite of all this, Ben Bella's Algeria became the second largest recipient in Africa of Soviet aid (after the UAR—a country of great concern to the USSR—which was taking over half the total). In December 1962, Moscow granted a first loan of 500 million French francs, and signed an agreement to enter into commercial exchanges during 1964. A varied sequence of agreements followed in 1964, of which the most important was the granting of a second loan of 625 million Algerian dinars to allow the completion of the Annaba (formerly Bône) steelworks, which was to have an annual capacity of 350,000 tons of steel. Moscow also undertook to set up at Bou-Merdas, near Algiers, an 'African centre of hydrocarbons and textiles' which would train 50 technologists annually for the textile industry and 2,000 Africans for the petroleum industry. A further 300 Soviet doctors were to be sent to Algeria, which also received further grants for the training of Algerian students in the USSR. A 19,000-ton tanker was to be delivered to Algeria, together with 550 tractors and 12 repair shops. Russia moreover was to train 200 specialists in agriculture. Official Algerian sources listed the following projects stemming from Soviet loans, which totalled 1,650 million Algerian dinars: 28 small irrigation dams (15 in Kabilya, 6 at Tiaret, 5 at Sétif and 3 at Constantine) which would lead to the irrigation of 8,500 hectares of land; hydraulic drillings to provide 22,000 cubic metres of water for irrigation in the southern regions; 30,000 hectares of cotton and sugar beet plantations; 10,000 hectares of animal food crops; 5 agricultural experimental stations; 2 centres (at Tiaret and Constantine) for artificial insemination; a factory for the production of fabricated aluminium products with an initial capacity of 400 tons per year, together with Soviet technicians to prospect for copper, lead, zinc and mercury in the Aurès, Tlemcen and Kabilya regions.

The next most important technical assistance from the socialist world came from Yugoslavia, who gave a credit of $7·3 million and signed agreements for commercial exchanges and for technical and scientific collaboration on July 24, 1963. This Yugoslav assistance was to be used for the construction and commissioning of two textile factories at Valmy and Tlélat, and for the erection of a tannery and a fruit juice plant at El Asnam. Other projects, initiated later, included the development of lead and zinc mines at Khierz el Youssef and Djebel Gester. Some projects are still under consideration, including a shipping company and shipyards, and the development of farms and industrial units in the Soummam Valley. There is also extensive technical co-operation. The Yugoslavs have given great help in the medical and educational fields; two training centres are to be opened, one for agricultural studies, the other for training in industrial self-management. Commercial exchanges are based on the complementary nature of the economies, Algeria providing petroleum and vegetables, Yugoslavia providing tractors, building equipment and—shortly—ships and buses.

Compared with all this, China's assistance seems that of a poor relation. A loan of 25 million French francs was made in 1963, and an agreement for technical and scientific collaboration was signed between the two countries on October 20 of the same year. For a long time, foreign observers in Algiers could not tell for certain if the Algerians had seen the colour of the Chinese money, and suspicions were encouraged by the length of time that Peking was letting lapse before making loans that it had announced elsewhere in Africa. But the Algerians quickly realised that they could make good propagandist use of these Chinese gestures. At the conference of the Afro-Asian People's Solidarity Committee at Moshi in January 1963, the Algerians fully supported China in overt opposition to Soviet doctrines. They even went so far as to take the side of the Chinese when the latter objected to the Turkish poet, Nazim Hikmet, when he rose to make a speech which the Chinese had learned from a stolen advance copy would support the USSR. 'Who is Nazim Hikmet to speak for Turkey? He represents himself, and not the Turks', the Chinese delegate protested—thereby ironically enough voicing precisely the view that the Turkish government held on the great communist poet. When, to his great embarrassment, Nazim Hikmet could not make his speech or remain a 'Turkish' delegate, he slowly worked his way along to the adjacent ranks of the Soviet delegation with which he had come from Moscow. Whereupon the Chinese delegate again stood up to ask: 'But now we see this Nazim Hikmet behind the Soviet flag. We are still at a loss to understand. Is he in fact a Soviet delegate?' Hikmet, a quarter of a century before had written, after doctors had warned him about a heart ailment: 'But the other half of my heart, Doctor, beats in time with the army that is marching along the Yellow River.' He had, in fact, been more popular in China than anywhere. But now he was compelled to withdraw from the ranks of the delegates to mix with the observers, and then disappear entirely. This was callous treatment for an ailing man (he died shortly afterwards) who had been so valiant and eloquent a fighter for communism.

The Algerians at the meeting were so zealously pro-Chinese as to support the Peking delegation over the Hikmet affair. But at a meeting of the same body exactly six months later, held this time at Nicosia in Cyprus, the Algerian delegate, Mohammed Sahnoun (later to be his country's representative at the OAU), turned the tables completely and gave his full support to the Soviet line. He was frank enough to admit in private the reason everyone had surmised. 'After all, Moscow is in much the better position to assist us economically.' The first Soviet loan of 500 million francs followed shortly afterwards, clearly demonstrating to many Algerians the relative values of Russian and Chinese economic aid. And when Peking offered Algeria her first merchant ship, Moscow countered with the promise of providing her first oil tanker, of 19,000 tons capacity.

Other communist countries as well as Russia, Yugoslavia and China provided economic assistance in various forms. Bulgaria signed, on February 22, 1963, agreements for finance, trade, and scientific and technical co-operation. A loan of $6 million dollars was made by Bulgaria in May 1963. Further agreements between Sofia and Algiers were signed in April 1964. In March of the same year, Hungary made financial and trade agreements. In 1963, Czechoslovakia and Algeria signed agreements regarding trade, loans, technical and scientific co-operation (December 21). Further agreements were signed on May 14, 1964, and on July 17 negotiations concluded for a Czechoslovak loan to Algeria of $15 million, repayable in ten years at a rate of interest of 2·5 per cent. This loan covers equipment for the sector of industrial self-management, and for transmitters and studios for the Algerian broadcasting service. With Poland trade and technical agreements were made in March 1964. Keeping a foot in the Chinese camp, on April 14 of the same year Algeria signed trade and financial agreements with Albania.

But in the face of the urgent economic needs of the country, all this economic aid did not account for much. The great fanfare of propaganda which preceded and accompanied every man and every consignment from the communist countries did little to help. The inadequacy of such aid greatly disturbed those Algerians who failed to understand Harbi's point that, be the aid on the most massive scale imaginable, it could only be regarded as augmenting the help which the Algerians needed to provide for themselves through their own efforts and sacrifices. But, above all, it was the quality of the assistance which led to the loudest complaints. This was perhaps inevitable, since the Algerians had become accustomed to French standards; they had been greatly pampered in an economic sense by France, who had given them everything on a plate. Before raising their voices in such loud complaint, the Algerians would have done well to look at themselves and add up what they had achieved in the technological and economic spheres by their own efforts.

The first complaint arose over the doctors, most of them from communist countries, who by the end of 1965 numbered over a thousand. The language barrier alone would have led to serious difficulties here; moreover, the Algerian patients, pharmacologists and hospitals were accustomed to French practices. Before long the communist (and, as we have seen, the Egyptian) doctors became known as the 'vets', and a *fellah* would often travel for days, and spend a lot of money, in seeking out a French doctor, to show him the prescription that he had been given and ask anxiously: 'Are you certain that this man is not going to kill me?' It was more in the service of propaganda than of professional duty that hundreds of doctors came to Algeria from a country like Bulgaria (and also architects and even instructors in the French language!), for many of the so-called 'doctors' had only very limited medical training.

Yet many were a credit to their calling. There was something distastefully redolent of a pampered people in the way the Algerians treated these doctors from overseas, for while Algerian doctors were doing all they could to remain in comfort in the towns, it was the Bulgarians who were donkey-trekking, equipped with practically no medicine, to look after the mountain villages of Kabilya. But the official attitude to communist assistance was changing, and any charge was good ammunition. At the higher official levels, this change began when the Algerian ambassador in Sofia, Omar Oussedik (who was very pro-communist until given this appointment), wrote to his ministry to complain that 'while these so-called doctors are being paid in our country in foreign currency and all make enough money to run cars, here I have to apply with six carbon copies for any building repairs to be done to the embassy and then have to wait for months for anything to happen'.

There is some substance in Oussedik's charge. For most experts from communist countries (Yugoslavs and, to some extent, Russians excepted), working in Algeria was something of a holiday. Certainly Switzerland became a carpark for the vehicles that the experts (in Tunisia and Morocco as well as Algeria) had been able to buy. In 1963, at least two communist doctors working in Algeria were known to have defected in Switzerland; they did not dare to do so in Algeria for fear of the local authorities. It was thanks to the complicity of Nekkache, Ben Bella's minister of Health, that communist countries were able to make such inroads into the medical profession in Algeria. Formerly an ALN officer with pronounced national-socialist tendencies, he came to be still more hated by the army because he 'betrayed' it by becoming one of Ben Bella's closest lieutenants. Nekkache was among those who resisted arrest and was wounded during the rising of June 19. After this, the Boumedienne government proceeded to put the Ministry of Health's house in order, and many of the privileges of the foreign doctors ceased.

Things went awry even in the case of Yugoslavia, whose relations with Algeria had been genuinely friendly. When a sudden need for tractors arose in Algeria, due to exceptionally good weather and a bumper harvest, the Algerian press and radio mounted a vast propaganda campaign, to which Yugoslavia very quickly responded with the dispatch of 500 badly needed tractors. But soon the

Algerians were bitterly reproaching the Yugoslavs as 'revisionists', saying that they had demanded payment in American dollars. 'If it is to come to that', said the Algerians, 'we might as well have Fergusons—anyway, they are far better'.

In the field of higher education, too, it was to be the Western aid that proved superior. The statistics given here (compiled by Algerian sources at the end of 1964) demonstrate that there were fewer Algerian students in Eastern communist countries on official scholarships than was generally believed to be the case. They are also interesting in showing that other Arab countries, and the UAR in particular, were quite unable to provide for Algeria's needs in respect to higher scientific and technological education.

ALGERIAN STUDENTS OVERSEAS

	Engineering	Sciences	Medicine	Law & Economics	Literature	Totals
Western states	349	100	50	143	44	686
Eastern states	146	34	26	28	10	244
Arab states	5	1	0	65	543	614
Totals	500	135	76	236	597	1,544

Since the war period, when the communist countries were the first to offer scholarships to Algerian students, the latter had been concerned at the ideological implications involved in such aid. This suspicion was later to spread throughout Africa, particularly in view of the fact that the Black African students were far from happy in Moscow in the years 1962 and 1963. The Russians tried to solve this problem by asking Poland to take more students, since there ideology was separated from normal higher education and taught in separate establishments. Moreover, in Poland there was a more liberal atmosphere; if a Polish girl went out with a Black African it was regarded as something between themselves and not a party political matter. But Warsaw only provided a symbolic number of scholarships because, as the Poles said, they had not got enough room in their universities for their own students. Moscow was also greatly interested in military education. A military course lasted three years, and it has been estimated that at least 1,000 Algerians have been sent to Moscow for such training.

Algerians grew increasingly resistant to communist propaganda—most of it imposed through Algerian media—and started to say, in effect, 'we want better quality aid and less propaganda about it'. A significant event occurred in this connection vis-à-vis the United States. Because of her strained relations with Ben Bella, America never provided 'official aid' for Algeria. But from the beginning of the country's independence to the present day, there has been a substantial flow of 'humanitarian aid' for Algeria, at first disbursed as unofficially as possible through the Quaker organisation. It consisted of basic items like flour, sugar, milk and soap, and proved to be vital to Algeria. By 1962 the United States was feeding 3½ millions, or one-third of the total population of the country. The attitude of the State Department in this respect was unexceptionable. It was hard for American officials to stomach the fanfares of welcome heralding any odd parcel of communist aid, while the American aid was never even mentioned. Ben Bella did not at all relish the idea of American assistance, yet he could not do without it, so he got out of this difficulty by never referring to help from the United States, except to denigrate it as 'imperialist penetration'. (Such was his description at the economic seminar of the AAPSC held in Algiers in 1965.) The days were long since past when the poor in India had almost to swallow an American flag with American flour. The Americans were now wise enough to remain discreetly quiet. What mattered was that the Algerian people were perfectly aware of the source of these supplies. This sensible attitude on the part of the United States was to bring its own rewards later. The extent of the aid from America in the form of commodity supplies between independence and June 1965 is indicated by the table on page 190, based on official figures disclosed in detail for the first time.

Of the aid from Western Europe, it was the West German contribution which took most solid shape. Algeria, with DM 45·1 million, was the second largest recipient of the Federal Republic's foreign aid (after Liberia). An agreement for economic collaboration signed with Bonn on October 4, 1964 envisaged a further loan of DM 70 million to reconstruct the port of Annaba (formerly Bône), which had been destroyed when the *Star of Alexandria*

AMERICAN COMMODITY AID TO ALGERIA
(FY = financial year)

	Tons	World Price $	Ocean Freight $	Totals $
FY 1963				
Wheat	181,519	12,343,292	2,722,785	15,066,077
Flour	81,179	7,143,752	2,536,844	9,680,596
Oil	23,710	20,390,600	1,043,240	21,433,840
Milk	4,354	862,092	135,116	997,208
Totals	290,762	40,739,736	6,437,985	47,177,721
FY 1964				
Wheat	273,628	19,427,588	4,104,420	23,532,008
Flour	22,501	1,890,084	703,156	2,593,240
Oil	13,126	11,288,360	577,544	11,865,904
Milk	5,971	1,486,779	322,434	1,809,213
Totals	315,226	34,092,811	5,707,554	39,800,365
FY 1965				
Wheat	118,995	9,519,600	1,963,417	11,483,017
Flour	6,015	505,260	187,969	693,229
Oil	6,402	5,307,258	281,688	5,588,946
Milk	457	156,294	24,678	180,972
Totals	131,869	15,488,412	2,457,752	17,946,164
GRAND TOTALS	737,857	90,320,959	14,603,291	104,924,250

—a UAR cargo boat carrying ammunition—blew up, and to irrigate 6,500 hectares in the plains of Marnia (the birthplace of Ben Bella). The Italian concern Ifregraria was entrusted with the task of improving the agriculture in 60,000 hectares of the plains of Annaba. And, as we shall see in chapter 9, private British capital enabled Algeria to embark on an authentically revolutionary project in the field of oil.

Ben Bella's allegiance to Nasser led him to interrupt the economic relations between West Germany and Algeria following the Cairo-Bonn crisis of 1965: an action on his part which was entered as a charge in the secret dossier maintained by Boumedienne on the head of state. But it was obvious that Western states could do far more for Algeria than countries of the communist bloc. The following Table* shows that in matters of trade—for economic assistance includes trade as well as technical help—Algeria ranks as a very poor last in Russia's dealing with African countries, however interested Moscow may be in Algerian affairs.

SOVIET TRADE WITH AFRICAN COUNTRIES
(in million roubles)

	1962		1963	
	Imports	*Exports*	*Imports*	*Exports*
United Arab Rep.	65·7	93·0	111·2	121·7
Ghana	15·0	8·9	19·4	15·0
Sudan	9·6	9·4	15·5	12·2
Morocco	5·4	5·1	9·1	8·8
Guinea	2·4	18·0	2·1	12·7
Mali	3·9	7·7	2·7	11·0
Tunisia	2·0	1·7	2·5	3·7
Algeria	0·1	0·7	0·6	4·6

The reader will easily understand why Algeria finally turned to France when seeking economic aid to help her to return to the standards of 1961, and to remedy an economic situation that promised catastrophe. Where the communist countries erred was in not recognising that this would ultimately be inevitable. Another major miscalculation, on the part both of Moscow and of Ben Bella, who was dealing much too off-handedly from the communist pack, was their failure to appreciate the greater respectability and sense of purpose that the leader of the ANP, Boumedienne, conferred on the term 'Algerian nationalism'. For the delivery of arms was a major factor in the Soviet assistance to Algeria: a factor which was to react against Moscow and Ben Bella with a vengeance.

* Source: *Europe-France-Outremer*, No. 419, December 1964; authorised quotation.

9

FRANCO-ALGERIAN ENTENTE

ALTHOUGH France today is not all-important in Algeria, she exerts
sufficient influence to constitute, in conjunction with the Algerian
character, a major obstacle to a socialist revolution.

Throughout the world, many people oversimplified the Franco-
Algerian relationship and labelled Algeria as 'another Cuba'. In
fact, Algeria never was and probably never could be a 'Cuba'. When
confronted with the revolution there, the French attitude was very
different from that of the United States in similar circumstances.
Where the intransigence of the United States cornered the Cubans
and thus encouraged their adoption of extreme revolutionary attitudes, France stretched a helping hand to the Algerian revolutionaries and thereby involved them in 'capitalistic' compromises. The
economic factor was used in diametrically opposed ways by the two
powers. In the hands of the United States it was an instrument for
crushing Castroism by wrecking the Cuban economy; in French
hands it became a means for Algeria's national survival and to that
extent a strengthening of the new regime. It succeeded in this
respect, but from a 'revolutionary' point of view French influence
after independence inhibited radical economic and social policies—a
fact generally overlooked, especially by the Algerians themselves.
Co-operation with France opens up various possibilities for Algeria,
ranging from a continuation of economic dependence on the greater
country, amounting almost to neocolonialism, to a mutually advantageous partnership capable of fostering the progressive social and
economic evolution of the smaller country. The one thing it cannot
lead to is a socialist revolution, for French assistance, sustaining as
it does the natural Algerian desire for a higher standard of living, at

the same time saps the existing will for revolutionary work and sacrifice.

While many in the West, not being well-informed of the actual situation, mistakenly feared 'another Cuba in Africa' (modern commercial journalism is largely responsible for this misapprehension), on-the-spot observers in communist embassies in Algiers knew there was no real parallel between the two revolutions, and they referred—in private—to French influence as marring the revolutionary fervour of the Algerians. They refrained, however, from airing this view in public, though well aware of the tacit Franco-Algerian entente. Unable to take any positive action, communist representatives resigned themselves to accepting the relationship as useful to de Gaulle—and therefore anti-American. The Chinese alone attempted to direct the Algerians on to the tougher but orthodox road of socialism, explaining to them the negative aspects of the Franco-Algerian relationship. But it is doubtful if the Algerians understood, or wanted to understand, the true revolutionary dialectic of the Chinese in this matter. Mao Tse-tung made a public allusion to the relationship in an interview he gave in 1963 to *Révolution Africaine* (when it was edited by Mansour Vergès who had gone, together with Djamila Bouhired, the Algerian war heroine, on an official mission to Peking). The Chinese leader remarked significantly: 'One hears that in Algeria you still have French military interests and, more particularly, big French economic interests.' The hint was obvious, and for Chinese-style socialists would have been a directive for a nation-wide campaign; but it needed far more than maoist insinuations to dislodge the Algerian 'revolutionaries' from the comfortable niche of 'neocolonialism' (as Peking would call it) on which they had perched themselves.

The Tripoli Programme and the Evian Agreements were opposed in spirit, the latter acting as a brake in those matters where the former sought to accelerate the process towards socialist revolution. As it turned out, the Algerians (with a few exceptions, like Mohammed Harbi) chose to compromise in favour of the more conservative Evian Agreements. Even the army, which had opposed the Agreements—except for the clause granting Algeria self-determination—at the last Tripoli meeting of the CNRA, opted for the compromise. Here is not the place to argue whether, in making this choice, the

Algerian leaders took the 'easy way out', or whether, on the contrary, they acted with a clear grasp of realities. Ben Bella himself opted for capitalistic 'realism' while loudly proclaiming 'socialist revolution'. It is perhaps not surprising that in the end he was hoist by his own petard.

It is necessary to understand something of France's motives in assisting the underdeveloped world in general in order to appreciate the Franco-Algerian 'entente', which hinged on a tacit partnership between de Gaulle and Ben Bella: a partnership which influenced the latter's actions at every turn. France gives proportionately more assistance to underdeveloped countries than any other country adhering to the Committee of Aid for Development of the OECD, as can be seen from the following percentages of Gross National Product devoted to overseas aid: France 2·41; Holland 2·08; Belgium 1·48; Portugal 1·37; Britain 1·32; Germany 1·17; United States 0·97; Japan 0·93; Italy 0·78; Canada 0·38.* The factors governing this high percentage of French aid, of which Algeria gets the lion's share, have been explained in the Rapport Jeanneney, an official government publication.[1] They can be summarised as follows: the benefactor reaps economic advantages since practically all transactions are within the French franc zone; it is an obligation of 'human solidarity'; it increases French prestige. In this last connection, the report says: 'France has never, in the course of her history, resigned herself to retire within herself; she has always felt the need to act well beyond her hexagon. If she fails to satisfy this inclination, she suffers the risk of feeling herself diminished and of sinking into apathy.'

The Rapport Jeanneney observes that France has not much to fear from the competition of communist countries in the Third World, and belittles the apprehension of some that, should countries in this sector be neglected by the West, they would 'go over' to the Eastern bloc and so provoke the economic suffocation of the West. It grants that such a danger exists, but warns against exaggerating it. It bases its analysis on the following premises: 1. Developed countries find their main economic outlets in satisfying their own needs, the underdeveloped countries offering additional outlets only. 2. Communist

* With the exception of the statistics about the Sahara, all the facts and figures cited in this chapter are taken from the Rapport Jeanneney 1964: see reference for note 1 below.

countries have weak economies and could not easily replace Western countries in the Third World. Centralised and planned exports and imports offer some advantages for communist countries, but these are not very interested in the raw materials which the underdeveloped countries have to offer. The report notes that, even where communist countries have made 'political' purchases of Egyptian cotton, Cuban sugar or North African fruits, they have later tried to sell these on the world market, thereby causing a fall in prices detrimental to the original producers. 3. Moreover, in numerous cases Soviet exports are in competition with those of many underdeveloped countries—'as in the case of petroleum', it observes with an eye on Algeria. 4. Whatever the theoretical superiority of their structures and the attraction of their promises, communist countries cannot excel the West in technical assistance. 5. A massive adherence of the Third World to the Eastern bloc is rendered even less likely by the Sino-Soviet dispute.

General de Gaulle, on whose instructions this report was made, regarded Ben Bella as another feather in his cap. Every time the Algerian leader commended France for 'co-operating with a revolutionary country like Algeria' (as he did from the OAU rostrum in Addis Ababa in May 1963), de Gaulle's prestige rose in the Third World. The tacit entente was, in fact, a Franco-Algerian complicity. Ben Bella knew that as long as he played the Algerian game on the lines de Gaulle desired, he could rely on the assistance of capitalist France while still continuing his revolutionary and socialist utterances. We saw in chapter 3 how ready Ben Bella was to protect France's atomic tests in the Sahara, well aware of the importance de Gaulle attached to them. We also saw in chapter 4 how, after having refused the GPRA's demand to close the barrages again, France co-operated with the Ben Bella-Boumedienne alliance to the extent even of allowing French troops to give occasional discreet assistance to ALN units entering Algeria. It was natural for the French government to seek to extend its 'co-operative attitude' to the military for it knew only too well that the army constituted the country's only organised force. How the French proceeded in this field is now, for the first time, disclosed.

As French troops began to withdraw in accordance with the time-table fixed by the Evian Agreements, they converged from the south of the country on three main points: Oran, Algiers and

Constantine; from these they were to disembark for France. Although they took their arms with them they left behind them many tons of varied equipment. ('Enough picks and shovels, for instance, for Ben Bella to equip all the youth brigades he can raise', a French officer told me.) They also left vehicles and workshops in good order, and barracks fully equipped even down to the bedding. The handing-over process was the beginning of the Franco-Algerian co-operation in the military field. The Armée Nationale Populaire was particularly glad to receive this legacy in view of its sudden increase at the liberation beyond the size of its parent, the ALN. At first, the arrangements were made on a local basis, the commander of a departing unit making over material and barracks to his ANP counterpart. But soon the French sought to have these arrangements made official at a higher level.

The first contact between Colonel Boumedienne and the French high command in Algeria came on December 28, 1962 when Boumedienne asked the French officer he was dealing with to convey to his superior and to the French government his belief in 'Franco-Algerian co-operation'. The colonel added that he was 'speaking in the name of the ANP as well'. He drew attention to the remarkably low number of clashes between the two armies since independence, and said this was generally regarded as an international example of good behaviour. The former enemies were now 'facing each other without sentiments of hatred. They are more or less ready to work, or at least to coexist together in a spirit of mutal understanding.' Boumedienne further stated that he would welcome immediate co-operation with the French on two particular points. 1. Any transport vehicles the French could leave behind, however old, and even if they would last only a couple of thousand kilometres, would be welcomed by the ALN. Lamentably short of equipment, it had urgent security missions to perform throughout the country which were very necessary to establish the law and order which both France and Algeria desired. 2. The ANP was anxious to take over as quickly as possible French barracks and training camps, particularly in the region of Algiers, where Boumedienne had the task of curbing the Wilaya IV bands, as well as that of consolidating his position vis-à-vis the Political Bureau. The colonel assured the French that, given the barracks and training camps in the Algiers province, he could turn the roaming armed bands 'into disciplined soldiers'. In return, the French officer pressed Boumedienne for a solution to the problem of the Algerian officers and NCOs serving in the French armed forces. He replied that their integration in the ANP was a delicate question which 'would need time to solve'.

All this happened less than six months after formal independence. A little over a year later, at the FLN congress in April 1964, Boumedienne rose to the defence of those Algerian officers and NCOs who had served in the French forces and were now integrated in the ANP, explaining: 'I need trained men to build an army.' He had already reached an agreement with France whereby the latter would start at once to train an Algerian gendarmerie and would also leave some French army doctors in the Sahara. A few Algerian officers were also sent, very quietly, to military schools in France.

Before making a present of her surplus equipment to Algeria, France tried to obtain a written request from the Algerians, but Boumedienne avoided doing this. It can now be disclosed, however, that when the French expressed willingness to make over to the ANP a large number of battledresses and *ghanduras* (capes), Ben Bella on February 4, 1963 sent to the French premier, M. Pompidou, a confidential letter expressing Algeria's willingness to extend co-operation with France to 'military matters'. Only the day before he had already assured the French, privately but officially, that his government would never present the big French companies with a fait accompli of nationalisation. 'Algerian socialism', repeated Ben Bella, 'does not involve marxism or even systematic nationalisation. The private sector will continue to exist.' It goes without saying that the French did not take these assurances completely literally, but they did not miss the implications. They were in a very good position to appreciate them since much of their aid to the new Algerian state consisted of injecting capital.

Even more important than the material aid that France gave Algeria, however, was her invaluable assistance in providing trained personnel. The high proportion of Frenchmen in the upper ranks of the Algerian civil service may come as a surprise to many people. In 1964, they formed 43 per cent in the administrative grade (Grade A) and 77 per cent in the senior Executive grade (Grade B). France also sent over 15,000 teachers (the Algerians would have welcomed several thousand more). The following table shows the role played by the 4,683 Frenchmen in the various branches of the Algerian administration.

FRENCH PERSONNEL IN ALGERIAN CIVIL SERVICE
(1964)

Departments	Grades					Totals
	Ungraded	A	B	C	D	
Office of Premier	2	4	4	13	8	31
Justice	18	57	63	51	8	197
Interior	31	225	367	171	89	883
Agriculture	6	45	76	147	109	383
Finance	2	77	138	257	150	624
Commerce	1	2	8	4	2	17
Industry	—	12	13	21	24	70
Reconstruction	1	105	165	329	250	850
Labour	7	8	30	17	7	69
Health	13	39	71	104	92	319
Post & Telegraph	50	265	547	233	38	1113
Ex-Mujahidin	—	1	1	2	—	4
Youth & Sport	—	5	17	29	50	101
Information	—	—	—	1	1	2
Totals	113	845	1500	1379	828	4663

Algeria has received from France more official assistance in respect to 'technical personnel' than any other country. Out of a total of 46,121 such personnel (including teachers) in service throughout the 'Third World', Algeria has received 19,555. (The next largest recipients are Morocco and Tunisia which together have received 11,373.) These figures relate to French 'public' aid only and do not include other French personnel from which Algeria's private sector benefits: oil, gas and industry, for example. Nor do they include the personnel of companies nationalised before independence, such as the SNCFA (the railway system, employing 1,625 Frenchmen), the EGA (the gas and electricity service, employing 380 French technicians) and so on. The largest category of the 'technical personnel' sent abroad by the French government is made up of teachers. These, in 1964, numbered 33,495 in all countries and were distributed as follows: Algeria 14,872; Morocco 8,916; Black Africa 4,385; Tunisia 2,293; Cambodia-Laos-Vietnam 898; Latin America

418; Middle East 271; Asia-Oceania 152; all other countries 1,290.

Quite apart from the Algerian students in France on official French scholarships (numbering 523 in the academic year 1964–65), 613 Algerians went to France during the same period on various technical courses. All these efforts—the supply of French personnel and the training of Algerian technologists—are directed towards overcoming the most serious obstacle to the development of Algeria: the lack of even the minimum essential number of trained personnel. The gravity of the problem can be judged from the manpower requirements in agriculture alone. (See Appendix III, Table 4, page 279.) It is natural that France should play the leading part in training Algerian personnel in view of the ties of language and habits. With the development of the European Economic Community, France is in a better position to give such help. Thanks to grants from the European Development Fund, 14 new agricultural training centres were planned in Algeria for 1965 in addition to the 17 already in being.

Another field in which France is playing the major role is that of providing financial assistance. Under the Evian Agreements, the French government undertook to extend for a three-year period assistance amounting to 10 million francs, from which 20 per cent was to be set aside for compensating French settlers for their losses, and the rest was to be divided equally between projects agreed on with France and projects initiated by the Algerian government at its own discretion. By 1963 public financial assistance by France to Algeria alone amounted to 1,368,000,000 francs (approximately £99½ million). In 1962–33 the *total* British public aid to Africa (in the form of grants and loans) amounted to £64½ million. Algeria in 1962 accounted for 52 per cent of all French aid to underdeveloped countries. The importance of this aid is made clear by the fact that, in 1964, the Algerian budget for equipment essentially depended on it.

This aid stems, of course, exclusively from public money. What of the direct and indirect gains from the investment of French private money? The significance of these gains is indicated by the fact that in 1964, out of the 5·5 million francs devoted in the Algerian budget to equipment, 3·7 million was derived from revenue accruing to the state from the French exploitation of the

Sahara.* In 1965, again, the main sources of the equipment budget were to be French public aid and revenues from the exploitation of oil and gas in the Sahara. Out of a total of 967 million dinars, the French contribution totalled no less than 670 million dinars, of which 270 million was represented by taxation on oil and gas. The Sahara is thus seen to play a role second only to French assistance in the economic life of Algeria.

The Sahara constitutes in itself a separate and quite monumental subject. Before Algerian independence, France and international organisations would officially refer to 'Algeria-Sahara', to draw a clear territorial distinction between the north and the Sahara. Even now that France, with the coming of independence, has given up any hope of a de jure partitioning of the country, many documents still refer to 'Algeria-Sahara', probably out of habit.

In fact, the Algerian nationalists prolonged their war for two years to ensure that there should be 'one Algeria' which included the Sahara. Had they been prepared to accept any kind of partition, or any kind of special status conferred on the Sahara that would have made it less integrally Algerian than the northern part of the country, France would have been prepared to agree to a cease-fire at least as early as 1960. Yet even though the Algerians fought so hard to include the Sahara as an integral part of their country, their failure to understand the social and economic possibilities of the area was even more marked than their similar failure in regard to the northern areas. Over and above the factors operating in northern Algeria, there was a tacit agreement about the Sahara between the French and the Algerian leaders which was taken to even greater lengths than the 'complicity' over the north. For one thing, the nationalists never carried the fighting to the Sahara during the war, not only because of the technical problems involved, but, also, as we shall see, because of the very full role played here by mutual complicity. Algeria fought for the Sahara on

* Consistent with French practice, the general budget of the state of Algeria comprises two superimposed budgets: one for administration and the other for equipment. The first is covered by taxation and the second by 'extraordinary' levies. In 1965 the income from taxation for administration was 2,830,791,000 dinars against expenditure of 3,052,580,267 dinars—a deficiency of 221,789,267 dinars. In the same year, the budget for equipment showed an income of 967 million and expenditure of 1,365,500,000 dinars—a deficit of 398,500,000 dinars.

the battlefields of the north, and at the conference tables, but the Sahara and all its resources only became fully Algerian in mid-1963. Algerian sovereignty began to take effect only with the new oil and petroleum agreements signed in mid-1965; and, clearly, for many years to come the Sahara will not be fully Algerian in any de facto sense. As for 'revolution': so far as the Sahara is concerned, it seems to be buried deep under the sand.

Mirage in the Sahara

In the spring of 1963 a group of journalists of the Algerian radio and television services toured the Sahara—the first Algerians to do so since independence. A Polish correspondent and myself were among the party. Land Rovers and other equipment necessary for the expedition were provided by Claude Cheysson, director-general of the Organisme Saharien.* (An able official of the Quai d'Orsay and a man of great integrity, devoted heart and soul to the economic development of the Sahara's resources, Cheysson is one of the most outstanding exemplars of the very best type of progressive senior French technocrat.) During the expedition—which was not without its difficulties, for while it is easy enough to travel in a north-south direction along the established routes, journeying from east to west is still not a light undertaking—everyone in the party was very forcibly struck by the unmistakably French character of the Sahara.

This was pointedly brought home to us at the town of In Salah in the northern part of the Sahara. The Polish journalist, Tadeusz Jatkowsky, irritated at the lack of interest in the Sahara shown by most Algerians, said to the préfet of the town: 'But tell me, Monsieur le Préfet, where are the Algerians? And where, especially, are the young people? We have now been touring the Sahara for more than a fortnight and the only person we have seen who was not a Saharan was a German hitch-hiker, a student from Hamburg. How long is it going to be before the Sahara attracts the youth of Algiers from the cafés and street-corners? Or, if it comes to that, from Paris?' In fact, everything our party had seen in the Sahara was the result of French effort, undertaken by Frenchmen aided by the labour of

* Abbreviation for Organisme Technique de Mise en Valeur des Richesses du Sous-Sol Saharien, replaced in December 1965 by the Organisme de Co-opération Industrielle.

the *Targui*, the indigenous inhabitants of the Sahara. The only sign of human energy that was not French in origin was a shrine of a *marabu* with a small Algerian flag on top of it. The reply of the préfet, a local man, conveyed the dilemma and, perhaps it is not too much to say, the tragedy of the Sahara. 'Ah, les gens du Nord: they don't understand the Sahara. And they don't like what little they see of it. All they want to do is to exploit it at long distance.' This, however, came a little too close to the attitude of the French, with their concept of two distinct territories in Algeria: the 'North' and the 'South'. The subject was quickly dropped, and my Polish colleague turned to watch the Algerian cameramen who were busily engaged in photographing the sand roses they were seeing for the first time. He could not resist saying after a while: 'Come on, there are other things of interest here. When I next go to Tunis, I'll bring you some sand roses from the *suq*. You'll be able to photograph them in comfort in Algiers!'

In spite of the two years of bloodshed which the Algerian nationalists imposed on themselves and their countrymen for the sake of possessing the Sahara, from almost the very start of the revolutionary war they evinced a well-nigh total lack of constructive interest in it and a quite astonishing ignorance of it. In the early stages of the armed struggle, nationalist operations were confined to the northern region of the country. Then, on October 23, 1957—the third anniversary of the revolution—the Comité de Coordination et d'Exécution of the CNRA issued an order of the day announcing that henceforward military operations, hitherto limited to a line north of the Sahara, would be extended 'to all of the national territory'—clearly implying that the Sahara was to come within the revolutionary nationalist orbit. But in fact there was little actual fighting there as a result of this decision. On October 17 an ALN unit based on Tozeur in Tunisia destroyed two oil tankers on the road to Edjeleh in the eastern part of Algerian Sahara. Three weeks or so later, on November 9, there was a clash some 70 km from Timimoum near the Moroccan border when the ALN attacked a French oil prospecting party escorted by legionnaires. (News of this engagement was discreetly suppressed by the nationalists for the French troops, under Colonel Bigeard, wiped out the Algerian unit.) There was no sequel to these incidents. A factor in the decision not to bring the Sahara fully into the war against the French was the Libyan government's concern, no less strong than its sympathy with the nationalist cause, that oil operations close to its borders should not be interrupted by military activities in the eastern Sahara.

There were, of course, other factors. The biggest problem in conducting military operations in the Sahara was the terrain itself. It was much easier for the French to locate and destroy ALN units in the open ground of the Sahara than in the mountains of the Aurès or Kabilya. Although oil and natural gas installations, especially the pipelines, are extremely vulnerable to sabotage, the Algerians, for all that they had both the men and the equipment for such operations, never touched these installations. They decided (rightly or wrongly does not concern us in this context) to let the French operate the pipelines unmolested, and this in spite of the fact that they knew many of the oil installations in the desert were strongholds of the OAS. The GPRA certainly protested very strongly when Tunisia agreed to allow the French to run a pipeline from Edjeleh to the Tunisian port of La Skhirra, asserting that by this action the muslim neighbour was 'helping the French war effort'. A fair point to make—yet the fact that oil installations remained intact assuredly did not help the Algerian war effort. At the back of their minds, however, the Algerian nationalists had the idea that one day these installations would be theirs, and so took the view that to destroy them would jeopardise their country's economic future. Similar economic considerations influenced the French government and the French oil companies, who were more persuasive than the Algerians could possibly be in restraining the OAS diehards from damaging the installations in revenge for the nationalist victory. The outcome was a tacit agreement between the two contending parties that operations in the Sahara were taboo.

Without entering into the tortuous complexities of international oil politics, it may be mentioned that 'complicity' in these matters took other forms than keeping war out of the Sahara. Two of the most significant are still largely unknown. 1. The Esso organisation in Tunisia, notwithstanding its membership of a cartel which contains French interests, supplied oil to the ALN through an agreed intermediary. Similar arrangements existed in Morocco. When the Algerians were given the opportunity of getting their supplies, on better terms, from an alternative source (the Italians), they flatly refused. 2. The GPRA, and later the Ben Bella government, refused to modify the wholly French-dominated structure of the Saharan oil and gas industry. The only exception was the case of the third pipeline, to Arzew, which had been built by British capital. (We shall see later why British interests were involved.) In these matters Algerian attitudes were governed by more than immediate practical considerations. France's presence in Algeria was a fact and could not be replaced without having the whole oil industry turned over to American or Soviet domination. This would be too extreme a step to be contemplated, if only because the French buy Algerian oil and gas at a premium above world prices. France refines 95 per cent of Algeria's oil and takes 85 per cent of the total production at a price which is 20 per cent above the world market price.* Though paying higher prices, France has the great advantage of settling her oil bills with Algeria in French currency. The financial advantage to Algeria is such as to intensify her economy's integration with that of France.

It would be pointless to debate who would have taken over Saharan oil exploitation if the French had been ejected, but it is very much to the point to emphasise that the Algerian government notably failed to do what would have been expected from a genuinely revolutionary regime: namely, to diminish foreign holdings in a major national industry and to Algerianise national resources as widely and as quickly as possible. This failure, of course, did not prevent Algerian leaders from descanting during and after the revolution on 'our oil and gas resources' and of the part these would play in 'our revolution'.

The Sahara posed two main problems to the Algerian leaders, one industrial and commercial, the other sociological. Perhaps the greatest measure of the failure of their 'socialist revolution'— indeed, of their national revolution pure and simple—has been their inability to give these problems, of paramount importance, appropriate and intelligent attention. They inherited them at independence exactly as the French had left them, for during the war the organisers of the Algerian national insurgence had given very

---

* By the Franco-Algerian agreement of July 1965 for 'co-operative association', France undertakes to buy Algerian oil at the following prices: $2·08 per barrel f.o.b. Bougie; $2·04 per barrel f.o.b. La Skhirra; $2·095 f.o.b. Arzew (where the third pipeline, owned by the Algerian state company SONATRACH, began functioning in 1966).

little thought to the future organisation of the country and its economy, beyond vague asseverations of belief in 'socialism'. Indeed, were it not for de Gaulle's support after independence for interstate arrangements over oil (arrangements detrimental, be it noted, to private French interests) and for the work of men like Claude Cheysson, Algeria's position vis-à-vis the Sahara and its resources would be far worse than it actually is.

To take the sociological problem first. Intimately related to economic activities in the area, this is crying out for a truly revolutionary solution. The challenge it presents is as complex as it is fascinating, and it can be discussed only very briefly here.[2]

With an area of 2 million square kilometres, the Sahara represents 87 per cent of all Algerian territory. Its population at the beginning of 1964 was estimated to be around 750,000: 7 to 8 per cent of the total population of the country. Distances between the inhabited centres vary between 600 and 1,500 kilometres. Water supplies are inadequate and the climate is extremely rigorous. In consequence, notwithstanding its great potential wealth, the Sahara makes a large contribution to the ranks of Algeria's unemployed—in 1964 no less than 120,000. Meanwhile the Saharan population increases at the rate of 2·7 per cent per year and is expected to reach one million towards 1975, having been as little as 590,000 as recently as 1960. So in twenty years' time, there will be another 550,000 Algerian mouths to feed in the Sahara alone. Will the Sahara become sufficiently developed to support a settled industrial population? If not, how can its increasingly grave social problem be prevented from crushing the northern part of the country under an impossibly heavy burden? Though the French oil companies have remained in the Sahara, and will no doubt extend their activities (though this does not necessarily mean that they will employ more people), nevertheless the withdrawal of the French army and civilian administration has made the economic problem of the Sahara more acute. Together they accounted for 58 per cent of the salaries paid to Saharan workers, compared with only 27 per cent in the case of the oil and gas industries. In certain regions, like that of Colomb-Béchar, the French administration and army accounted for no less than 82·5 per cent of all the salaries paid to Saharans, since part of the responsibility for maintaining the road network of the Sahara, with the use of local labour, fell to the military. To the question of how far the Algerian army and administration can take over the role of their French counterparts, particularly in the field of public works, statistics provide an answer. Before independence, the able-bodied population of the Sahara totalled about 200,000 of whom 58 per cent were engaged in agriculture in the sectors of Laghouat and El Oued in the eastern Sahara, and at Adrar and Timimoum in the west. The sudden growth in the number of unemployed to 120,000 sustains the inference that at least 100,000 (or one-seventh of the entire population) have lost all sources of income, and that the income of others has been drastically cut. It is obvious that, unless something is done quickly to remedy the catastrophic situation which has resulted from Algeria's change of flag, there is a strong possibility that the *Targui* (who had in fact shown very little interest in independence) will look favourably on the French concept of an Algeria partitioned into 'North' and 'South' as distinct and governmentally detached regions.

The contribution of Ben Bella and his colleagues—or of Algerians in general—to the Sahara and its sociological challenge can be assessed very simply. Their so-called 'revolutionary' approach revealed nothing either of the Soviet concept of the assimilation of virgin territories or (a hard charge for Algerians to swallow) of the Israeli vision and energy which are conquering the Negev. And yet the Sahara had been fully conquered and assimilated by the French. When at long last, towards the end of 1963, Ben Bella finally visited the northern towns of the Sahara, it was only to make fine speeches about oil. The vast majority of Mediterranean Algerians take no interest in the Sahara beyond sitting back and calculating from afar the royalties Saharan oil will bring in. The only occasion on which they showed any real interest was when the ALN joined up with Modibo Keita's forces to curb the dissident nomadic Touareg in Mali: a move hardly calculated to increase the northerner's popularity in the Sahara. Ben Bella fondly hoped that the revolution would at last reach the Sahara—out of the blue—when it was reported that China was interested in building a trans-Saharan road to link Algeria with Mali. But it has fallen to the French to produce economic and sociological planning which attempts to alleviate the growing problems of the Sahara. One does not have to be clairvoyant to predict that the affinities between the Sahara and the French will grow increasingly close.

The picture is very different in the case of the other great problem of the Sahara: the extraction of oil and gas. The problem here is primarily one of the shortage of trained personnel and of the failure of the Algerians and their government to face this problem, especially in the southern part of the country. The difficulties are all the greater since the oil industry has its own highly specialised technical and administrative expertise.

A measure of the regime's ignorance of these technicalities was seen when Ben Bella sought to put at the head of oil and gas matters a man with experience of this field. His choice fell on the very young Ahmed Ghozali, whose experience of the industry—though probably unique among Algerian nationals—was no more than that acquired from a few years' service as a junior official in a French oil company. Ghozali started his climb upwards when Ben Bella made him, on December 12, 1964, state under-secretary for Public Works. (After the coup of 1965, he was dismissed by Boumedienne who alleged that his appointment was based on 'favouritism', Ghozali having been born in the same town as Ben Bella.) Yet during and after the war, the Algerians were offered on a plate a unique opportunity for training personnel in the oil industry by the late Enrico Mattei of Italy, the founder of the state oil organisation Ente Nazionale Idrocarburi (ENI).

Mattei, killed in an air crash on October 28, 1963, was a highly controversial figure both in his own country and overseas. He became the nightmare of the international oil cartels when he began to cut into their huge profits by offering better terms than the fifty-fifty arrangement of the private companies. He was a genius, and his memorial is what he has achieved in the industrial and social revolution of Italy, as well as of Africa. But like most geniuses, he had much of the dictator in him, and he liked to run a one-man show. As a result he took all his secrets with him at his death; these included the details of his abortive attempt to assist the Algerians. From what I have been able to gather from close associates of Mattei and from observations during the Algerian war, the relations between ENI and the Algerians were far from being as sinister as is generally imagined. (The first meeting of GPRA and ENI representatives—between Abdelhafid Boussouf and Dr Mario Pirani—took place in my house, which was occasionally used for private meetings by Algerian leaders.) The Western oil companies, already seeing in

H

Mattei their grimmest bête noire, took a really dark view of the whole affair, especially when it transpired that the founder of ENI had met Ben Khedda in 1958 in a town in Siberia! But, in fact, this encounter was no more than a coincidence, both men being held up there for several days by a November snowstorm while Ben Khedda was returning from Peking and Mattei was on his way to China. There was, it is true, talk on general matters between them, but no arrangements were made, although Mattei did make an offer of assistance to Algeria.

The legend of 'the communist Mattei' (in fact he was a leftwing Christian Democrat) and of his 'penetration of Algeria' luxuriated, and stories were rife of his supplying arms and money to the Algerian insurgents. Mattei did indeed provide some financial aid and medical supplies, and smoothed over the administrative difficulties in the way of members of the FLN wishing to enter Italy. The antagonism shown to Mattei, particularly by the French, began in 1957, when he went to Paris to give a lecture at the Centre de Politique Etrangère. He turned down offers from the French to collaborate with them in Algiers, and told Guillaumat, now in charge of oil and gas under de Gaulle, that he would never send ENI employees 'to work under the protection of machine guns'. In the event it seems that Mattei may have been mistaken in refusing the French offer but, like many others at the time, he overestimated the capabilities of the Algerian revolutionaries. ENI's interest in Algeria continued, and with it the legend of Mattei's sinister influence. In August 1961, his organisation set up a public relations office in Tunis, with the full approval of Taieb Boulharouf, the head of the GPRA mission, then in Rome. Dr Mario Pirani, who is now head of the press bureau of the ENI headquarters in Rome, was put in charge of this office in Tunis.

ENI's first concrete approach to the GPRA was made in 1961 when it offered to train any number of young Algerians at every level, without any charge or conditions whatever. It also said that, if things would thereby be made easier for the GPRA, it would train as many as possible in its installations in the United Arab Republic and Tunisia. Yet strange to say, the GPRA, who all the time was sending army officers and airmen to be trained in Czechoslovakia and China, were not prepared to fall in with this suggestion. Oil was taboo! Mattei's organisation nevertheless tried hard to persuade the nationalist leaders of the prime necessity of starting to train young men with good university qualifications for the administrative, economic and political aspects of the oil industry, so that Algeria could as soon as possible produce technicians and administrators able to stand their ground against the supremely skilled experts whom France would call on in negotiations to determine the future of Algerian oil. But the GPRA continued to turn a deaf ear, with the result that the revolutionary leaders at Evian had no alternative to accepting French terms for the economic control of the Sahara. Thus the new state, suffering from a woeful lack of qualified men to cope with the situation, inherited the problems of the oil and gas industry with all the economic, political and social complexities deriving from the colonialist period: a situation which, as we shall see, continued for nearly three years after independence.

The Algerian government's position as an oil-owner is one of the happier French bequests at independence. The French state handed over to the new state its 40·51 per cent share in the production of the Société Nationale de Recherches Petrolières en Algérie (SN REPAL), which amounted to 5 million tons of oil a year. This percentage, however, Algeria decided to take in money, not in material. This decision was not taken for lack of alternative proposals. Belatedly, as the negotiations with France were in train, the Algerian nationalists approached the Italians for advice. This was given: namely, that they should adopt a positive oil policy—a quite feasible policy in view of the richness of Algeria's holdings. ENI held it to be a necessary condition for the development of such a policy (in Algeria herself, to start with) that the new government establish a domestic low-price system for home-produced oil by taking the SN REPAL percentage in material instead of cash. The advice was not followed, the Algerians preferring to sell their oil at high prices to France and taking payment in French currency. A corollary of this was the new regime's approach to the control and exploitation of the national assets. Independent Algeria followed French law regarding natural resources, whereby the subsoil is the property of the state (in contrast to English and American law which regards it as the property of the landowner). Hence the Algerian state became owner of the mineral rights of the Sahara. The exploitation of these rights it conceded back to the French companies already operating in the

Sahara. (After June 1963, the Algerian share of the production was increased to 50 per cent.)

The ENI offer to train Algerian personnel was repeated, after independence, on June 10, 1962, when several branches of Ben Bella's administration were approached. It can now be stated that ENI, in an attempt to make this offer more acceptable, went so far as to say that the scholarships would be offered not by the company but by the state of Italy, thereby attempting to dispel French suspicions of ENI and of Mattei. (These suspicions began to evaporate when de Gaulle, who was trying to set up in France an institution on the lines of ENI—the Union Générale de Pétrole—made approaches to the Italians over the much more important question of gas supplies to Western Europe.) However, once again the Ben Bella administration turned a deaf ear to ENI. Ben Bella eventually attempted to justify his attitude—which was really conditioned by his fear of the large French oil interests and by sheer ignorance—by maintaining that 'ENI is no longer what it was under Mattei: it is now the tool of the capitalist Italian government'! In 1963, his government signed an agreement for a 1,250,000-ton refinery to be built by ENI in collaboration with the Algerian government, which required Italian investment amounting to 115 million francs. But this has turned out to be no more than a blatant attempt to blackmail France. The Algerians wanted to amend the agreement so as to get ENI to build a much bigger refinery. The Italians rejected this as 'utterly uneconomic'. Ben Bella's reply to the Italian objection was typical of the man. 'If you call yourselves our friends, put the extra production on the Italian market—give us some room there.' It proved very difficult to make Ben Bella understand the futility of his suggestion—Italy's own refineries are not working at full capacity. His next move was to announce a deal with Moscow whereby the Russians were to run an 'African Institute of Hydrocarbons' in Algiers, with the intention of training both North Africans and Black Africans to 'revolutionise' the oil industry of the continent. Far from giving the French the fright intended, the agreement proved a dead letter and the USSR's oil and gas centre was never founded. It was left to France to set up such an organisation, which was actually established before the overthrow of Ben Bella.

This is not to imply that the Algerians should have abandoned the French in order to embrace ENI or anyone else, but to show that, in rejecting the offers of ENI, Algeria squandered a golden opportunity to train the technologists she so badly needed. Ben Bella got no further than sending a purely token contingent to train at ENI's Metanopolis, near Milan. What an opportunity the Algerians missed can be seen more clearly from the programme of help the Italians were prepared to organise. This programme was offered to the Algerians during the war and repeated in 1962.

Higher Studies in Petrol Technology : nine-month courses for engineers, physicists and chemists, geologists and statisticians; in politics, economics, commercial and legal studies; scholarships worth 60,000 liras a month.

Institute of Management and Technology : five-week courses for managers; special courses of about six months in sales, engineering, refining, etc.; special courses for trainees in administration, management, accounting, etc.

Experience in the Field. 1. *In geophysical techniques.* (i) A stay with operating units of about a year for engineers and geologists. (ii) A similar stay for industrial experts and surveyors. 2. *In refining techniques.* A similar stay for about eight months for engineers and chemists. 3. *In pipeline techniques.* (i) Courses on operational, maintenance and compression problems with experience of operating units lasting from four to eight months. (ii) Courses for electro-technicians and radio-technicians of from one to three months. (iii) Courses for workers on regulation of gas pressure, care of instruments, general maintenance, welding, etc., of from two to four months for the theoretical part and of four to six months for the practical. 4. *In drilling and production techniques.* (i) Theoretical and practical courses for industrial experts and surveyors. (ii) Theoretical and practical courses for workers in production and maintenance.

The grievous shortage of trained personnel in Algeria is starkly revealed by statistics. At independence in 1962, the total number of Algerians employed by the oil and gas industry was 4,139, of whom 9 were engineers, 118 were technicians, 255 were white-collar workers and 3,757 were operatives. By mid-1964, thanks to strenuous efforts (which, however, ran the risk of jeopardising the quality of the personnel), the figure reached 5,698; but (as is shown in Appendix III, Table 12) the aspirations of nationalist politics could not provide reinforcements for the higher echelons of the industry, especially among the technical ranks.

The absence of any policy for the oil and gas industry and its problems, the hesitations, contradictions, blunders, threats and promises—all this led to a slowing up of development, especially in exploration. The production of oil failed to follow the vigorous upward trend hoped for with independence, and for which the French companies in the Sahara were technically ready. (See Appendix III, Table 13.) Though oil production rose, the rate of increase was appreciably less than in Libya, Algeria's direct competitor. While the earlier oilfields were getting 'old', important new ones, such as El Agreb-El Gassi and Gassi Touil, were hardly being exploited at all. The fall-away was especially notable in prospecting. By January 1965, the amount of geophysical (seismic) research had fallen away by 72 per cent compared with the same month in 1964, and drilling had been reduced by almost a half. The number of seismic teams employed in exploration has declined steadily since 1961. In that year 257 teams explored 395 metres; in 1962, 190 teams (333 metres); in 1963, 159 teams (379 metres); in 1964, 113 teams (236 metres).

In the meantime, the outer world was not prepared to wait for the Algerians to get themselves organised. In Libya, a big boom in oil production led to output's nearly doubling, reaching 41 million tons by 1964. Libyan oil is well sited geographically, both in relation to wellheads and to the coast, whereas Algeria's two main oilfields are 600 and 800 kilometres respectively from the coast. Experience has shown that 400 drillings in the Sahara have produced only 600 tons of oil per square kilometre as against 8,000 tons in the Middle East. The discoveries in the Sahara have certainly been considerable, but the reserves are not very great, and for every ton of oil extracted there must be 2 tons of exploitable reserves. The proven reserves of the Algerian Sahara are 500 million tons, representing about 1 per cent of the world's known reserves (about 7,080 billion tons); this is to be compared with Libya's 7·82 per cent. Western Europe is primarily dependent on the Middle East for its oil, with Algeria exclusively supplying France. French imports of Algerian oil represent 13·7 per cent of the oil supplies coming to the Common Market countries, as against 61·7 per cent from the Middle East.

In fact, the real importance of the Sahara lies not in its oil but in its natural gas reserves, which are estimated at 20,000 billion cubic metres: 7 to 8 per cent of the world's known reserves. Algeria is the fourth largest source of natural gas, after the United States, Russia and Iran. Many experts think that Algeria has missed the boat over natural gas as she has done over oil.

Once again, it was a question of ignorance and political meddling. Ben Bella did not want the gas pipelines to go via the most economical routes, through Tunis and Morocco. He spoke of a supply of gas that would help to feed Black Africans: a singularly fatuous and utopian suggestion in view of the fact that Black Africans do not use gas. Then he said that Algerian gas would be used to meet the needs of Algeria; but Algerian consumption hardly amounts to 400 million cubic metres a year. But probably his biggest blunder was his mishandling of negotiations over gas with the Italians. In early 1962, ENI told the GPRA that its major interest in Algeria now centred on gas supplies. Private discussions were held between Dr Mario Pirani and Ben Khedda, the latter assisted by Hafid Karaman, the head of the GPRA mission in West Germany. The Italians brought the question up again after independence. Instead of accepting the ENI proposal that the gas be carried across the Mediterranean by refrigerated liquid methane tankers, Ben Bella sought to get accepted a much more ambitious plan for a pipeline laid on the sea bed. This he wanted to go via Tunisia and Sicily to the Italian mainland. The Algerians said that they would see to the piping and liquefication of the gas, and, subsequently, to its marketing in Italy. The Italians rejected this scheme. And there matters rest at present. Italy is the largest consumer of gas in Western Europe. The Algerians missed a major opportunity.

As a result of this deadlock, the industry stagnated to the point where, at the end of 1963, 90 out of 106 gas wells in the Sahara had been shut down or abandoned. The Italians and others turned their attention to Libya, which began the large-scale production of gas, selling it cheaply. On October 22, 1964, the minister in charge of the petroleum industry in Libya announced that by 1967 the largest liquefaction plant in the world, built by Esso at Marsa Brega, would be in operation. Agreement in principle, he added, had already been reached for the supplying of Libyan gas for fifteen to twenty years to Italy and Spain—another customer the Algerians had been fondly eyeing. Nor was Libya Algeria's only rival. Large reserves of gas were discovered off the coast of Holland, giving Western Europe—Britain included—high hopes of workable reserves in the North Sea. Algeria was paying a high price for her procrastination and for thinking she could call the tune in the oil and gas industries of Western Europe and Africa.

But Algeria did achieve one thing after independence of which she can justifiably be proud: the establishment of her own pipeline and transport system for petroleum products. This—for once, authentically revolutionary—development was achieved largely with the help of capital privately provided from Britain after France had refused to grant the Algerian government a 20 per cent share (probably to be increased to 33 per cent) in the pipeline being built between Hassi-Messaoud and Arzew. Very much against the advice of the Organisme Saharien, the French companies took a stand which smacked of the obduracy of French capitalists during colonial days, expecting that the Algerians would give in. But capitalism is not indivisible! In Algeria 1964, a contract for the building of this pipeline was placed with Constructors John Brown of London. A consortium of British merchant banks, led by Kleinwort, Benson Ltd, made a loan of £18·6 million repayable in eleven years at 5½ per cent interest over the first seven years. Another loan, of 7·5 million francs, was raised in Kuwait, and by June 26, 1964 Algeria had started to build her own pipeline. Britain's participation in this venture led to the first large overseas purchase of Algerian gas, to supply London. In 1963, a fifteen-year contract was signed with the British Gas Council for the delivery of about one billion cubic metres annually; two methane tankers of 12,000 tons each were specially built to transport it.

The stagnation in the Algerian gas industry ended when, after twenty months of tortuous negotiations, Algeria in July 1965 signed an agreement for 'co-operative association' with France. This agreement (embodied in a document 150 pages in length) is effective for fifteen years, subject to revision after five years and extendable to forty years. The French side of the agreement is very much in line with de Gaulle's policy of creating companies in which the state has a majority holding. Examples of these are the Bureau de Recherches Minières (BRP) and the Régie Autonome des Pétroles (RAP), which are the main arbiters of the oil and gas policies of

France. After them comes the Compagnie Française des Pétroles, which is one third publicly owned. Together BRP and RAP form the French side of the Association Coopérative (ASCOP), the company set up under the terms of the Franco-Algerian agreement. Other companies may participate in ASCOP if the French government approves of them. France and Algeria have equal interests in it: an arrangement highly unpalatable to private French interests which criticise it as favouring Algeria far too much. It has been likened to 'a horse and a skylark harnessed together', with France as the horse.[3]

Even *Moudjahid* (the daily paper published under the eye of Boumedienne's government, which had hailed the agreement with such enthusiasm) cautiously stated that 'the agreement does not give everybody cause for satisfaction'. Indeed, the Algerians could scarcely describe their participation in the agreement as consistent with the 'revolutionary' talk about the exploitation of Saharan resources. Certainly it gave the Algerian state a greater share in the benefits of oil and gas exploitation and more participation in the administration of the industry; but it also provided very strong safeguards to French public and private interests, according France as a purchaser of Algerian gas a privileged position against any countries other than Algeria's neighbours. (This exception, however, has so far remained hypothetical.) Moreover, the Algerian government undertook to confirm that the oil and gas wells of the Sahara should remain in French hands. The socialist and anti-Boumedienne group, the Organisation de la Résistance Populaire (ORP), was not without reason in denouncing the agreement.

Still, revolutionary or not, the Franco-Algerian agreement was the best thing the government in Algiers could do in the circumstances. The Algerians as a whole decided that it was better to settle for larger royalties and for a progressively advantageous arrangement than for revolutionary actions which would remain utopian. There were, moreover, implications in it which went far beyond oil and gas: it meant the possibility of industrialising all Algeria. France is now firmly settled in the saddle in Sahara for a good many years to come; but at the same time she has undertaken to supply Algeria with a yearly credit of 200 million francs, starting in 1966. Of this, 160 million francs are to be reimbursable in twenty years' time and bear an interest rate of 3 per cent. A further loan of 200

H*

million francs per annum is to be made to encourage Algerian exports. Both these loans are to be for the benefit of the Organisme de Coopération Industrielle (OCI) which has taken the place of the Organisme Saharien in sponsoring industrialisation. What other power, sober-minded Algerians may ask, could offer Algeria assistance on this scale and on these terms? Small wonder then that, whatever reservations they may have, the reply of the great majority of Algerians to the question 'Franco-Algerian co-operation?' is a resounding *Yes*!

10

BOUMEDIENNE TAKES OVER

EARLY on the morning of June 19, 1965, passers-by noticed tanks along Algiers' Franklin Roosevelt Boulevard, in which the People's Palace and the Villa Joly, which Ben Bella still used as a residence, are situated. To most people the tanks were merely objects of mild curiosity, the new weapons of their independent country—probably part of the scenery of *La Bataille d'Alger*, then on the point of being filmed in the capital by the Italian producer, M. Pontecorvo. This unobtrusiveness was unlucky for Ben Bella for it helped to minimise the reactions, at least in Algiers, when it became generally known that there had been an army coup and that Ben Bella had been taken prisoner.

Officers of the ANP had for some time been heard privately expressing the opinion that 'Ben Bella is nothing . . . he has no force to back his power . . . we could take care of him in a few hours and no one in the country would raise a voice in his defence'. The former minister, Abdelhafid Boussouf, expressed the same opinion to me on several occasions. In a public statement on June 21 in Geneva to the French and Swiss press, he said that, while Ben Bella's downfall may have astounded the world, a great many Algerians were not particularly surprised. This was no boast but the strict truth.

The ANP officers were proved right. The ease with which Ben Bella was overthrown was all the more remarkable as the coup took place at a time when world attention was focused on Algiers where delegates and journalists had already arrived in their thousands to attend the Second Afro-Asian Conference due to open on June 25. A few days later, the heads of states and governments of over sixty

Afro-Asian nations, and U Thant, the secretary-general of the United Nations, were due to arrive as the guests of Algeria. It was at this point that Ben Bella—to so many people one of the emerging 'world figures'—disappeared in a couple of hours in the most humiliating fashion. And Algeria hardly stirred. According to eye-witnesses, the action took place as follows:

03.30 hours. A unit of the ANP quickly took over from the police guarding the Villa Joly. Some raised voices were heard. Residents—Algerian, French and foreign—in the immediate vicinity reported there was a sound of breaking glass and the light suddenly went on in Ben Bella's apartment on the top floor of the Villa Joly. A few shots were then heard, and shooting continued sporadically till daylight in the expensive residential districts on the hillslopes of the capital.

07.45 hours. In Paris, at the headquarters of Agence France Presse in the Place de la Bourse, a flash shook the sleepy subeditors, announcing that tanks had been seen at strategic posts in Algiers, and particularly around the Villa Joly.

08.05 hours. ANP soldiers in combat dress occupied Radio Algiers, which began to broadcast military marches (including the French *Sambre et Meuse*) and patriotic songs. The town was absolutely calm and only two tanks remained outside the Villa Joly. Passers-by were unaware of what was happening. But world news agencies were now very much on the alert, especially after the developments at Radio Algiers.

08.20 hours. The ANP took over Dar-El-Beida airport. The Tunisian and Moroccan borders were reported closed on the Algerian side.

08.30. A correspondent of Agence France Presse who managed to put through a telephone call to the Villa Joly was answered by a charwoman: 'I do not know anything. I am getting on with my work', she replied.

09.00 Radio Algiers announced 'a very important statement to be made soon', inviting listeners to stand by.

09.18. Agence France Presse reported that some fifty diplomatists of the French embassy were trying in vain to contact 'any' Algerian official. Military guards were reported around the villas of ministers and other prominent people.

09.30. The French news agency reported: 'It is learnt from non-official but generally well-informed sources that President Ben Bella has been overthrown.' The atmosphere remained quite normal in the capital and traffic at Dar-El-Beida was unaffected. But an aircraft with yet another load of Chinese for the Second Afro-Asian Conference returned to Cairo instead of landing at Algiers, apparently after a radioed warning from the Chinese embassy in Algeria. Customers began to rush to the markets to stock up with foodstuffs.

09.40. All communications with the outside world were cut. Radio Algiers continued to repeat its announcement every five minutes inviting listeners to stand by.

11.40. Radio Algiers again repeated its announcement, and this time asked particularly that all 'state functionaries and security officials' stand by.

12.05. Radio Algiers announced the formation of a 'Council of the Revolution' but gave no names.

12.09. Radio Algiers broadcast the following 'Proclamation of the Council of the Revolution', signed by Colonel Boumedienne.

PEOPLE OF ALGERIA!

On November 1, 1954, our country began a revolution which was to bring about, by armed combat and sacrifice, the end of more than a century of colonial domination. On July 5, 1962, Algeria finally recovered her liberty and independence, having paid the price of one of the heaviest sacrifices that history has ever known.

The political crisis which then immediately followed reflected in a violent manner the numerous and inevitable internal disagreements built up during eight years of war. The country was then on the edge of the abyss and, once again, it was only through the loyal and disinterested attitude adopted by all sincere militants that we escaped civil war. But the problems were not resolved.

After three years of national sovereignty, our country finds itself a prey to shadowy intrigues and to conflicts of interests and factions, resurrected so that the government might have recourse to the old game: divide and rule. Sordid calculation, political narcissism and morbid love of power have been exemplified by the systematic liquidation of the cadres of the country and the criminal attempt to discredit the *mujahidin* and resistants. L'Armée Nationale Populaire, worthy heir of the glorious Army of National Liberation, will never allow itself, whatever the manoeuvres and temptations, to be cut off from the people from which it sprang and from which it draws both its strength and its raison d'être.

People of Algeria!

The men who have today decided to answer your anguished appeal, feeling that in doing so they are realising your dearest wish, have taken it upon themselves to regain for you the freedom that had been usurped and the dignity that had been trampled upon. It was high time that the evil should be pinpointed, circumscribed and denounced. It was even more imperative to act in order to bring this dramatic situation to an end. However confused the scene, the government cannot be allowed to dispose of the country and the public affairs in its charge as if they were personal and private property.

The accusations are weighty and significant. The misdirection of the national heritage, dilapidation of public property, instability, demagogy, anarchy, lies and improvisation have been the methods of the government. By threats, blackmail, the violation of individual liberty and uncertainty as to the future, attempts have been made to reduce some to docility and others, through fear, to silence and resignation. Personal power, all the national and regional institutions of the party and the state are at the mercy of one man who delegates power to suit himself, whose actions are dictated by unsound and improvised tactics, and who imposes policies and men according to the mood of the moment, whim and caprice.

People of Algeria!

Your silence is not cowardice. If the tyrant, now overcome, thought you were sunk in profound lethargy, events have now shown him that punishment has come in the measure that he tricked and betrayed you, and took advantage of your confidence, sincerity and support.

People of Algeria!

A Council of the Revolution has been created. It has taken all necessary measures to ensure that institutions may function normally and public affairs proceed. Moreover, it will try to create favourable conditions for the construction of a serious, democratic state, with its own morality and governed by law: a state which will survive governments and men. The institutions of the party and of the state must function harmoniously, each within its own limitations, and with strict regard to revolutionary legality. With confidence and stability re-established, the Council of the Revolution will work towards order and the reconstruction of the national economy. This will only be possible if dialectic and empiricism are banished and if the ways and means are defined objectively and understood by all.

In this field more than in any other, the love of luxury must be replaced by integrity, improvisation by steady work, impulsive reactions by a state philosophy—in a word, realistic socialism based on the country's needs must replace day-to-day, publicity-seeking socialism. It goes without saying that fundamental rights cannot be altered and the gains of the revolution must be respected. Nevertheless, only rigorous measures and a firm policy can pull us out of the mire into which we are sinking, and which is already characterised by a fall in productivity, lower profitability and a withdrawing of funds.

The radical transformation of our society cannot take place without taking into account our faith, our convictions, the secular traditions of our people and our moral values. In this new phase of the revolution, the whole nation, united in confidence and serenity, must work so that our institutions may regain their values and that we may rediscover political stability and fraternity, that we may consolidate the revolution on a better-understood basis of democratic centralisation and that we may build a truly socialist society.

People of Algeria!

Algeria is on the eve of an international conference, the most important that can be held in a country of the Third World. The prestige gained by our revolution since November 1, 1954, and which has perhaps led to our being chosen for this assembly, will never let us lose sight of the confidence placed in our country by the peoples of Asia, Africa and Latin America. But international conventions, however desirable, cannot authorise one man cynically to exploit them to his own ends and to the detriment of the interests of his country. The sincere friendship and fraternal respect which we owe these peoples and their leaders obliges us to denounce the machiavellian manoeuvres of the diabolical dictator who hoped to gain so much from this event, not by reaffirming our common ideals of solidarity, liberty and peace, but by extending his personal power and lulling the national conscience. Now that his deceit, adventurism and political charlatanism have been unmasked, Ben Bella, in submitting to the fate which history has reserved for despots, will have understood that no one has the right to humiliate the nation, or take the generosity of our people for irresponsibility, or to take advantage in a shameless fashion of illustrious guests to cover up crimes and high treason. Perhaps he did not understand that Algeria's relations with her friends, allies and partners, and with all peoples who love liberty and justice, were above men and political fluctuations.

In the foreign field, now more than ever, our country will make a point of loyally honouring any agreement undertaken to date. In future, our actions will no longer be dictated by subjectivism. They will be the external projection of our internal policies, directed to the erection of a stable state and a prosperous economy. Considerations of personal prestige will no longer make us forget the essential, which is to strengthen our national independence and develop our economy that we may first help the disinherited.

In accordance with the fundamental philosophy of the FLN, our diplomacy will be efficient and realistic, and will draw its inspiration from the principles laid down in the Tripoli Programme and the Charter of Algiers.

People of Algeria!
The heavy burden inherited from the long period of colonial rule and eight years of suffering have been seriously aggravated by the negligence of the state and by stupid optimism. The situation may not be beyond repair but it is one of anguish. Only a national effort to achieve the essential objectives will help us to clear the way to salvation and happier prospects.

There can be no redress, and certainly no miracle, without work, seriousness, clear objectives and unity. Our country, which has been so severely tried, demands that we should rise once more, individually and collectively, to shoulder our historic responsibilities, that the revolution may triumph once and for all.

For the Council of the Revolution:
HOUARI BOUMEDIENNE.

Subsequent events proved that the coup was handled in the most masterly way. Not without a certain pride, *Le Monde* on July 14, 1965, noted that the 'un-Mediterranean discretion and efficiency' of the authors of the coup was a tribute to the former French cavalry school at Bou-Saada in which Algerian officers of the French army were trained—officers who now held high positions in the ANP, and who were known as 'the military officers' by their colleagues of the wartime guerrilla units. The best known of the 'military' officers were: Commander Chabou, the chef de cabinet at the Defence Ministry; Colonel Slimane Hoffman, in charge of armoured units; Abbas, assistant chief of staff; Bencherif, in charge of the Gendarmerie; and Draia, in charge of the Compagnies Nationales de Securité (CNS). Colonel Draia was personally in charge of Ben Bella's security and, shortly before his deposition, the Algerian leader had asked him to recruit his personal bodyguard exclusively from Saharans—becoming known as the 'Guarde Noire'—as these were less likely to be infected by 'northern' politics. Draia was one of those who made the arrest at pistol-point. Ben Bella also made the mistake of trusting Commander Mahmoud Guennèz, a member of parliament who was in charge of the Milices Populaires which Ben Bella had created with the specific purpose of counterbalancing the ANP. It became clear after the event that Guennèz had given his loyalty to Boumedienne, under whom he had served in the wartime HQ at Ghardimau. Another piquant case was that of Colonel Tahar Zbiri, whom Ben Bella had appointed chief of general staff against the wishes and behind the back of Boumedienne. Zbiri was also among those who made the arrest. In an interview later on with a special emissary of President Nasser, Hassanein Heykal (the Egyptian journalist-cum-diplomatist), Boumedienne was asked if there had been any particular significance in the fact that he had ordered Zbiri to make the arrest. *Al Ahram* reported that Boumedienne (who rarely smiles) permitted himself a smile when replying: 'Yes, to show Ben Bella how his machinations against me had failed!'

Ben Bella's overthrow caused more emotion outside than inside Algeria; and here perhaps is another parallel with Lumumba. Algerians on the whole took his abrupt removal from the scene with the same apathy they had displayed towards all events since the great tide of popular enthusiasm broke during the 'Summer of Shame' in mid-1962. Certainly, there were a few disturbances—and shots were heard in Bône, Constantine and Oran—and the official communiqué of June 23, stating that 'the whole operation has been conducted without the shedding of a single drop of blood', was an exaggeration: but much less so than reports in the European communist press of 'blood-baths'. As some 1,318 political prisoners of the Ben Bella era were being freed, small groups of people— mainly small children, but including students and women—began to demonstrate in Algiers, shouting '*Yahya Ben Bella*' and 'Down with Boumedienne'. (As we saw in chapter 5, the one bright spot in his regime was the emphasis on education: hence the support of the students. We shall see in chapter 11 why the women were against Boumedienne.) But the ANP showed great skill, not only by refraining from any brutality, but also by making itself as scarce as possible at the height of the crisis and then disappearing from the scene completely. Life went on as usual.

What provoked the putsch of June 19, 1965? The times when

Ben Bella and Boumedienne needed each other, and therefore could co-operate, were over. Previously, when Ben Bella went abroad, he left the country to Boumedienne, who had become vice-president, and the official 'second-in-command'—although some witty and perspicacious journalists had labelled him Number 1a! After a year or so in power Ben Bella began to feel sufficiently secure to try to squeeze out Boumedienne. In 1963, he brought about the resignation of one of Boumedienne's best men—the minister of the Interior, Medighri—without provoking any strong reaction. But when he tried to repeat these earlier tactics against Bouteflika, the foreign minister and another of Boumedienne's best men, the army leader saw the writing on the wall. Bouteflika, finding himself in the unsatisfactory position of having the work of his ministry in fact carried out by Ben Bella's office, had already tendered his resignation some time before; but Ben Bella, following his previously successful line of action, had at first refused it, though ready to accept if it were offered a second time. In this way, no one could accuse him of having precipitated the resignation. Boumedienne at this point stepped in and forbade Bouteflika to resign: there was to be no repetition of the Medighri affair. Ben Bella's tactics were thus thwarted and it became a case of an impatient premier pressing a recalcitrant foreign minister for his resignation. A short but very sharp encounter followed between Ben Bella and Boumedienne. The latter is reported to have burst into Ben Bella's office to tell him curtly, 'Bouteflika will not resign', and then withdraw, slamming the door.

Abdelaziz Bouteflika, now Colonel Boumedienne's righthand man and the player of a key role in the overthrow of Ben Bella, is a very sympathetic young man, with a ready smile and unassuming, friendly manners. He was born in 1935 at Oujda in Morocco. His parents, themselves from Tlemcen, owned and operated Turkish baths. He was one of the young Algerians who interrupted their studies (secondary level in his case) to join the anti-French resistance. He fought in Wilaya V and became secretary of COM-OUEST under Colonel Boumedienne. He remained at the Oujda headquarters of the ALN, with the rank of commander, till the end of the hostilities and was entrusted with the task of opening a new front in the Sahara. To enlist support for this, he made several trips to Mali, Guinea and other African countries during 1961. During the war he was known by the nickname of 'Si Abdelkader'. It was he who, in February 1962, secretly (although the French knew about it) contacted Ben Bella in his château prison at Aulnoy, to establish the first contacts in the name of the ALN. He has been foreign minister since September 1963.

The ANP decided to strike when it did to prevent Ben Bella from using the Afro-Asian Conference as a cover for internal plotting against Boumedienne. Ben Bella had indeed planned to do just this. The army leader deliberately chose the eve of the conference as the moment for his coup. His aim was to forestall a new attempt by Ben Bella to rally the (non-Boumedienne) opposition and then, with the new prestige and strength stemming from the conference, to get rid of the army leader. Ben Bella, it seems, was planning to make a spectacular gesture by freeing the veteran leader, Ait Ahmed and either to produce him at the Afro-Asian Conference, or to stage a grand public reconciliation with his former opponent on the anniversary of the Algerian independence in July. This would have been a prelude to getting rid of Boumedienne. According to private information at the time from several authoritative Afro-Asian sources, what the deposed Algerian leader had in mind was to form a sort of 'inner club' of selected heads of states who would run the conference from the side-lines. Ben Bella, with his eye on his July rendezvous with General de Gaulle, also had the intention of administering the United States a 'big blast' over Vietnam to try and regain his lost influence in Africa. The axis with Nasser was to be re-emphasised with a view to driving into a corner the Tunisians and Moroccans.

Neither Ben Bella nor anyone else dreamed that the ANP would be daring or imaginative enough to reverse the tables by exploiting for its own ends such an international gathering as the Afro-Asian Conference. This explains why Ben Bella was so confident to the end. Late on the night of June 19, I was in Tunis talking to President Bourguiba's own advisers, among whom was his son, the Tunisian foreign minister. The Tunisians were certainly very worried, for they feared (rightly) that the clash between Ben Bella and Bouteflika, which they knew about, 'might make Boumedienne decide at last to take the long-expected potshot at Ben Bella'. But no one ever thought for a second that Boumedienne would strike before or during the Afro-Asian Conference, or dreamed that his tanks were gathering for action at the very moment of the discussion in Tunis. Ben Bella had been out of Algiers for a week, touring the Oran province, and Boumedienne had made full use of the president's absence. He was helped by the fact that his troop movements could readily be explained by the need to protect the sixty-odd heads of states and governments who were due to arrive in Algiers. When Ben Bella returned to the capital from Oran, flying in the special IL 18 given him by the Soviet Union (which also provided two crews of seven men to operate the aircraft), he granted a press interview which reflected his rose-tinctured mood. Among other things he said that self-management in Algeria was going 'better than in Yugoslavia', and expressed optimism over the outcome of the Afro-Asian Conference.[1] Everything seemed as it should be. On getting out of the plane at the airport he found waiting to greet him, as was proper and normal, his foreign minister, Bouteflika, wearing his customary boyish smile, and another minister, Cherif Belkacem (another young supporter of Boumedienne). The normality of these events made the coup a total surprise and helped to give it an air of great and skilful daring.

Before the coup, it was generally held that Boumedienne was not 'power-thirsty' in the sense of seeking honours and acclamation. This is still valid now that he has seized power. He seems genuinely to have tried to resist the pressure of his lieutenants to make him take the post of premier. No one doubts that Colonel Boumedienne has his own very definite ideas as to how Algeria should be run and the Arab revolution be promoted. But he is a complex person-ality, and his great will and determination are coupled with reserve and secrecy. He has always avoided public appearances, and since he has become premier these have been limited and devoid of all pomp and show. At his first public function after the coup—which was appropriately a graduation ceremony at a military school—the television team were told not to direct the cameras at the speaker. Viewers could hear Boumedienne's dry voice but not see him. 'The cult of personality has now been replaced by the cult of imperson-ality', Jean Lacouture commented in *Le Monde*, while *The Times* on June 28, 1965, noted: 'The style of Mr Ben Bella has been replaced by a faceless machine.' This was the new order of the day: Down with the cult of personality and forward with collegial rule! An attempt to analyse Boumedienne's version of 'collegial rule' will be made further on.

Ever since his wartime days at Ghardimau, Boumedienne had been preparing to direct the Algerian revolution and, if necessary, to take over full powers, and he had been patiently manoeuvring the army into a position of strength. It was to this end that the ALN's advance through Algeria had been retarded to allow time for the establishment of army-controlled administrations along the routes of the units converging on Algiers: a process which was not completed without a number of political and armed clashes. It was to this end also that Boumedienne after the war had so rapidly accepted 'the military officers' into the ANP. He realised that what was needed above all was competence in administration and organisation. When defending at the FLN congress in July 1964 those Algerians who had been officers in the French army, he said— not without a touch of xenophobia: 'The revolution having entrusted me with the task of building an army, I do this with those who are the most capable. I prefer to work with Algerians, however late they may have joined our revolution, rather than with foreign experts.' The general staff of the ANP was largely created out of these officers.

One of the first tasks of the new general staff was to reorganise the country's 'politico-military' organisation. First of all, to put an end to the Wilayas, seven new regions of military administration were set up, designed as far as possible to cut across the divisions of the Wilayas. The new regions were as follow. *First Region:* Algiers; Ténes to the west, the Sergou plateau to the south, and Bouira-Aumale to the east. *Second Region:* Oran; the Ksour mountains and the Djebel Amour to the south. *Third Region:* Colomb-Béchar and Reggane. *Fourth Region* (the former turbulent Wilaya IV): from Laghouat to Touggourt. *Fifth Region:* Batna; here nothing was changed of the former Wilaya I, the cradle of the revolution. (Any change would have been resented and perhaps opposed.) *Sixth Region:* Constantine. *Seventh Region:* Kabilya; for obvious ethno-political reasons, the boundaries of the former Wilaya III were left unchanged. Another important step was the creation of the gendarmerie, consisting largely of former *mujahidin* who were no longer suitable for the modernised ANP. By the end of 1965, the strength of the gendarmerie was about 40,000.

While all this was being done, the ANP was persistently and systematically insinuating its own men into all levels of the administration, particularly in key ministries, in the police and the intelligence services. It was also active in another field, quite unconnected with security. Even today, very little is known about the many farms and other properties throughout Algeria which are run by the army and used for training young men in paramilitary skills as well as for economic production. No one knows how much Algerian land is under the exclusive administration of the army.

The man responsible for these achievements, Houari Boumedienne, is one of Algeria's lesser-known leaders, and his best friends—all army men—have by their silence contributed to the mystery surrounding him. He is an extremely thin man, with prominent cheek-bones and red hair (hence the nickname of 'Houari', meaning the 'red-haired', which he has kept as a public name). He looks very much like a German romantic of the last century. Born in 1925 at Guelma, in the department of Bône, he studied literary Arabic at the theological universities of Zeitun (Tunis) and Al Azhar (Cairo). He was teaching Arabic when he joined the revolution. From Cairo, he went to Algeria and secretly landed with a small group of men near Oran. He was singled out by Abdelhafid Boussouf, whom he replaced in 1957 as the head of Wilaya V. His close friends have told me that, in contrast to his public manner, Boumedienne when among friends is good company and laughs a good deal. He is not as ascetic as he appears, though a very devout muslim. But the silent colonel is not all that mysterious. He certainly made no mystery of the army's attitude to the civilian leaders of the revolution, from Ferhat Abbas to Ben Bella. When the ALN first paraded for Ben Bella and his companions on their release from French captivity on March 23, 1962, at the Ben M'hidi camp at Oujda in Morocco, everyone was staggered to find the ALN displaying revolutionary slogans. A huge one, right over the troops being reviewed by the two leaders, clearly warned the 'historic leaders'.

ON NE PEUT TROMPER UN PEUPLE TOUT LE TEMPS!
LES PROMESSES POUR PLAIRE, LES MENSONGES, ONT POUR
ENNEMI LE PEUPLE!
L'HISTOIRE ABAT LES PRETENTIONS IMPATIENTES
ET SOUTIENT LES LONGUES ESPERANCES

In his speech that day, Boumedienne announced that the army was supporting Ben Bella because it thought he was the best choice; but he emphasised that this support would be withdrawn the day Ben Bella deviated 'from the correct revolutionary paths'.

Everyone knew that Boumedienne meant what he said on this occasion, and that he would never just give blind support. But looking back on events, it is difficult not to conclude that Boumedienne himself was not without a certain political opportunism. How else can one account for the unreserved support he gave Ben Bella so soon after publicly expressing these reservations? When Ben Bella was trying for the highest post in the country, he enjoyed the full support of Boumedienne. The army's organ, *El Djeich*, in September 1963 said on the occasion of the election of Ben Bella to the presidency of the republic: 'In saying yes to the patriot Ahmed Ben Bella, we express our loyalty to the revolution of November 1, 1954 and to the building of socialism.' In the same month, addressing in Arabic a conference of the FLN cadres, Houari Boumedienne said:

We have chosen him [Ahmed Ben Bella] as candidate for president of the republic for his faith and trust in the socialist revolution. I say this, dear brothers, to clear up some misunderstandings and to show up the manoeuvres aimed at separating the ANP from the FLN. The choice of brother Ben Bella by the people and the army is not dictated by mere sentiment. We have decided that brother Ben Bella is qualified to occupy this post because we consider him the only man capable of assuming it. We have chosen him . . . because we are certain he will remain a sincere militant.

The issue of *El Djeich* cited above also reproduces an interview granted by Boumedienne to the Syrian daily *Al-Baas*, in which, among other things, he said that Ben Bella 'was the first defender of our cause and was able to preserve the unity of the people and of its revolutionary army'. It is true that Ben Bella changed later, but Boumedienne is open to the charge of having made some errors of judgement!

But, of course, in public life the whole truth is rarely spoken, and—in spite of his verbal support—Boumedienne never ceased to build up his position under cover. Admittedly, it is very possible that if Ben Bella had not become so much of a dictator, Boumedienne might well have been satisfied with his position as 'Number 1a'. But Ben Bella overplayed his hand. What is now clear is that there were secret conflicts from the beginning. Boumedienne admitted this in an interview with the Egyptian press after the coup. Ben Bella also knew it only too well. On one occasion in 1964, he introduced the colonel to an Egyptian journalist representing *Al Ahram*, saying with a smile: 'Here is the man who plots against me. . . . How are the intrigues, Colonel?' To which Boumedienne replied shortly: 'Very well, thank you'—but not without a blush!

Boumedienne is by no means the 'terrible' dictator of legend. Although he does not hesitate to take life if he thinks it necessary, he is not bloodthirsty and he likes an appearance of legality. He is very serious, patient, determined, intelligent and a good planner. These qualities showed themselves as soon as he took power. There was no great repression and, in fact, an atmosphere of confidence settled over the country during the weeks after the coup. Well aware of the Algerian dislike of the uniform, Boumedienne kept his army in barracks and ordered officers to wear civilian clothes even at official functions. But the lack of parade did not prevent the military from tightening its hold on the country, and the Council of Revolution consisted essentially of former or serving army officers. There were originally only two civilians on it. The army representatives were by no means all loyal supporters of Boumedienne; they were in fact drawn from five different military groups and constituted a cross-section of Algeria's new military caste. The Council was composed as follows:

1. *The five regional military commanders:* (i) Commander Said Abid, in charge of the First Military Region from June 1964. He is a former assistant of Colonel Tahar Zbiri, whom he had succeeded as head of the former Wilaya I. (ii) Commander Chadli Bendjedid, currently in charge of the Second Region. He led the ANP's first mission to China in September 1963 and heads the military tribunal. (iii) Commander Soufi Salah, at present in charge of the Third Region. He is a former member of the Constituent Assembly from Bône and a noted Islamist. (iv) Commander Amar Mellah, in charge of the Fourth Region. He replaced Colonel Chaabani who was executed as a 'traitor'. (v) Commander Abdallah Belchouet, in charge of the Fifth Region. During the war he headed an ALN opera-

tional HQ which covered the Algerian sector of Soukh-el-Ahras from Tunisia.

2. *General Staff Officers:* (i) Colonel Ahmed Boudjemane, alias Abbas, assistant chief of general staff and commander of the Cherchell interservice military college. (ii) Colonel Tahar Zbiri, chief of general staff and commander of the former Wilaya I. (iii) Commander Abderrahman Bensalem, member of the general staff and of the military court. (iv) Commander Moulay Abdelkader, alias Chabou, Boumedienne's director of cabinet at the Ministry of National Defence.

3. *Former Wilaya commanders:* (i) Colonel Mohand ou El-Hadj (former head of Wilaya III, Kabilya). (ii) Colonel Saout el Arab (former head of Wilaya II, Constantine). Arrested in 1963 by Boumedienne, he was then sent in semi-exile as military attaché to Cairo where he could do no harm. (iii) Colonel Youssouf Khatib, alias Si Hassan (former head of Wilaya IV, the Algérois). (iv) Colonel Bouhadjar, alias Si Othman. In charge of the Moroccan border during the war, he was arrested by Boumedienne in October 1963 and released on order of Ben Bella to become the co-ordinator of the FLN for the region of Oran.

4. *Security Officers:* (i) Colonel Ahmed Bencherif, in charge of the gendarmerie. He headed the military tribunal which condemned Colonel Chaabani to death. (ii) Colonel Ahmed Draia, the head of the CNS and a member of the military court. He was in charge of Ben Bella's security and is also a member of the Central Committee of the FLN.

5. *'Civilian' (ex-army) Officers:* (i) Abdelaziz Bouteflika, the well-known minister of Foreign Affairs, alias Commander Abdelkader during the war. (ii) Cherif Belkacem, minister of National Education, known as Commander Djemal during the war. (iii) Ahmed Medighri, the minister of the Interior, expelled by Ben Bella, and a member of the wartime Ghardimau HQ. (iv) Commander Ali Mendjli, member of the ALN wartime general staff. (v) Commander Ahmed Kaid, alias Commander Slimane, member of the ALN war-time general staff. (vi) Colonel Mohammedi Said, alias Si Nasser, second vice-president of the Council of Ministers under Ben Bella. (vii) Mohammed Taibi, alias Commander Larbi, formerly in charge of national security, then ambassador to Cuba. He is a member of the Central Committee of the FLN. (viii) Moham-

med Sakah Yahiaoui, member of the FLN Central Committee.
(ix) Commander Mohammed Benhamed.

6. *Civilians:* Bachir Boumaza (minister) and Ali Mahsas (minister). Mahsas was Ben Bella's most faithful companion, but he turned against him after the coup.

In contrast with the exclusively military background of the Revolutionary Council and in an evident attempt to broaden the base of his support, Boumedienne tried to draw the members of his government as far as possible from civilians. (See Appendix III for a complete list of the government.)

Abdelaziz Zerdani became minister of Labour: a major surprise, and certainly an answer to accusations from the Algerian left that Boumedienne was a 'fascist'. Zerdani, a member of the FLN Central Committee and director of the Algiers daily *Le Peuple* (which closed down after the coup), is exactly the sort of man who was under strong attack from the army during the first FLN Congress. It was the drive to get rid of Ben Bella's 'leftwing advisers' that began the conflict which ended on June 19. During the rupture between the UAR and West Germany, Zerdani supported recognition of East Germany (now, with the Cubans, Boumedienne's harshest critic). He wrote an article for Mohammed Harbi on the theme "Algeria-China: More than Friends". His place in the government was partly due to his personal friendship with Tahar Zbiri, but it was also a sign of Boumedienne's attempted catholicity of choice. Among the Kabyle ministers (another sign of Boumedienne's peace-making), there was Abdennour Ali Yahia. A leftwing trade unionist, he was one of the general secretaries of UGTA. He was involved until 1963 with Hocine Ait Ahmed's Kabyle resistance. Belaid Abdessalam is perhaps the most interesting of all. He replaced Bachir Boumaza in the key Ministry of Industry and Energy, Boumaza going to Information. Abdessalam was originally a follower of Ben Khedda, but has since held technical posts in the administration. In particular he has handled the oil negotiations with France, where he is highly regarded as a man of integrity.

Rabah Bitat was the only 'historic leader' included in the new cabinet. He got the nominal 'Number 2' position of minister of state. Mohammed Khider, who was in Madrid when the putsch occurred, showed great enthusiasm; Boudiaf in Paris was more reserved in his reaction. But neither these, nor other former GPRA figures like Ferhat Abbas and Ben Khedda, were called in. The West, including the French, would have been particularly pleased to see Ferhat Abbas join the new team, but it was evident that the ANP retained its strong prejudice against the GPRA 'bourgeois' and the 'historic leaders'.

A month after the coup, Boumedienne consolidated his network by announcing the formation of a new executive secretariat of the FLN to replace Ben Bella's Political Bureau. The five members of this new body were drawn largely from the army: Colonel Mohand ou El-Hadj, Commander Larbi and Colonel Youssouf Khatib, alias Si Hassan. Cherif Belkacem, alias Commander Djemal—the former minister of Education—headed this secretariat, which explains why this most faithful lieutenant of Boumedienne's had not been included in the government. From several pronouncements made by Boumedienne, it became obvious, if further proof was needed, that Algeria was to be governed by the army. On July 5, he defined the role of the FLN party (which Ben Bella had wanted to be supreme and had confused with the state) as one of 'elaboration, orientation, animation and control, but not one of supremacy over the state'. The state, whichever way one looked at it, was the army, headed by Colonel Boumedienne and his lieutenants.

It is typical of revolutions and counter-revolutions that, once the idol of yesterday has been overthrown, people will vie with each other in claiming that they have always supported the new victor. The speed and lack of reticence with which many people made the switch in Algeria disgusted many observers. Men who only a day before had been singing the praises of Ben Bella at the tops of their voices (one thinks particularly of the former cabinet minister, Mohammedi Said) were the first to brand him 'a fascist and a despot'; others, like Amar Ouzegane who, as a minister, had praised him to the skies, now used their pens to vilify him; still others, like Boumaza and Mahsas, who had shared his life in power as ministerial collaborators as well as friends, now could not denounce him loudly enough. But in a manner typical of post-war Algeria, these convulsions only affected restricted circles close to power; the population as a whole remained apathetic.

On August 12, the Milices Populaires, which Ben Bella had fitted with baggy trousers purchased from the Middle East, were disbanded. As they had been instituted specifically to 'combat counter-revolution', the political significance of their dissolution escaped no one, although the official reason given was 'an economic measure of austerity'. After this the government announced its main aims: 1. reform of the FLN; 2. convocation of an FLN congress; 3. preparation of a new constitution; 4. preparation of communal and national elections; 5. social and economic reform. While these things were being worked out by the army, it was announced on September 14 that a 'congress of all officers of the ANP' would meet under the chairmanship of Colonel Boumedienne. This extraordinary congress would 'study the situation after the revolution of June 19'.

The coup took on an international importance out of proportion to its true significance. This was partly because its victim had been making such a great reputation for himself in the Third World and partly because of the spectacular way in which it wrecked the Second Afro-Asian Conference. The two foreign interests most affected by the affair were the communists and the United Arab Republic. Opinion is divided as to which suffered the most: the Chinese communists, the USSR or the UAR; but all agree that for these the downfall of Ben Bella was all the more catastrophic for coming as a complete surprise.

Cairo was baffled. Only a few days before the overthrow of Ben Bella, President Nasser's confidant, Mohammed Hassanein Heykal, in an analysis in *Al Ahram* of the world situation on the eve of the Afro-Asian Conference, praised Algeria for setting 'the revolutionary example'. In less than ten days, in the same paper, Heykal expressed bitter disappointment and tried to put up a last-minute defence for Ben Bella—'the hero of the Arab struggle'—in protest against the silence with which the rest of the Arab world had greeted his downfall. Strangely enough, the only African leader who echoed this cri de coeur was Sékou Touré. The events were catastrophic for the UAR not only because the one man on which they had based their entire Algerian policy had disappeared overnight, breaking Nasser's most important and (as he had thought) solid, foreign political arm, but because this happened at a time when the UAR's policies were proving disastrous almost everywhere: in the Yemen, Iraq, the Sudan and most of all in Syria. 'Never since its inception has the Nasser regime appeared as weak as it does now', commented an experienced observer of the Middle East.[2]

Moreover, the Egyptians handled the Algerian situation so tactlessly that they greatly aggravated their own situation, confirming the criticism by the Algerians (and others) that Nasser considered it his natural right, as leader of the Arab world, to interfere in the domestic affairs of the other Arab countries. Cairo blundered beyond all imagination when, on learning of the coup in Algeria, it immediately despatched Marshal Amer and Heykal to try and save the Ben Bella regime. When this proved a failure, Nasser asked Boumedienne to deliver to her Ben Bella and his assistant, Abderrahmane Cherif, with the assurance that they would not be 'politically active against Algeria in Cairo'. This demand, which proved—if further proof was needed—the role Cherif was playing, infuriated the Algerians. Boumedienne put the Egyptian request to his Revolutionary Council which tartly observed that 'Algeria is neither Syria nor the Yemen'. Anti-Egyptian feeling in Algeria reached new heights when a group of Egyptians were arrested and accused of having, on June 25, placed a bomb in the conference hall of the Club des Pins in which the Afro-Asian Conference was to take place. It was already known that Nasser wished to have the conference postponed in order to avoid supporting the Boumedienne regime by his presence in Algiers. About this time, the car of the Egyptian embassy in Algiers was stopped and searched by Algerian soldiers while the ambassador and another high official from Cairo were on board. It is significant that the Egyptians refrained from any official protest. Boumedienne later ejected many Egyptians from Algeria.

The overthrow of Ben Bella seemed likely to have internal as well as external repercussions for the United Arab Republic. *Le Monde* reported that, after Ben Bella's downfall, murmurs against 'Nasser's socialism' were frequently being heard in Egypt. In the past Boumedienne had not attempted to hide his opinion of Nasser, and when passing through Damascus airport early in 1965 he openly criticised Nasser's 'cult of personality', the Egyptian 'bureaucracy' and the UAR's 'saloon socialism'. No wonder that of all the Arab regimes, it was the Ba'ath of Syria—arch-enemy of Nasser—which rejoiced the most when Boumedienne came to power. Many saw another repercussion of the changes in Algeria, and the rise there of more conservative Islamic forces, in the revolt in early September of the Muslim Brotherhood. This was an affair of which the last has not yet been heard, although the Egyptian security announced arrests by the hundred. The change of power in Algeria could hardly have proved more disastrous to Egypt both internally and externally, and it may well be that the future will show that the failure of the Nasser-Ben Bella axis sounded the death-knell of the more aggressive form of Nasserism.

The communists had only fragile roots in Algeria, but at least they had something on which to base their opposition to the putsch. The local communist party and Algerian socialists of all shades at once went underground and began to organise demonstrations against Boumedienne. This provided ammunition for the French and Italian communist parties which published in *Humanité* and *Unità* greatly exaggerated versions of pro-Ben Bella 'resistance'. These two communist papers even went so far as to appeal openly for an anti-Boumedienne revolt. These tactics were unwise as well as unsuccessful, for they provided Boumedienne with a pretext for open hostility towards communism—an hostility which otherwise he would, for tactical reasons, have been chary of displaying. Ben Bella had been the only Algerian to try to restore the name of communism in Algeria, and he had allowed the secretary-general of the French communist party, Waldeck Rochet, to make an official visit to Algiers in the summer of 1965, when he thanked him for the French communist party's 'assistance to wartime Algeria'. It was logical that the communists should put up a struggle for the only man who had been foolish enough to attempt to rehabilitate the French communist party in Algeria—an attempt very distasteful to Boumedienne and most other Algerians. But it did not explain why the Italian communists, who generally evince more intelligent attitudes, joined the French in the 'save Ben Bella' campaign. The only explanation seems to be their ignorance of conditions in Algeria and the desire not to be outdone by their rivals in France. Both parties must be considered responsible by the communist world for forcing the Boumedienne regime to become more anti-communist than necessary.

It was, however, equally logical that there should have been an element of anti-communism in the Boumedienne coup, for it had been directed not only at the deposed leader but at those advisers, Algerian and foreign, who were pushing Ben Bella further to the left. Although it had not attracted much notice at the time, on

April 16, 1965—the anniversary of the death of the famous Sheikh Ben Badis—the president of the Algerian *ulama*, Mohammed Rachid Brahimi, had distributed a clandestine tract in which the fight for 'Islam and the renaissance of the Arab language' was called for.

The hour is grave. Our country is sliding nearer and nearer to hopeless civil war, an unprecedented moral crisis and insurmountable economic difficulties. Those governing us do not seem to realise that what our people aspire to above all is unity, peace and prosperity and that the theories on which their actions should be founded are to be found not in foreign doctrines but in our Arab-Islamic roots.

The hour has come when those responsible must set an example of sacrifice; honesty and competence must alone count; and the general interest must be put first. The hour has come to rediscover the much-abused term of fraternity and to return to those principles of consultation so dear to the PROPHET. The hour has at last come for the children of Algeria to gather together to build a city of justice and freedom, a city where GOD will have his place.

This tract had been very favourably received by army headquarters so it was not surprising that the *ulama* were, on June 21, the first to come out in support of the coup. Their association's official communiqué stated: 'The *ulama* of Algeria solemnly proclaim their solidarity with and their absolute support of the Council of the Revolution. They exhort the Algerian people, Arab and Muslim, men, women, young and old, to close the ranks and unite as one man behind the Council of the Revolution'.

It was well known that Boumedienne's xenophobia was directed mainly towards communists. When the new daily, *El Moudjahid*, appeared on June 21 it was noted that the communist editor of *Alger Républicain*, whom Ben Bella had destined for it, was denied any part in the running of the paper. Boumedienne's secret police quickly established the fact that the youth demonstrations in favour of Ben Bella were being organised and exploited by the PAC. The new government's first proclamations ignored the favourite self-management and anti-imperialist themes of Ben Bella's day, but urged co-operation with France and 'Islam'. The trend was only too clear. The left could hardly be expected to like it.

The first round was fired by *Unità*, albeit hesitatingly, on June 21. The Italian communist organ said it was still too early for definite judgement; too little was known of Boumedienne's personality, and communists would have to see whether 'pro-Chinese tendencies would emerge during the Second Afro-Asian Conference', which *Unità* still thought would take place. This was the editorial opinion, but in its other columns the Italian communist paper greatly exaggerated the pro-Ben Bella demonstrations. Two days later, its French equivalent, *Humanité*, branded the deposition as an 'anti-communist coup'. Thereafter the animosities between the new regime and the French and Italian communist parties came out into the open. However, although it was anti-communist, the new regime did not wish to be labelled as such, for it was still hoping the Afro-Asian Conference would take place. It made only one non-Algerian arrest and expulsion, and that was of the correspondent of *Humanité*. But the antagonisms then widened and the Algiers office of the Cuban news agency, Prensa Latina, was closed on charges of subversive propaganda. Fidel Castro reacted vigorously and in the course of a televised statement he called the coup 'perfidious and ignominious', and said: 'Ben Bella stood for revolution but not Bouteflika, the minister of Foreign Affairs, whose insubordination marked the culminating point of the putsch. Bouteflika is not a revolutionary, he represents the right, he is an enemy of socialism, an enemy of revolution. Bouteflika is a reactionary.' This blast was made on June 27, and shortly afterwards the Cuban ambassador was recalled.

In the meantime, there were reactions from various other communist quarters. The Bulgarian and French communist parties issued a joint communiqué condemning the coup, and even Belgrade —while maintaining a reserve at governmental level—in its press reproduced articles from *Humanité* and *Al Ahram*. Boumedienne was also attacked violently on Yugoslav television. The first official reaction from the European communist countries came from Budapest where, on June 27, *Magyar Nemzet* said that 'popular resistance to the army is only beginning'. Meanwhile (as stressed in a despatch of June 22 from *Le Monde*'s Moscow correspondent), the Kremlin was maintaining a 'revealing silence' even though, on June 22, a group of Algerian students had demonstrated in the Soviet capital and asked for a revolt 'against military dictatorship'.

(Similar demonstrations took place in Cairo, Tunis and Paris.) What attitude should Moscow adopt towards Ben Bella who only recently had been made a 'Hero of the Soviet Union'? The question was indeed tricky for not only had China become the very first country to recognise the Boumedienne regime, but, contradictory as it may seem, Boumedienne had himself been a main factor in the Soviet penetration in Algeria. The Russians now had to establish who had used whom in the past, they the colonel, or vice-versa! The question affected Russia's international policy as well as its fight with Peking, for already Tirana was accusing 'the imperialists, Khrushchevists and Titoists' of having launched 'a campaign of lies and of provocations following the recent changes in Algeria and of grossly interfering in the internal affairs of that country'. *Zeri i Populit* drew a parallel between 'the Algeria of today and Albania after the death of Stalin'.

Practically all Moscow's contacts with Algeria, from the very beginning, had been made through Boumedienne. This relationship with the ANP had been Russia's first major political action in Africa after the fiasco of its attempts in the Congo in 1960. Observers had noticed that, since this failure in the Congo, the USSR had had no coherent policy worth the name in Africa where her actions were dictated by Chinese moves and intentions. It was two years before the Russians began to take in Algeria a political interest which appeared to rest on sounder calculations. Their plan here was to base Soviet policy on an Arab coalition, which they hoped would resist Chinese penetration. The main axis of this Arab front would be Cairo and Algiers. In Algeria the Russians intended to repeat their successful Egyptian tactics and start with the supply of military equipment. Their task was facilitated because Algeria, a new country with a revolution in perspective, needed equipment which the West, even France, was not willing to give at this stage. Further, Moscow had to earn the forgiveness of the Algerians for having supplied Morocco, before Algerian independence, with the tanks which had largely accounted for Boumedienne's subsequent defeat at the hands of the Moroccan army. So the Russians proceeded to concentrate on the military angle in their penetration of Algeria and they early established a firm hold on the Algerian armed forces. During the war of independence, Moscow had already shown interest in the Algerian army. Of the very first batch of twenty to twenty-five ALN officers sent to Cairo for military training, a number had gone on to the Soviet Union at the latter's suggestion. It is not without interest to note here that the Russians trained these Algerians as specialists in submarine detection. This was of little use to the Algerians for they could hardly hope to take on the French fleet. But it made sense from the Soviet point of view as, together with the submarines and other naval craft later supplied to the UAR, it provided a contact which might eventually realise the age-old Russian dream of penetrating to the warm waters of the Mediterranean. Similarly, by training Algerian pilots, the Russians hoped to secure a foothold in the Algerian airforce of the future, as indeed happened.

Shortly after independence, it was learnt that the Russians had already advised the ANP not to dismantle the French fortified lines, since Morocco and Tunisia might become 'bases for American imperialism and aggression.' These and similar warnings made sense to Algerian ears. When the question of partial clearance of the millions of mines left by the French along the borders was raised because so many Algerians were being killed, the Russians offered to send a team of mine disposal experts, for they wanted to have their finger in every military matter in Algeria. (The ANP had contacted a private Italian firm for the job.) When one of the Soviet team unfortunately stepped on an old French mine, great play was made of the 'Soviet blood shed for Algeria'. The war with Morocco provided the Soviets with an ideal opportunity for dumping huge quantities of armaments in Algeria.

But others had realised what the Soviets had not: that Boumedienne was much too nationalist-minded to let himself be unduly influenced. Indeed he was already thinking up ways and means of avoiding dependence on a single source of armaments. (See chapter 11). Late in October 1964, in an unsigned article in the French daily *France-Soir*, I noted that diplomatists of an Eastern European country stationed in Algiers had sent to their government a very confidential report expressing doubts as to the soundness of Soviet hopes based on Boumedienne. This report feared that the Soviet arms supplied to Boumedienne 'may one day be used against us' (i.e. the communists). It was not necessary to be a great prophet to come to the same conclusion, but it goes to show that the theoretical knowledge gained by the Soviet diplomatists and journalists

in their various specialised African institutes did not necessarily fit
in with African realities. The Russians can be terribly misinformed.

Moscow broke its 'revealing silence' on June 24, when the Soviet
papers carried a despatch from a Western news agency, retrans-
mitted by TASS, in which it was said that 'popular' resistance to the
army putsch had been going on for 'four days'. The day before, the
Algerian ambassador in Moscow, Ahmed Ben Yahia (later transferred to London), had had a two-hour talk with top leaders in the
Kremlin, but the TASS communiqué which followed was quite
neutral in tone. The Russians must by then have realised that the
main leftwing opposition to Boumedienne, the Organisation de
Résistance Populaire (ORP), whose clandestine tracts were being
fully reproduced in the French communist press, was not worth
publicly supporting.* Raison d'état prevailed in Moscow because
of China, one supposes, and in Algiers because it did not suit the
new regime, which had made a friendly first gesture towards the
USA, to disturb the balance of the neutrality it wanted to observe by
taking an antagonistic attitude to Moscow.

Peking adopted a very different line from Moscow. The Chinese
attitude was dictated by expediency. At that time, China was
chiefly concerned with the fate of the Second Afro-Asian Conference
and was anxious that the coup should not prevent this from taking
place. The Chinese communists went as far as they could short of
actually labelling the Boumedienne regime a progressive one, and
granted it immediate recognition and support. Even without the
coup, the Second Afro-Asian Conference had very little chance of
succeeding, so divided was the communist world. The Chinese
realised this but hoped to 'purify' the Afro-Asian trend, the better
to control it. However, they were fighting a losing battle, for it
should have been clear from the disorder into which Ben Bella's

* On September 21, a spokesman of the new regime announced the arrest of
Hocine Zahouane, head of the Commission on Orientation of the Political
Bureau of the FLN under Ben Bella, and of Bachir Hadj Ali, Moscow-oriented
first secretary of the PAC. These two men were leaders of ORP and were arrested
as such. This followed a few days after the arrest of six Frenchmen and a
Frenchwoman implicated in the ORP. The French officially expressed dis-
satisfaction at their citizens' getting involved in internal Algerian affairs and
satisfaction at the gesture of the Algerian government in having at once turned
over to the French embassy for expulsion, according to the Evian Agreements, a
French army technician doing a civilian job who had been among those arrested.

downfall plunged the Afro-Asian world that the conference could assuredly not take place. Yet the Chinese effort to rescue the conference was understandable for, as the *Far Eastern Economic Review*, an expert journal on Chinese affairs published in Hong Kong, said: 'The postponement (to November 5, 1965) of the Afro-Asian conference at Algiers . . . was the worst setback yet for Chinese diplomacy in the uncommitted world.'[3]

Moreover, Peking thought that while Ben Bella leant, if anything, towards Moscow, Boumedienne—a man reputed 'plus pur et dur'—might well look towards China. (For one thing, during the Indo-Pakistan war and on the occasion of Marshal Chen Yi's visit to Algiers, *El Djeich* expressed the solidarity of muslim Algeria with muslim Pakistan.) These were only theories, however, though it is true that China would now be regarded in Algeria with a more favourable eye than Russia. Sukarno's Indonesia lost no time in echoing the Chinese by recognising the new regime and the leader of the Indonesian Communist Party, Aidit, on June 22 accused Ben Bella of having conducted 'a rightwing policy opposed to the aspirations of the Algerian people. . . . We must thank Colonel Boumedienne', added Aidit, still hoping from distant Jakarta that the Afro-Asian Conference would take place as scheduled. (This was shortly before September 30, when dramatic events in Indonesia were radically to upset the political situation in this huge archipelago.)

The West welcomed the coup in Algeria but—with the exception of the rightwing French papers, which went into ecstasies—the European and American press were astonished and cautious. Most of the Western governments took the same line, except for the Foreign Office, which for reasons hard to fathom blundered heavily by announcing very early that it would recognise the new regime, only to correct this later and say the matter was 'under study'. The Algerians eventually came to the rescue of the Foreign Office and other embarrassed governments by saying that Algeria need not again be recognised by countries which had already established diplomatic relations with her since independence. The *Guardian* expressed its dislike of military dictatorship, and *The Times* remarked that to put a bankrupt economy back on its feet needed other qualities than those needed for the prosecution of a guerrilla war. Editorially the *New York Times* was glad to see the end of Ben

Bella but thought it too early to welcome Colonel Boumedienne, who 'may prove to be another Nasser, another Marshal Ky or even another Fidel Castro'; and the State Department received with cautious courtesy the new approaches from Algeria. On June 27, President Johnson received a personal message from Boumedienne (as did the Pope), and subsequently satisfactory talks between Bouteflika and the American ambassador in Algiers, Porter, led to a State Department declaration on July 9 that the United States was ready to 'explore with the Algerian government new roads of mutual co-operation'. The Bonn government, with which Ben Bella had broken off relations to follow Nasser's example, remained silent; while in East Germany, students demonstrated against Algerian 'military dictatorship'.

Most of the Middle Eastern countries, except Syria who vied with China in giving the Boumedienne regime her blessing, waited for 'clarification', but India and Turkey quickly recognised the new regime—'as it is in power', Ankara added. No one can have embarrassed the new head of government as much as Saigon, however, for Marshal Nguyen Cao Ky even expressed willingness to go to Algiers at the head of a thirty-man delegation to attend the Afro-Asian Conference. North Vietnam was more reserved, delaying the departure of its delegation for Algiers 'pending the clarification of the situation'.

It was in Africa, however, that reactions were the strongest and the most confused. At the start, Algeria's two neighbours were full of apprehension. They knew only too well Boumedienne disliked them and they returned the sentiment. Ben Bella had not liked them either but they felt there was much truth in the old saying, better the devil you know. . . . Morocco reacted by reinforcing her border garrisons, and the country's leftwing opposition took a critical view of Boumedienne. 'The mentality of the putsch is a reactionary and anti-popular one', commented on June 26 *L'Avant Garde*, the journal of the Union Marocaine du Travail. President Bourguiba called together his officers to warn them of the necessity for armies to remain 'la grande muette'. 'Coups d'état and revolutions are symbols of decadence and underdevelopment, even when the coup appears to be the lesser of two evils', Bourguiba said. 'Always bear in mind that once this particular door is opened it is difficult to close it again.' Tunisia and Morocco, however, were the first countries to which Boumedienne despatched special emissaries to give assurance of his good intentions. He missed no opportunity of repeating these good intentions in public, calling King Hassan 'Majesty and dear Friend'.

Puzzled, Africa south of the Sahara divided along two lines of thought. The leaders of 'British' Africa, in London at the Commonwealth Conference, demanded the postponement of the Afro-Asian Conference, saying that they would not participate if it took place—a stand in which they were supported by Asian members of the Commonwealth. They also announced they would not recognise the new government and even started agitating for the liberation of Ben Bella. The fear of military coups, especially among the Eastern Africans where mutinies were still fresh in memory, was behind this reaction. President Nkrumah proceeded shortly thereafter to dismiss his general staff in order to keep a tighter personal hold on his colonels! French-speaking Africa reacted much more favourably and the indefatigable Tshombe, then an official of the French-speaking African family, declared that it was 'an internal affair in which we must not meddle', adding, not without humour, 'we are always ready to help the Algerian leaders provided that they try to agree among themselves and do not try to meddle in the problems of other countries'.

The many French-speaking African states had good reason to rejoice at the overthrow of Ben Bella whom they were accusing, together with President Nkrumah, of training subversive elements to overthrow them. In addition, most of the French-speaking Africans were not unhappy to see the Afro-Asian Conference fail. There was also another reason for their not opposing the new Algerian regime. As noted at the very beginning of this book, while the world stood amazed, de Gaulle described the fall of Ben Bella as a mere 'péripétie', and the new regime lost no time in assuring France of its good intentions. Loyalty to Islam and co-operation with France were the very first official statements made by the new rulers of Algeria. The French-speaking Africans, more at sea than ever, thought it best to follow the lead from Paris and take a favourable view. Here may be seen a marked further benefit to the Algerians of their 'special relationship' with France.

The very first action of Boumedienne's regime vis-à-vis the outside world (if France can properly be regarded as 'outside') was

Bouteflika's solemn assurance (June 20) to a representative of the French embassy that 'Algeria would respect the security of Frenchmen and co-operation between France and Algeria'. He added: 'The policies of co-operation between France and Algeria constitute an original and exalting experiment based on the common will of these two countries to serve the interests of their peoples while respecting their integrity and independence. These policies will be maintained and developed in the most harmonious and advantageous way.' The next day he repeated these assurances in an interview given to the French radio and television—the first interview granted by the new regime. 'I have given my most faithful assurances to the chargé d'affaires, and the French ambassador, M. Gorse. I have given instructions to the Algerian chargé d'affaires in Paris to give similar assurances to the secretary of state for Algerian Affairs, M. de Broglie. Co-operation with France is the cornerstone of our foreign policy. This co-operation expresses in an original and most exalted form a remarkable example of co-operation between two powers.' On the occasion of France's Quatorze Juillet celebrations, Boumedienne sent a personal message to de Gaulle in which he said: 'Croyez à l'amitié de l'Algérie.'

The Second International Fair of Algiers, held in September, would have been a very poor affair, although there were big Russian and Chinese stands, if France had not participated. The great attractions were a French oil derrick transported from the desert and the transmission, for the first time, of colour TV by the French SECAM system. Using the opportunity provided by the fair, Boumedienne launched a pressing appeal for an 'urgent interim plan of industrialisation'. The agreement on 'co-operative association with France who has undertaken to help us' had been signed a few days previously, and Le Monde reported an Algerian minister as saying: 'After all, we [Algerians and French] understand each other best.' And indeed co-operation with France was as vital a part of Boumedienne's policies as it had been of his predecessor's.

There was one more foreign reaction which cannot be passed over without comment: Israel's. Although Tel Aviv rightly observed that Boumedienne 'is still more rabidly anti-Israeli than Ben Bella,' the Jews expressed satisfaction at the turn of events. 'For', explained Abba Eban, vice-president of the Israeli Council of Ministers, on June 26, 'the Arab world drifts further from Nasser's unitarian concepts.' Certainly Nasser still appeared the greatest loser in the affair, together with the communists.

While Moscow may have rejoiced at the postponement of the Second Afro-Asian Conference, and was using the time gained to prepare an attack on the Chinese idea of a 'purer' Afro-Asian gathering to prepare for an enlarged three-continent conference of the Third World in Havana in 1966, Soviet policy suffered a great setback in the postponement of a pro-communist rally that was to have been held from Ben Bella's Algerian platform. On July 21, Moscow announced that the World Youth Festival due to open in Algiers on July 28 would not take place. The Soviet disappointment must have been great, for some 120 countries had been due to take part. The hope of influencing the youth of the Third World vanished for 1965, since no other suitable place for the festival could be found. Also postponed was the Conference of Afro-Asian Women, sponsored by the Cairo-based, pro-Soviet Afro-Asian People's Solidarity Committee, scheduled for November 5, 1965.

The many hopes that had been pinned on Ben Bella were scattered to the winds in a most tragi-comic way. Algiers, which was going to be the platform for the aspirations of the revolutionaries of the Third World, became the scene of a burlesque. Heads of state en route for the conference tried to find suitable pretexts for changing their destinations without too much loss of face. Delegates who had already reached the Algerian capital in their thousands scrambled for everyone's target: a seat on any available plane. Contemplating this unbelievable stampede, *Le Monde*'s correspondent, Jean-François Khan, reported that a cinema in Algiers was that very day advertising *La Grande Illusion*.

11

PROBLEMS AND PROSPECTS

A NEW PERIOD opened in Algerian affairs on June 19, 1965. Ben Bella's 'ideology' was replaced by Boumedienne's concept of 'the nation'. This concept of a group of army officers had all the characteristics typical of rightwing nationalism, but it also represented something more: it reflected the view of the great majority of Algerians who, to transpose Khrushchev's words in Budapest, were greatly in favour of a 'ghoulash' brand of nationalism.

This nationalist mood was one which could easily generate a spirit of xenophobia. Boumedienne had unmistakably demonstrated that he was against foreign influences and was for a 'strong Algeria run by Algerians'. Hostility to foreign influences was evident, for example, in regard to socialism. Speaking to the Bouzerah Military School of Communications on September 28, 1965, Boumedienne said of 'the socialism we want' that 'we shall never want it to be imported from abroad'. This was in harmony with the feelings of Algerians as a whole, most of whom—especially the *fellah* and the muslim bourgeoisie—also approved of his emphasis on Islam and on the 'retour aux sources'. On the other hand, all this was highly disquieting for progressive and Western-oriented elements in Algerian society.

To an outsider, Boumedienne-type nationalism may seem to consist of little more than empty slogans; and, indeed, for a good many Algerians it was hardly more than a vague notion. Yet it accorded well with a widespread desire for that national identity which, as was mentioned in chapter 1, has been hard to seek in Algeria. Two voices are discernible in the country where 'national identity' is concerned. We find *Jeune Afrique* saying, on December

21, 1965: 'Unity and identity—it will be a long time before Algerians assimilate these ideas necessary for the creation of an Algerian people.' But Boumedienne in his Bouzerah address showed no such reservations. The socialism Algeria wanted, he said, 'will spring from the people, from its past, its history and its civilisation'. His view consorted well with the spirit of the Soummam Congress, to which he was always ready to refer since, as we have seen, it was strongly opposed to the 'personality cult'.

Beginning with its issue of October 9, 1965, *Al Ahram*, the Cairo daily, published a long series of interviews that Mohammed Hassanein Heykal had had with Boumedienne immediately after the overthrow of Ben Bella. In these, Boumedienne denied that Ben Bella was a 'socialist' or an 'Arab revolutionary nationalist', and asserted that he was no more than a mere professional politician.

For him socialism was merely a means of avenging himself on those who opposed his personal power. One day he would proclaim Castro's type of socialism. The next day he would call himself an Algerian socialist; on other occasions, a muslim socialist. It was demagogy. . . .

In what way could the nationalisation of small restaurants and hairdressers help Algerian socialism? Arab? Ben Bella was Arab in Cairo, but not in Europe. One day he told me that we must not represent ourselves as Arabs in Africa because Arabism was unpopular; we must represent ourselves as African muslims.

Turning to his predecessor's squandering of public money, Boumedienne declared that, whereas the state of Algeria had decided to allocate 2 billion French francs to the Afro-Asian conference which was to be held in Algiers, 'Ben Bella, simply for reasons of personal prestige, had increased this sum to 15 billion francs. . . . Revolutionary action? Two million Algerians are unemployed. The net agricultural revenue in 1961, before independence, was between 100 and 128 billion francs; but in 1964 it fell to 10 billion.'

Certainly, it was Boumedienne who had introduced the first seeds of Castroism and Nasserism into Algeria, but it is equally true that he made haste to reject such concepts immediately he found that they were alien to Algerian interests and sentiment. Apart from a few true revolutionaries, Algeria ardently desired—in a 'bourgeois' way, perhaps—order, peace, and an easier and better life. Boumedienne was ready to identify himself with this desire of his countrymen, in contrast to the volatile Ben Bella who had only agitated them with his schemes.

Although by the beginning of 1966—that is, about seven months after the coup of June 19—there did not seem to be any great enthusiasm for the new regime, Algeria certainly now appeared to be on the road to becoming better organised and administered. Boumedienne had effected something of a détente in Algeria, and the greater stability of the new regime was reflected in attitudes to the country abroad, where both friendly and unfriendly states soon concluded that independent Algeria under the new dispensation had become something 'solid', something more serious to be reckoned with.

Even so, Boumedienne's regime was not without serious weaknesses and anomalies, some of them inherited from its predecessor, others of its own making. Of the latter, the most glaring was to be found in the continued assertion that Algeria was still a revolutionary state, heading towards socialism. One of the regime's most grotesque tenets, forcibly reminiscent of the much-decried demagogy of Ben Bella, was that it was not anti-communist, and that the military putsch was no 'coup de barre à droite'—as both *El Djeich* and *El Moudjahid* had frequently implied in articles after the overthrow of Ben Bella. Boumedienne's 'revolution'—initiated by a small clique, with no element of popular participation, and carried out by army officers who then assumed absolute power—is, in fact, a classic example of 'counter-revolution'.

The return to first principles, though in many ways a necessary and healthy concept, nevertheless involved reactionary features, with far too much emphasis on the conservative aspects of religion. With the ending of the war against the French, the *ulama* ceased to be identified with a revolutionary cause, as they had been when the the common enemy was both foreign and christian. Regarding themselves as an elite superior to any other class, and suppressing the development of independence of thought, they tended after the establishment of the new state to become an influence retarding progress. Their attempts to appear progressive only led them to introduce even more absurdities into the 'Islam-socialism' theory, until they reached the point of saying that there was nothing in the pages of Marx that had not already appeared in the Koran. In fact, they were using the 'socialism-within-Islam' theory to increase their sway over the people.

This was particularly manifest in the increasing hostility of the more reactionary elements to the civil and social equality of women. The emancipation of women had, of course, been one of the major slogans of the Ben Bella era; but in practice it had been a slogan and little more. Ben Bella had even reduced the symbolic number of female parliamentary deputies, for all that women—largely because of the war—formed well over 65 per cent of the total population of Algeria. While Ben Bella was still in power, Algerian delegations attended communist congresses of women, yet, as *Révolution Africaine* pointed out, not a single woman was present at the first UGTA congress in Algiers, either in the executive committee or in the secretariat.[1] General illiteracy among women was put forward as an excuse for their exclusion but, as *Révolution Africaine* again pointed out, women members were not to be found on the committees even of student bodies.[2] Here illiteracy could hardly be advanced as an excuse. Even party cells refused to admit women who had been militants in the maquis, or former communists.

The cry of revolt of Algerian womanhood against the submissive role to which they were condemned—in spite of the would-be-'socialism' of new Algeria—is poignantly emphasised by Fadela M'Rabet's revelation that, in 1964, no less than 175 young Algerian girls had chosen suicide rather than marry the man selected for them by their parents.[3] In criticising views expressed by *Le Monde*, which she considered to be biased against Algerian women, Mlle M'Rabet wrote, in a letter to that paper:

What freedom have we received from the Ben Bella government? I do not speak of the Constitution, nor of the Charter of Algiers— dead letters so far as we are concerned—but of the concrete measures which the previous [i.e. Ben Bella] regime could well have taken. The greater number of marriages are still forced unions; fathers are still all-powerful, and can interrupt at will the studies of their daughters (in order to marry off or cloister them), and husbands have complete freedom to repudiate their wives or to marry four. Abandoned wives, with children to support, are too numerous to count. . . . And if, to have freedom, one must be able to earn one's living, what freedom is possible to Algerian women ? There are less than a thousand salaried women employees in agriculture, and still fewer in industry; they are just as scarce in administration. Let those who accuse us of invading the ministries look at the statistics. In the PTT, which employs by far the greatest number of women, female personnel total only one-eighth of the whole, numbering about 1,400; 110 women work in the administration of the Ministry of Education, 68 in the Ministry of Foreign Affairs, 26 in that of Youth (out of 200), and 20 in that of Tourism. And most of these are either charwomen or typists.[4]

Such was the situation under Ben Bella.

But the status of 'our socialist sisters' was to be lowered still further after the Boumedienne coup, when the *ulama* and many conservative army officers started complaining about the decline in 'standards of modesty and morals', about unduly short skirts, and so forth. The few women who occupied public posts were dismissed, and this despite Boumedienne's assertion, on August 21, that he had no intention of suppressing the rights of woman. 'We recognise her rights because she played her part in the struggle. . . . We have seen her, machine-gun in hand, and not only at ceremonies at the Majestic and the Place des Martyrs.' This referred to political meetings held by Ben Bella. Yet Boumedienne's words on this subject had no more substance in them than Ben Bella's.

The instigators of the coup were so preoccupied with 'order' that Cherif Belkacem, co-ordinator of the FLN, later justified their actions in *Jeune Afrique* by saying that 'bringing in the masses' would have led to chaos. In fact, notwithstanding their claims of 'collegiality', the new leaders of Algeria were manipulating the country according to decisions taken in their own tightly restricted conclaves (note the composition of the Revolutionary Council on pages 230–2), and had little regard to the good opinion of outsiders, either Algerian or foreign. Though taking advantage of the widespread disillusionment with Ben Bella, the new regime had none of the characteristics which arouse popular enthusiasm, and which are essential ingredients of a true revolution. On the contrary, the great mass of the population remained as apathetic as before, while everything was decided, promulgated and enacted by 'higher authority'—that is, Boumedienne and his supporters. It seemed very much as if one club, the 'BB', had simply been replaced by another, the 'B'.

Organised political bodies were not destined to flourish after Ben Bella's overthrow. On December 10, 1965, Boumedienne addressed a meeting of the cadres of the FLN—still, on paper, a political party. He attacked 'those who are trying to separate the army from the party', contending that 'the best way of solving problems is to tackle them within the confines of the party, and not to publish outside it statements critical of the state'. He added that 'the *total* autonomy of the national organisations must come to an end'. (Our italics.) This was followed by the regime's taking exactly the same measures as had been taken in the past to muzzle the UGTA and, in particular, the students' organisation. The seemingly endless debate as to 'what is the party?' continued, with Boumedienne giving the following definition: 'The FLN is not, and must not be, a party of the masses, but rather one of the cadres, whose valuable contribution to the state must be by the mobilisation of the masses and the effective participation of the people in the tasks of the nation.' The ingrained dislike and fear of the masses was only too evident. The muzzling of the press, tight enough under Ben Bella, was intensified by putting all publications (except *El Moudjahid* and *Révolution Africaine*, which were run by the party) under the control of the Ministry of Information. French newspapers—effectively Algeria's only windows on the outside world—were frequently seized.

Even more than in Ben Bella's day, repressive acts were taken against the political left, and in particular against the communists. Boumaza, minister of Information, announced at a press conference, on September 24, 1965, further arrests of communists—some hundred or so, including seven from the banned *Alger Républicain*. He intimated that communist resistance in Algeria was 'benefiting from a certain collusion abroad'. All this was in spite of assurances by Boumedienne, Boumaza and others that the regime was not anti-communist. It would take far too long to list all the anti-communist statements made by the regime, together with the replies provoked from communist parties overseas, especially those of France and Italy. It is enough to quote *El Moudjahid* which, during its controversy with *Humanité*, said of the French Communist Party: 'The so-called heirs of Lenin seem rather to have followed the lessons of Goebbels.' Accusing the PCF of having 'betrayed the Algerian revolution', and the Algerian Communist Party of 'never having had a national attitude', *El Moudjahid* threatened to publish documents which would establish 'the complicity of the so-called French Communist Party and the so-called Algerian Communist Party with colonialism'.[5] It went on to say:

> The leaders of the first [the PCF] will be scandalised by our opinions. They will protest noisily and parade their anti-colonialism . . . they will accuse us of supplying grist for the imperialist mill. *Humanité* has already denounced 'the anti-socialist nature of the present regime, evidenced by the violent anti-communist onslaughts of the Algerian press'. But doubtless soon *Humanité* will run out of arguments to explain and justify itself.
>
> Algeria is not communist. In neglecting this truth, the previous regime, seeking for reasons of expediency the support of the renegades of the PCA before being devoured by them, committed a grave error of judgement. In building the socialist edifice, we will not neglect the support of marxism. In fact, it does not seem possible that a developing country can afford to ignore the scientific and economic aspects of marxism. But to ignore the inherited traditions of our Arabo-Islamic past, to ignore certain aspects of our national culture, is to cut Algeria off from all that gives her originality, from that which was at the root of our uprising, and from that which will enable us to realise an authentically revolutionary socialism.[6]

Even before the dispute between *El Moudjahid* and *Humanité* reached this level of intensity, it was obvious that relations between the Algerian leadership and the communists were very bad. They had been none too good for the past twenty years but, as noted by Philippe Herreman, 'they had never been as bad as after June 19'.[7] If the protests of Boumedienne and his supporters that they were not anti-communist are to be taken seriously, one would have to adopt a novel theory of leftwing revolution: a leftwing revolution conducted against the left itself!

In harrying and imprisoning leftist elements, the new regime demonstrated another point of similarity with its predecessor. Political prisoners were put to torture with the same zeal as by the much-denounced Ben Bella and, earlier, by the colonialist regime. It would seem that torture had become accepted by Algerians as a commonplace political weapon. *Unità* and *Humanité* denounced the use of torture with especial fervour because it was communist elements who suffered most from it, but protests were by no means limited to the international communist press. Pierre Vidal-Nacquet, a French intellectual and a member of the Central Committee of the League for Human Rights, who had always strongly opposed its use, no matter by whom, observed that torture was now being applied in Algeria 'even more systematically than was previously the case'.[8] The Algerian government attempted to suppress the campaign in the French press against torture by releasing the French citizens who had been captured as members of opposition groups in Algeria. They all promptly publicised what they had undergone in prison at the hands of the Algerians. Vidal-Nacquet wrote of his interview with one of them:

> I have questioned at length my friend, Albert Roux, a militant trotskyite whom I knew when he was making up thousands of parcels for Algerian prisoners. His story, alas! is exactly the one we heard so often during the war: arrested without a warrant and without proof; torture graded according to the different ranks of the police (from simple violence to strangulation, electric and water tortures as formerly recommended by Inspector Guillaume). Nothing is missing, not even the hypocritical warnings of 'We are gentle, but the others . . .'; and the regrets expressed by the military authorities: 'The police are like that.'
>
> We know that most of the European victims of these police operations have been expelled, but the others, the Algerians, remain. We are no longer directly responsible for their lot. But if we do not speak out, who will take an interest in their fate?[9]

It was perhaps significant of a special mentality in a once-colonised people that the regime, having bowed to pressure and released the French prisoners, then revenged itself by continuing to maltreat its own citizens, especially leftwing intellectuals, like Mohammed Harbi. And this at the very moment when Boumedienne was solemnly stating (like Ben Bella before him): 'I say it in few words—in this country we shall have absolute justice or nothing; equality between all citizens or nothing.' (A speech on October 6, 1965.)

What made matters even more tragic was that, as under Ben

Bella, it was the military security forces who were the most ferocious in the use of torture. Official denials, like those issued by the Algerian embassy in Paris on September 28, 1965 specially for French consumption, convinced no one; nor did claims that talk of torture was mere 'communist propaganda'. The French government took formal cognisance of the situation in a statement by de Broglie, secretary of state for Algerian Affairs, on December 18, 1965.

> Some Frenchmen have been arrested in Algeria since the end of September 1965 for having, according to the Algerian authorities, sheltered Algerian fugitives, participated in a secret printing press, and helped to distribute the pamphlets of a proscribed political organisation considered as subversive by the Algerian government. Some of them have been held for over a month. The French government has at all times protested against these irregularities, particularly unlawful detention, for it is during these delays that cruelty occurs.

After recalling that seventeen prisoners had been freed and expelled in mid-November, de Broglie went on:

> The secretary of state for Algerian Affairs and the French ambassador in Algiers have made urgent representations to the Algerian government that all those of French origin be allowed to receive the visits of their lawyers and families, and where they have not become Algerians nationals, of their consul, according to the Vienna Convention on consular relations, signed and ratified by the Algerian government.[10]

The Boumedienne government, so solicitous of French opinion where economic questions were involved, gave a further demonstration of its complete disregard of public opinion in the case of Ben Bella. The new regime was very anxious not to make of Ben Bella another martyr of the Lumumba type. This could be well understood. But it was shown that, even in the twentieth century, the operation of the oubliette was still perfectly feasible—and this in the case of a man who had attracted world wide attention.

In a letter to *The Times* on July 19, 1965, Lord Brockway (formerly Fenner Brockway, MP), pointed out that, at the time of writing, Ben Bella had been overthrown some weeks, but no information had been given about him or about the intention to bring him to trial.

'This is a matter which concerns not only the people of Algeria, but all of us in other countries who wish to see democratic processes in that country.' Similar statements had been made throughout the world, by press and governments. But the day following publication of Lord Brockway's letter, a government spokesman in Algiers said no more than that Ben Bella was 'well-treated and in good health'. *Al Ahram*, concluding the series of articles already mentioned, noted on October 10 that the case of Ben Bella remained undecided, and quoted Boumedienne as saying: 'We shall make him wear clothes of exactly the right size, neither too loose nor too tight!'

But it required strong campaigning by the press throughout the French-speaking world (especially in *Le Monde* and *Jeune Afrique*) before Algiers agreed that Ben Bella be allowed at least to write to his mother.* This letter, dated November 9, was published but it showed strong signs of having been dictated. 'I send you this word to assure you about my fate. I am well and have no complaints about my treatment and the material conditions in which I live. My mother will soon be able to see for herself when she visits me. Or so I have been promised. Be reassured. I kiss you all. AHMED BEN BELLA.'

The writing, according to Maître Lafue-Veron, self-appointed advocate of Ben Bella, was the signatory's own. Yet, by the beginning of 1966, this constituted, together with a similar letter to one of his nieces, the sole sign of life from the deposed leader. He was generally thought to be imprisoned in an underground bunker in the former Admiralty building in the port area of Algiers,[11] having been previously confined in different parts of the country, including the Sahara, to prevent his being traced. (The *Christian Science Monitor* on January 26, 1966 disclosed that three attempts to rescue Ben Bella had been made by Egyptian commandos.)

Ben Bella's trial, and the White Book which Boumedienne said would be published about him, are still to come. An open trial or a

* An editorial in *Jeune Afrique* is said to have finally forced the hand of Algiers. In it, Bechir Ben Yahmet wrote: 'His disappearance as through a trapdoor, his being denied the most elementary of human rights, that of communicating with his mother, of being defended and attended to—this is one of those scandals which our epoch is beginning to take for granted. As a result, those in power are inclined to think there is no day of reckoning—which, fortunately, is an error!'

published document would only serve to renew interest in him and shed unwelcome light on the workings of Boumedienne's mind. Any renewal of interest in the deposed leader would be awkward for the new regime for, as long as he remained alive, there would always be the possibility, however remote, of his staging a come-back. Moreover, Boumedienne came to realise that his promised White Book would lead to 'diplomatic complications'.[12] This would certainly be so. Such a book would show that Boumedienne had, in fact, been more opposed than was Ben Bella to a peaceful settlement of the territorial disputes with Morocco and Tunisia, over which the military leader had accused the civilian leader of 'treason' and of 'giving away our land'. Nor is this all. Boumedienne's accusations of 'adventurer', 'secret deals' and 'personal diplomacy' would reveal that he had been opposed to close co-operation with the UAR. It would also prove embarrassing to the new regime's relations with the communist countries. It can be disclosed here that one of the charges against Ben Bella was that the embassy in Algiers of a communist country had blackmailed some of his opponents and threatened them with physical liquidation if they did not toe the Ben Bella line.* Boumedienne, not surprisingly, preferred to keep these things secret, in spite of his promises of 'full light' after the coup.

Although this oubliette treatment was no more than the treatment Ben Bella himself had meted out to his adversaries, the intellectual and diplomatic worlds would continue to look askance at the Boumedienne regime as long as Ben Bella did not get some kind of hearing. One of the best comments on the case was made by the chief editor of *Jeune Afrique*, Georges Henein, after a number of world-famed intellectuals—including François Mauriac, Jean-Paul Sartre, Bertrand Russell and Lelio Basso—had appealed to the UN Commission of Human Rights on Ben Bella's behalf. Henein wrote:

There is a general malaise in the Third World, which is a malaise of liberty. It is easier to spotlight the misfortunes of a head of state or of a well-known politican than those of a little provincial teacher who fails to return home one night, or of an obscure

* The source for this information—an authoritative Algerian one—allows the author to say only that the embassy concerned was a 'European communist one, but not Yugoslavia or the USSR'.

trade unionist who disappears into the blue, or of a student picked up after a reunion, never to see the light of day again. Those who have fallen from power suffer so much in their downfall that the consequent discomforts are but secondary evils. . . . Their case is not as bad as that of the humble man who does not aspire to command but merely wishes to say his piece. We cannot accept that he should be punished merely for speaking out. . . .

Those leaders of the new societies of the Third World who recognise that liberty has been sacrificed, or shelved for the time being, invoke their economic obligations: to create work, construct factories and provide bread. But there is something dangerous and serious in this bartering of human rights for a meal. It is impossible not to fear that, in the end, both the meal and the means of asking for it will be gone.

Real decolonisation has not yet begun. For, to be truly decolonised, it is not enough to be a sovereign state. The people must be treated as responsible and of age, not as pawns and playthings. Better a law without police than police without law.[13]

Henein's words have a general relevance, but they are particularly apposite in the case of Algeria.

Ben Bella's regime of 'revolution' and of 'socialism' had left a deep mark on Algeria. The desire to continue in the role of 'fervent revolutionaries'—genuine in the case of a small minority now behind bars, but simply a pretentious charade for those in power—remained very strong. This was made obvious by the absurd parrot-cry of 'we are not anti-communists', and by the attempts to hold the Second Afro-Asian Conference in Algeria, whatever the cost and despite the fact that it had been wrecked by the coup. It was also clearly demonstrated by the persistent efforts by Algiers to avoid further deterioration in its relations with the communist parties (the PCF excepted) and with the communist states, Russia in particular.

Yet it was characteristic of the new regime that efforts to maintain 'friendly' relations with communist states went hand in hand with strong attacks on overseas communism, at least in the aftermath of the coup. Immediately after the overthrow of Ben Bella, Boumaza had publicly attacked communist countries in a speech to Algerian industrialists. 'The Bulgarian Communist Party talks about the uprising of June 19 and says that it has confidence in the struggle of the Algerian people for socialism. As far as we are concerned, the Bulgarian Communist Party can go to —— after the way it has behaved towards us.' He followed this up by stressing the continuation of socialism: 'We did not learn our Algerian socialism from the texts of the Bulgarian People's Party nor from the French Communist Party. Algerian politics is a living thing.' In this connection, *Africa 1965* rightly observed that 'the strong tendency towards nationalism in the new rulers—of far greater importance than the overstressed Islamic orthodoxy of Boumedienne—has turned against international communism, simply because it *is* international'. In the course of its feud with the PCF, *Révolution Africaine*, in its issue of September 26, 1965, said: 'Since June 19, they have not ceased pouring out torrents of insane abuse on the Algerians. What aim have they in mind? To force us into anti-communism and cause our relations with the communist countries to deteriorate? It is possible, but we shall not fall into the trap.'

And, indeed, strange as it may seem, Algeria did not. Many overtures were made to communist states and also, because of its rivalry with the PCF, to the Italian Communist Party. (The Italian party accepted an invitation to the third anniversary celebrations of independence, though its representative was not a party official but the local correspondent of *Unità*.) With the rapid waning of any of the enthusiasm still felt for Ben Bella, and with even Nasser becoming resigned to dealing with Boumedienne, the communist states decided it would be expedient to respond to these Algerian overtures, whatever their dislike of the new regime. Of the European communist states, it was the USSR, probably with an eye to the conflict with Peking, which first responded to the overtures of Boumedienne. This was in line with its policy elsewhere, as towards Baghdad and Cairo, for example, where good relations were maintained in spite of the treatment meted out to communists there.

The day after the coup, China had announced its 'total and unconditional support' of the new regime through its ambassador in Algiers, Tseng Hoa. The New China News Agency had also published in full the proclamation in which Boumedienne denounced Ben Bella as a 'diabolical dictator, an adventurer and charlatan'. Many then thought that Algeria would align itself with China: a feeling reinforced when the Chinese ambassador's reception of credentials was given precedence over the USSR and the USA, preceded only by France and the UAR. More evidence for this view seemed to appear when Algeria took the side of Pakistan in the latter's conflict with India. (In fact, this stemmed mainly from feelings of Islamic solidarity; Saudi Arabia, for example, acted similarly.) *Le Monde*, in its issue of July 6, 1965, attached some importance to a statement made by a group of young officers around Boumedienne. 'As to the USSR', they said, 'we respect her as a great power and hope to keep her as a friend. But, as a revolutionary inspiration, we consider her discredited. She has no power to inspire a socialism which she has liquidated. We are far more interested in China. Not that we wish to base our socialism entirely on hers, but her experience is the one in which we are most interested today.'

But others analysed the situation more shrewdly. Patrick Seale reported in the *Observer* on July 3, 1965:

> Many observers have argued that the eclipse of the European communists in Algeria has thrown the door open to China. Certainly a major obstacle to Chinese influence has been removed. Following the hostility of Cuba to the new regime and the chilly reserve of Moscow and Bulgaria, Peking has rushed in with warm expressions of support.
>
> The Chinese will spare no effort to turn these sentiments into political gains, but as yet there is no real chance of an effective Peking-Algiers axis. The new Algerian regime does not want and cannot afford to take sides in international disputes. It has powerful over-riding material reasons for remaining on good terms with France, the Soviet Union, the United States and Britain.

The simple fact of the matter was that China's initial burst of enthusiasm for the new regime had been due to its hope that the Second Afro-Asian Conference could still be held. Later, as we shall see, it became clear that Boumedienne's government was primarily interested in economic matters and that Algerian needs would be satisfied by the West and Soviet Russia rather than by China.

Moscow's hand of friendship was first extended on July 22. After a period of coldness between the two countries, the Foreign Ministry in Algiers released the text of a message from the Soviet government to Boumedienne in which Moscow reaffirmed its 'satisfaction in the ties of friendship which linked Algeria and the USSR'. It went on to reiterate 'the principle of non-interference in the affairs of other states', and underlined the Soviet desire to 'reinforce relations at all levels. . . . The Central Committee of the Communist Party and the Soviet Government express their satisfaction at the Council of the Revolution's reaffirmation that it wishes to pursue a policy of non-alignment while working to build up socialism and develop relations with socialist countries.' Two weeks later, Algeria replied in similar tone to the Moscow Note, emphasising that the technical agreements between the two countries were continuing unhindered.

All the same, Moscow could hardly remain a passive spectator of all the anti-communist activities in Algeria. On September 25, *Pravda*, in outlining the feud between Boumedienne and the left-wing opposition, observed that these were 'internal affairs of Algeria which Algerians alone could settle'; but it went on to say: 'The arrests . . . are alarming. They show renewed activity by forces that are apparently not desirous of solving by democratic means the problems and the inevitable disagreements between patriots during a period of transition.'

However, political expediency soon overcame any ideological scruples felt in Moscow, and on October 21 it was announced in Algiers that Boumedienne had received an official invitation to visit the Soviet Union. Boumedienne was anxious to extract all he could from this visit. Before departing, he said that he was going at the invitation 'of the Central Committee of the Communist Party of the Soviet Union'. In fact, he had been invited by the Russian government, not the party. Commenting on this, *Unità* observed (December 14, 1965) that Boumedienne's 'lapse' was evidence of his desire to renew relations with the USSR at the party level. *Le Monde* noted, four days later, that, although Boumedienne had received a friendly welcome in Moscow, his reception was markedly less enthusiastic than that accorded to Ben Bella—who had, indeed, been made a Hero of the Soviet Union. It was clear that it would only be with difficulty that Moscow would come round to the kind of happy interparty relationship of the days of Ben Bella.

Washington seems to have appreciated this. On July 16, a State Department spokesman had stated that the USA 'expects to have happier relations with Algiers'. According to the *New York Times* on January 4, 1966, the American food aid programme for Algiers had been reinstated after a lapse of six months. This was held to mark the favourable conclusion of a long and careful assessment of Boumedienne's policies. An agreement was made for the supply to Algeria of surplus food to the value of $12 million, together with credits to be used for paying for agricultural projects, as well as substantial technical assistance. It was not until after the overthrow of Ben Bella that Algeria publicly acknowledged the food aid from America. At a press conference on July 31, 1965, Boumaza said: 'We do receive American wheat. Do not some Eastern European countries also receive it? Was not the USSR unhappy some time ago because the US did not give her wheat?'

The desire to be regarded as 'revolutionary' and 'socialist' was so pressing for the new rulers of Algeria that, in trying to recreate the 'progressive' image, they were led at times to behave in a way reminiscent of Ben Bella. Considerable efforts would be needed to convince Black Africa of the purity of Boumedienne's intentions.

The unilateral declaration of independence by the white racialist leaders of Rhodesia was seized on by Algiers as a golden opportunity for currying favour with Black Africa. The foreign minister, Bouteflika, announced that the barracks of Algeria were being 'held in readiness to train troops' for the liberation of Rhodesia, and that Algeria would sever diplomatic relations with the United Kingdom. Yet this could hardly be considered strong action, even in Algeria where the British diplomatists were given a whole month in which to pack their bags (they had already seen what was coming and had destroyed their secret files). Some kind of pressure, it was arguable, needed to be brought to bear on Britain to impose more drastic sanctions on Salisbury. But it was not very intelligent of Algeria to sever relations with the country on whom the Africans of Rhodesia and Zambia were relying to solve the problem; and, in fact, no more than ten of the thirty-six African states took such a step. Again, Boumedienne publicly announced on December 23, 1965 that Algeria would fight against the creation of a new Israel in Africa, heedless of the fact that most of Black Africa, and certainly the more revolutionary states, maintained perfectly good working relations with Tel-Aviv.

All this did not amount to much. Indeed, it could perhaps be suggested that Algeria's main 'revolutionary' role in Africa since June 19, 1965 has been the coup's encouragement of military putsches in the continent. Colonels in other African states certainly do not seem to have been made more docile in their relations with civilian politicians by Colonel Boumedienne's ousting of Ben Bella! By the beginning of 1966, military coups à l'Algérienne had occurred in the Upper Volta, in the Central African Republic and in Nigeria, and Ghana was soon to follow suit with the army's overthrow of the seemingly impregnable Nkrumah. Such an association of their coup with these others was of grave embarrassment to the new Algerian leaders, and we find *El Moudjahid* on January 10, 1966 accusing the coup-making colonels of Black Africa of being 'latter-day Don Quixotes ... attempting to act a part on the stage of world politics, and, in so doing, severing their countries' affinities with China'!

Even so, one must in fairness say that, with the exception of the instances just cited, the foreign policy of Boumedienne's government over the post-coup period was consistent on the whole with Bouteflika's statement on June 20, 1965: 'The era of noisy speeches, of vulgar catchwords and of impulsive frenzy is over.' A manifestation of a more sober foreign policy was discernible in Algeria's contacts with the 'liberation movements', many of which had been undiscriminatingly encouraged by the Ben Bella regime. Boumedienne confined his attention to the more serious and stable among them: the ANC in South Africa, the FRELIMO in Mozambique and, particularly, the PAIGC of Amilcar Cabral in Portuguese Guinea. These continued to receive aid from Algeria, but such aid was now given with much less ostentation than under Ben Bella.

The new regime's serious intent was evinced mainly in its internal economic policy. The 1966 'budget de fonctionnement', totalling 3,200 million dinars (as against 3,052 million for 1965, of which 2,800 million had been spent by the time of the coup), provided for an increase in public funds for agriculture. Presenting the budget on January 4, 1966, the minister of Finance, Ahmed Kaid, described its main features thus: administrative reorganisation and elimination of waste; creation of a national bank to reorganise the credit system; and tax reforms in favour of the working classes. Denouncing 'corruption and speculation', he said: 'There is a danger, a serious danger, facing countries which have opted for socialism; it is corruption and theft.' As under Ben Bella, the allocation for national education was the largest item in the budget: 630 million dinars, or 21·5 per cent of the total. National defence accounted for 490 million dinars, or 15 per cent of the total.

Boumedienne frequently avowed that no more would there be two Algerias: a prosperous Algeria along the coast, and a poor Algeria in the interior and in the Sahara. But it was no easy matter to put to rights the economic chaos of the country; and, as was in many ways inevitable, his regime tended towards capitalist solutions. Algeria, like other countries in the Third World, had come to realise that social equality was not to be achieved by the mere shouting of socialist slogans. The closing of the inefficient 'Socialist Pilot Shops' set up under Ben Bella aroused communist criticism, but soon it was not only communists who detected the new trend: the abandonment of the very concept of 'self-management'. Industrial enterprises under 'self-management' were gradually returned to their former owners, some of them of French nationality —a development which led *Révolution et Travail*, the organ of UGTA, to appeal (on September 13, 1965) for 'increased vigilance'. The increasing agitation by the trade unions was suppressed, as were all other forms of opposition to the regime. But, though self-managing enterprises had done disastrously badly under Ben Bella, their failure lay more in their practice—the absence of proper credit and marketing procedures—than in the principles on which they were based. This, however, was not accepted by Boumedienne, and the principle of self-managing units was marked down for condemnation.

Boumaza stated on July 31, 1965 that Algeria would now 'look favourably on private investment from abroad, provided that it did not affect nationalised key sectors of the economy'. Earlier that same month (on July 3), Ali Mahsas said that, in regard to agrarian reforms, 'the agrarian revolution . . . does not aim at suppressing private property'. Furthermore, as was noted by *Oilgram*, an American specialised news-service, a striking feature of the new regime was its reliance on American consulting and contracting companies who worked for some time in complete secrecy, avoiding contact even with the rest of the Western business community in Algeria. (As many as twenty-four such companies were said to be active in October 1965, twelve of them on specific projects.)

While the practice of Algerian domestic policy was thus gradually taking on a distinctly more 'capitalist' character, the regime continued nevertheless to declare solemnly its 'socialist' principles, seeking thereby to maintain at least the outward show of 'self-management'. Yet 'this avowed adhesion to socialist principles would be unlikely to produce really effective results unless traditional attitudes in Algeria radically changed, and government and people alike accepted genuinely socialist practices'.[14] Only time can tell what effect Boumedienne's policies will have on the Algerian economy. In at least one notable instance—that of the continued strengthening of the armed forces, despite Boumedienne's avowals of a policy of 'austerity'—practice differs sharply from theory. Demobilisation after independence reduced the army from about 100,000 to around 60,000 men in mid-1965, but under both Ben Bella and Boumedienne military expenditure has been far too great for the country's economy to support. The parade of November 1, 1965 showed a large range of Soviet, French and West German equipment, including some Soviet ground-to-air missiles which were recognised by military attachés in Algiers as being of the most modern design.[15]

In its economic difficulties, the new regime right from the start looked to France for help—indeed, for salvation. Only France could give Boumedienne that assistance he needed for the planned interim scheme of industrialisation. Of particular urgency was the perpetuation (under a different guise) of the financial terms of the Evian Agreements which came to an end in 1965. When Bouteflika met de Gaulle on October 11, 1965—the first member of the new administration to be officially received by France's head of state—he asked for continued financial assistance, preferably for several years. Reporting the interview two days later, Le Monde stated that all the other major problems, including the early evacuation of the base (desired by Algeria) at Mers-el-Kebir, had been discussed, and took the meeting to indicate clearly that de Gaulle had given his personal approval to the new regime. It was confidently predicted that France would evacuate her base at Mers-el-Kebir much earlier than stipulated in the Evian Agreements, and would help in establishing an industrial complex there.[16] On January 12, 1966, the Organisation Saharien was dissolved and replaced by the Organisme de Coopération Industrielle (OCI), through which France would play the key role in plans for Algerian industrialisation.

As we have seen, in economic matters Ben Bella's Algeria was linked inextricably to France. Boumedienne's Algeria sought an even larger economic collaboration with the former colonial power. In a shrewd analysis of Franco-Algerian relations shortly before Bouteflika's meeting with de Gaulle, Philippe Herreman observed that closer collaboration had been encouraged by the new regime's rejection of 'imported socialism' and by its clear indications of goodwill towards France.

> This impression is founded on several things. Without wishing to become involved in Algeria's domestic affairs, the French government thinks that co-operation can only be facilitated by the reorganisation of the administration and the economic development being planned by the new team. . . . It also knows . . . that our technicians and instructors are in greater demand (provided they are not communists) than those of Egypt or other Eastern countries, who were rejected at the same time as M. Ben Bella for political intervention or plain incompetence. It is impressed by the new direction being taken by the regime which, wishing to judge by standards of efficiency rather than 'dogmatic socialism' . . . is calling a halt to nationalism, even returning enterprises to private hands, and is dismissing marxists from responsible posts. . . . It is trying to restore the confidence of the Algerian middle class and the foreign business communities which had been dissuaded from participating in the development of the country by M. Ben Bella's policies of 'socialist adventurism'. Since he has been at the head of government, Colonel Boumedienne seems to wish to establish even more firmly the policy he was already championing at the Ministry of Defence. He has asked and, it appears, obtained from Paris instructors for tanks and engineering, and has requested France to help Algeria to create a navy. A French naval mission has left for Algiers.[17]

In a New Year broadcast over Radio Algiers, de Broglie, the French secretary of state for Algerian Affairs, expressed high satisfaction at the exceptional degree of co-operation between France and Algeria, which 'had reached a level attained nowhere else in the world'.

The advantage in this remarkable state of affairs was not wholly Algeria's, to put it mildly. De Broglie had previously stated in public, when replying to critics of his policy, that the assistance rendered to France by Algeria was 'profitable to our economy', and that the agreement over oil and gas had not been reached without some heavy concessions by Algeria.[18] Earlier he had mentioned something about which the Algerians had kept quiet: 'Algeria has undertaken to renounce any intention of nationalising these industries. . . . We have safeguarded our interests.'[19] Though Boumedienne, like his predecessor, was anxious to diversify the country's economic outlets, Algerian trade with France increased. In October 1965, French official circles noted 'with satisfaction' that French exports to Algeria had reached 268 million francs for that month, and were expected to amount to 2,500 million francs for the whole of 1965.

For its part, however, Algeria—with some 20 million hectolitres of wine in stock—was expressing concern early in 1966 that France was willing to buy only 7·75 million hectolitres. France was no longer so dependent on Algerian wine supplies as she had been before the war, having taken steps to increase the quantity of the French national output. This was a serious matter for Algeria since industrial development depended to a large extent on a prosperous agriculture. As before, Algeria threatened to reduce her trade with France; but any sanctions against France could hardly fail to do greater harm to Algeria. Similar threats were made over oil and gas. At the end of 1965, the authorities threatened to send a delegation of oilmen to meet workers in the Italian oil industry—clearly in an attempt to persuade them to act against the interests of their own employers (in this case ENI) who had just signed an agreement to import gas from Libya. (Spain, another potential customer for Algerian gas, had made a similar agreement with Libya.) The Algerians detected 'plots' in these deals with Libya, refusing to see that their failure to do business was caused by high prices, by the pretentious wish for direct distribution within Italy, and by continuing dependence on the French economy. An Algerian oil delegation did, in fact, go to Rome in December 1965; but it spent its time trying to convince leftwing circles in Italy that Algeria was pursuing a 'revolutionary oil policy'. Such lack of business acumen increased still further the French domination of oil production in the Sahara. Of the 26·5 million tons of crude oil produced by Algeria in 1965 (Libya's production in the same year was 58·5 million tons), 66·4 per cent was absorbed by France and only 6·1 per cent by the Algiers refinery. Continuing the decline noted in chapter 9, drilling activities decreased by 19 per cent in 1965 as compared with 1964. However, the Algerians could take comfort from the increase of gas production during the same period by 149 per cent.

Another difficulty confronting Algerian policy stemmed from the need to 'keep well in' with public opinion in France. The complexity of the marriage between the two countries meant that the French left could not forgive Algeria her 'treasons'—especially the entente with de Gaulle—while the right resented having to swallow the bitter pill of Algerian independence. Since de Gaulle called the tune in France, Algeria set itself to court his goodwill. This proved to be none too easy, despite all the avowals of 'close collaboration'. Though the architect of Franco-Algerian co-operation, de Gaulle was intent on putting relations with Algeria on a conventional footing as soon as possible. Thus, for example, when his new cabinet was formed in January 1966, the office of secretary of state for Algerian Affairs was abolished, and relations with Algeria were made the responsibility of the Quai d'Orsay.

Courting de Gaulle's goodwill sprang from something more than official policy. The general enjoyed a wide measure of personal popularity in Algeria. Reporting the avid interest among Algerians in the French presidential election in late 1965, *Le Monde* commented:

> It is necessary to remember that, if General de Gaulle is popular in Algeria, it is primarily because he accepted Algerian independence and made the French accept it. It is also because he stands, in Algerian eyes, for a policy of co-operation. . . . Moreover, certain Algerians do not forget that many men of the left, and M. Mitterand himself, were opposed to the emancipation of Algeria when they were in power.

El Moudjahid, on the eve of the elections, stated explicitly that Algeria wished for de Gaulle's victory. Its explanation is very illuminating.

Algeria should doubtless feel closer ideologically to the French left. But how can we ignore the reality and take more note of intentions than of acts? How can we forget the attitude of the [French] Communist Party which, denying its international nature, has fallen into demagogy and paltry nationalism, and prefers the tactics of the moment to loyalty to its doctrines?

Whatever the future may hold, and still hopeful that the French left may recover its revolutionary fervour and its sense of proletarian solidarity, we believe it is de Gaulle who, in the short term, remains the most solid guarantor of Franco-Algerian co-operation.[20]

In his very first interview given to a French newspaper, Boumedienne had stated: 'There are no longer, thanks to the General, any problems between the Algerian people and the French people. We have known General de Gaulle as an enemy, and we know that, thanks to his vision of the future, he is now our friend.'[21] Algeria's new leader was the first of the very few to congratulate de Gaulle on the launching of France's first satellite from a French military base in the Sahara on November 26, 1965. Less than six months had elapsed from the overthrow of Ben Bella against whom one of the charges was that he had leaned too heavily on de Gaulle's support!

By the spring of 1966, the Boumedienne regime, though strongly grasping the levers of power, was far from being in complete command of the support of the Algerian people as a whole. Ben Bella seemed to have become more popular in his oubliette than ever he had been at the Villa Joly. This was largely a consequence of the inertia which was already beginning to characterise the new regime. Little seemed to be happening in the country itself, and Paris was dissatisfied because the Organisme de Coopération Industrielle was not functioning usefully. Another factor tending to enhance Ben Bella's popularity was the regime's continued use of the heavy hand against intellectuals, and especially against any move towards civil and social emancipation. On March 10, 1966, the police were called in to prevent a walk-out of women from a meeting where Boumedienne had implied in his address that women could not be given equality with men in the allocation of jobs. He warned the women of Algeria 'not to imitate the women of the West. . . . Our society is

Islamic and socialist . . . morality must be respected.' As an editorial in *The Times* remarked on the following day, Algeria was among the African countries that admired the West and Russia for their 'technological prowess', but drew the line at 'the emancipation of women, and the resulting assertion of their personal equality with men'.

Nevertheless, the Boumedienne regime maintained, and even intensified, its lip-service to socialism. At the ceremony in March to inaugurate the third pipeline (to Arzew), foreign guests were met by huge posters displaying socialist slogans. One reason for this fresh asseveration of the regime's 'socialist principles' was the fact that Russia, very discreetly, had recently greatly increased her technical aid to Algeria, especially in the provision of technical experts.

Beneath the apparent calm, however, political intrigues—which had been stigmatised by Boumedienne in his proclamation of June 19, 1965, as a deplorable feature of the Ben Bella era—began to start up again, this time among the colonels who formed part of the National Revolutionary Council. A good many colonels, and more especially regional commanders, had by this time come to the conclusion that Boumedienne had greater need of them than they of him. Never an outstanding political leader, he was finding his authority challenged by his military colleagues. It was even rumoured that Boumedienne might confine himself to more strictly military matters, and once more become 'Number 1a', leaving the ship of state to be steered by civilians. But such a change in the power-structure was strongly opposed by the trio of Bouteflika, Medighri and Cherif Belkacem, who had been responsible for the overthrow of Ben Bella, and who would be the first to suffer if there were any collapse of the new regime. Progress in Algeria continued to be impeded by unresolved political and social questions which overshadowed the whole country.

On July 31, 1965, it was officially estimated that, of Algeria's population of about 10·5 million, no less than 57 per cent were below the age of twenty, and that the urbanisation rate was as high as 6 per cent a year. With so young a population, and with the fervour of leftwing revolution so recently intense in the country, it is not improbable that attempts may be made to establish a more 'revolutionary' Algeria. But it is probable that, for some time to come, at least, the more conservative forces of Boumedienne could control such attempts. It is possible that the large armed forces maintained by Algeria may be unleashed to settle the territorial disputes with Tunisia and, particularly, with Morocco. This possibility will remain as long as Algeria refrains from seeking a political solution to these disputes. Between his coming to power and the time of writing, Boumedienne has shown no sign of seeking a political solution. If the new regime thinks it of over-riding importance to assert itself to the world as 'revolutionary' and 'socialist', the future may possibly see the armed forces of Algeria in action against the remnants of colonial rule in Africa.

Indeed, since the word 'impossible' does not exist in politics, there is still a chance that Ben Bella, as long as he remains alive, may stage a come-back—in which case he would certainly be supported by the more revolutionary elements in Algeria, however much they may have criticised him in the past.

But the strongest probability of all seems to be that Algeria will continue to be France's closest 'client-state'. This may arguably be the best thing for Algeria, though it must entail the continued evaporation of any genuine claim to an Algerian 'socialist revolution'.

APPENDIX I

CHART OF ORIGINS AND DEVELOPMENT
OF ALGERIAN NATIONALISM

NOTES TO CHART

1. OS founder members: Hocine Ait Ahmed, M. Boudiaf, Ben Boulaid, Ben Bella, M. Didouche, R. Bitat, Ben M'Hidi, M. Khider, Belkacem Krim.

2. CRUA: same founder members as for OS.

3. CNRA meetings: 1st, Soummam Valley, Algeria, August 20, 1956; 2nd, Cairo, August 1957; 3rd, Tripoli, Libya, January 13–15, 1960; 4th, Tripoli, August 6–27, 1961; 5th, Tripoli, February 22–26, 1962; 6th, Tripoli, May 27, 1962.

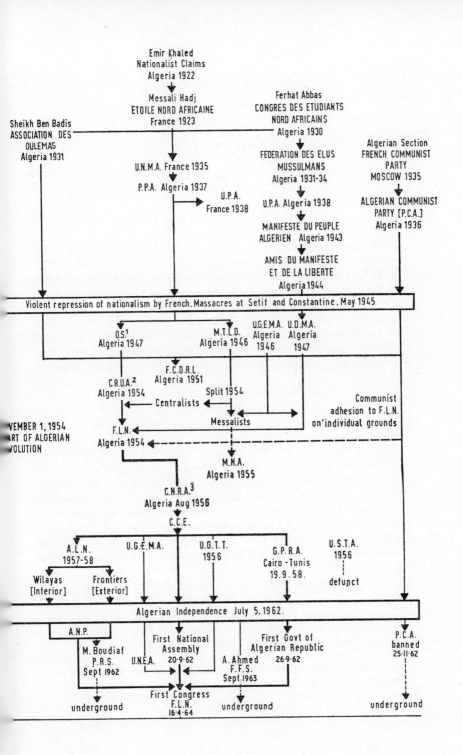

APPENDIX II
COMPOSITION OF ALGERIAN PROVISIONAL AND POST-INDEPENDENCE GOVERNMENTS

FIRST CONSEIL NATIONAL (CNRA)
(August 20, 1956)

Full members: Hocine Ait Ahmed, Abane Ramdane, Ferhat Abbas, Mohammed Boudiaf, Mostefa Ben Boulaid, *Belkacem**, Ahmed Ben Bella, Larbi Ben M'Hidi, Rabah Bitat, Mohammed Khider, Belkacem Krim, Mohammed Lamine Debaghine, *Mokrane*, Amar Ouamrane, Tawfik El-Madani, M'Hammed Yazid, Youssef Zirout.

Substitute members: Aissat, Lakhdari Bentobbal, Abdelhafid Boussouf, Mohammed Ben Yahia, Slimane Dehiles, Ahmed Francis, Mohammedi Said, Brahim Mezhoudi, Ali Mellah, *Mouloud*, *Mourad*, Ahmed Mahsas, Abdelhamid Mahri, Said Saddek, Tayeb Thaalbi, *Zoubir*.

FIRST PROVISIONAL GOVERNMENT (GPRA)
(Tunis-Cairo, September 19, 1958)

President of Council: Ferhat Abbas. *Vice-Presidents:* Belkacem Krim (also responsible for *Armed Forces*), Mohammed (better known as Ahmed) Ben Bella. *Ministers of State:* Hocine Ait Ahmed, Rabah Bitat, Mohammed Boudiaf, Mohammed Khider. *External Affairs:* M. Lamine Debaghine. *Armaments and Supplies:* Cherif Mahmoud. *Interior:* Lakhdari Bentobbal. *General Liaisons and Communications:* Abdelhafid Boussouf. *North African Affairs:* Abdelhamid Mahri. *Economic Affairs and Finance:* Ahmed Francis. *Information:* M'Hammed Yazid. *Social Affairs:* Benyoussef Ben Khedda. *Cultural Affairs:* Tawfik El-Madani. *State Secretaries:* Lamine Khan, Omar Oussedik, Mustafa Stomboli.

SECOND PROVISIONAL GOVERNMENT (GPRA)
(Tripoli, January 18, 1960)

At the same time as the formation of the 2nd GPRA, an 'Interministerial Committee for War' was formed, consisting of Belkacem Krim, Abdelhafid Boussouf and Lakhdari Bentobbal, known as 'the trio'.

* Names in italics are the wartime pseudonyms of personalities who had to remain anonymous.

President of Council: Ferhat Abbas. *Vice-presidents:* Belkacem Krim (also responsible for *External Affairs*), Mohammed Ben Bella. *Ministers of State:* Hocine Ait Ahmed, Rabah Bitat, Mohammed Khider, Mohammedi Said. *Armaments and General Liaisons:* Abdelhafid Boussouf. *Interior:* Lakhdari Bentobbal. *Economic Affairs and Finance:* Ahmed Francis. *Information:* M'Hammed Yazid. *Social and Cultural Affairs:* Abdelhamid Mahri.

THIRD PROVISIONAL GOVERNMENT (GPRA)
(Tripoli, August 27, 1961)

President of Council: Benyoussef Ben Khedda (also responsible for *Finance*. *Vice-presidents:* Belkacem Krim (also responsible for *Interior*), Ahmed Ben Bella, Mohammed Boudiaf. *Ministers of State:* Hocine Ait Ahmed, Lakhdari Bentobbal, Rabah Bitat, Mohammed Khider, Mohammedi Said. *Foreign Affairs:* Saad Dahlab. *Armaments and General Liaisons:* Abdelhafid Boussouf. *Information:* M'Hammed Yazid.

FIRST BEN BELLA GOVERNMENT
(September 27, 1962)

President of Council: Ahmed Ben Bella. *Vice-president:* Rabah Bitat. *Justice:* Amar Bentoumi. *Interior:* Ahmed Medighri. *National Defence:* Houari Boumedienne. *Foreign Affairs:* Mohammed Khemisti. *Finance:* Ahmed Francis. *Agriculture:* Amar Ouzegane. *Trade:* Mohammed Khobzi. *Industry and Power:* Laroussi Khelifa. *Reconstruction, Public Works and Transport:* Ahmed Boumendjel. *Labour and Social Affairs:* Bachir Boumaza. *Education:* Abderrahmane Benhamida. *Health:* Mohammed Seghir Nekkache. *Ex-Mujahidin and War Victims:* Mohammedi Said. *Youth and Sports:* Abdelaziz Bouteflika. *Habus**: Tawfik El-Madani. *Information:* Mohammed Hadj Hamou.

SECOND BEN BELLA GOVERNMENT
(September 18, 1963)

President of Republic and of Council: Ahmed Ben Bella. *Vice-presidents o Council:* Houari Boumedienne (also responsible for *National Defence*), Mohammedi Said, Rabah Bitat.† *Minister of State:* Amar Ouzegane. *Justice:* Mohammed Hadj Smain. *Interior:* Ahmed Medighri. *Foreign Affairs:* Abdelaziz Bouteflika. *Economy:* Bachir Boumaza. *Agriculture:* Ali Mahsas. *Reconstruction:* Ahmed Boumendjel. *Social Affairs:* Mohammed Seghir Nekkache. *Education:* Cherif Belkacem. *Habus:* Tawfik El-Madani. *Posts and Telecommunications:* Abdelkader Zaibek.

* Religious Endowments.
† Resigned next day, September 19.

Tourism: Ahmed Kaid (Commander Slimane). *State under-secretary for Youth and Sports:* Sadek Batel.

THIRD BEN BELLA GOVERNMENT
(December 12, 1964)

President of Republic and of Council:* Ahmed Ben Bella. *Vice-presidents of Council:* Houari Boumedienne (also responsible for *National Defence*), Mohammedi Said. *Minister delegated to Council Presidency:* Abderrahmane Cherif. *Justice:* Mohammed Bedjaoui. *Foreign Affairs:* Abdelaziz Bouteflika. *Agriculture:* Ali Mahsas. *Trade:* Noureddine Dellici. *Industry and Power:* Bachir Boumaza. *Reconstruction and Housing:* Mohammed Hadj Smain. *Labour:* Safi Boudissa. *Health, ex-Mujahidin and Social Affairs:* Mohammed Seghir Nekkache. *Education:* Cherif Belkacem. *Youth and Sports:* Sadek Batel. *Habus:* Tedjani Haddam. *Posts and Telecommunications, Public Works and Transport:* Abdelkader Zaibek. *Administrative Reform and Public Function:* Said Amrani. *Tourism:* Amar Ouzegane. *State under-secretary for Public Works:* Ahmed Ghozali.

BOUMEDIENNE GOVERNMENT
(July 10, 1965)

President of Council: Houari Boumedienne† (also responsible for *National Defence*). *Minister of State:* Rabah Bitat. *Justice:* Mohammed Bedjaoui.† *Interior:* Ahmed Medighri. *Foreign Affairs:* Abdelaziz Bouteflika.† *Finance:* Ahmed Kaid. *Agriculture:* Ali Mahsas.† *Trade:* Noureddine Dellici.† *Industry and Power:* Belaid Abdessalam. *Reconstruction and Housing:* Mohammed Hadj Smain.† *Public Works:* Abdennour Ali Yahia. *Labour:* Abdelaziz Zerdani. *Education:* Ahmed Taleb. *Health:* Tedjani Haddam.† *Ex-Mujahidin:* Boualem Ben Hamouda. *Youth and Sports:* Abdelkrim Ben Mahmoud. *Habus:* Larbi Saadouni. *Posts and Telecommunications:* Abdelkader Zaibek.† *Tourism:* Abdelaziz Maaoui. *Information:* Bachir Boumaza.†

---

* Attached to the Bureau of the President of the Council were the following General Directorates: *Interior* (directly under Ben Bella), *Information* (Salah Louanchi), *Finance* (Smail Mahroug), *Plan and Economic Studies* (M. Temam), *Legislation* (Ayache Benadjila). The 'chefs de cabinet' in the Ministries were disbanded, Ben Bella's Bureau nominating the secretary-general of each Ministry.

† Indicates membership of previous Ben Bella government.

APPENDIX III
ECONOMIC AND SOCIAL STATISTICS

Table 1

REGIONAL DISTRIBUTION OF ALGERIAN
INDIGENOUS POPULATION, 1963

Département	Population in 000s
Algiers	1,207·8
Titteri	809·1
El-Asnam	727·8
Greater Kabilya	807·4
Constantine	1,448·7
Annaba (formerly Bône)	749·9
Aurès	607·8
Sétif	1,156·7
Oran	706·2
Mostaganem	702·0
Saida	200·3
Tiaret	333·5
Tlemcen	383·8
Oasis	442·0
Saoura (Sahara)	170·6

Total population, excluding workers abroad: 10,453,600

Table 2

SOCIAL STRUCTURE OF THE INDIGENOUS POPULATION
(based on a UN report for 1964)

Sector	Population in 000s	
Urban:		
Active	1,200·0	
Non-active	2,150·0	
Total Urban Population		3,350·0

Sector	Population in 000s	
Rural:		
(i) Agricultural population		
Active	2,675·0	
Non-active	3,325·0	
Total agricultural population		6,000·0
(ii) Non-agricultural population		
Active	300·0	
Non-active	800·0	
Total non-agricultural population		1,100·0
Total rural population		7,100·0
Total population of Algeria		10,450·0

Of the active agricultural population, 2,100,000 are in the tradition sector and 575,000 in the modern sector, of whom 375,000 are seasonal workers and 200,000 are permanent workers. To the figures given in the Table should be added some 1,700,000 million Algerian workers abroad.

Table 3

UNEMPLOYMENT AND UNDEREMPLOYMENT OF THE
ACTIVE LABOUR FORCE

(figures based on a UN Report for 1964)

Sector	Persons	Equivalent Man-Years
Urban	800,000	800,000
Rural		
(i) Non-agricultural	250,000	250,000
(ii) Agricultural, traditional sector	2,100,000	1,596,000
(iii) Agricultural, modern sector	375,000	225,000
Totals	3,525,000	2,871,000

Table 4

MANPOWER REQUIREMENTS (AGRICULTURE) 1965–69

Estimates of the Algerian Ministry of Agriculture

		Personnel	Teachers
I. *Technical and Administrative Services*			
1. Monitors	3,250		60
technical services		1,000	
forestry		1,000	
rural engineers		1,000	
plant protection		250	
2. Technical Agents	3,000		50
technical services		600	
forestry		600	
rural engineers		600	
ONRA		600	
plant protection		300	
veterinary services		300	
3. Technical Assistants	1,400		70
technical services		300	
forestry		300	
rural engineers		300	
ONRA		300	
plant protection		100	
veterinary services		100	
4. Agricultural Engineers	755		60
technical services		145	
forestry		145	
rural engineers		145	
ONRA		145	
plant protection		30	
veterinary services		145	
Totals	8,405		240
II. *Socialist and Co-operative Farms*			
1. Tractor Drivers	12,000		60
2. Forestry, Vine, Irrigation Specialists	5,500		30

II. *Socialist and Co-operative Farms—continued*

3. Accountants	4,500	25
4. Farm Managers	2,600	50
5. Animal Husbandrymen	2,400	30
6. Mechanics	1,000	90
7. Food Processing Specialists	400	5
Totals	28,400	290

Table 5

ALGERIAN EXPORTS TO FRANCE

(in million French francs, c.i.f.)

	1960	1961	1962	1963
Food Products	1,672·8	1,555·6	1,677·7	1,071·2
Cereals and by-products	*46·9*	*33·3*	*10·0*	*26·3*
of which:				
semolina and ground cereals —wheat flour excepted	*45·5*	*29·9*	*6·9*	*20·6*
Fruit and vegetables	*370·7*	*392·0*	*429·9*	*405·3*
of which:				
fresh fruits	*196·7*	*256·8*	*269·5*	*277·7*
fresh vegetables	*148·7*	*106·0*	*126·1*	*88·3*
canned vegetables	*25·3*	*29·2*	*32·3*	*39·3*
Alcoholic beverages	*1,174·5*	*1,041·6*	*1,167·7*	*570·0*
of which:				
wines	*1,169·0*	*1,039·6*	*1,152·7*	*564·3*
Mineral fuels, lubricants and connected products	694·2	1,179·9	1,394·5	1,587·7
of which:				
crude petroleum	*693·6*	*1,155·0*	*1,300·3*	*1,511·0*
Other products	167·8	194·7	175·8	157·9
Totals	2,534·8	2,930·2	3,248·0	2,816·8

Table 6

ALGERIAN IMPORTS FROM FRANCE

(in million French francs, f.o.b.)

	1960	1961	1962	1963
Food products	1,129·0	1,145·4	823·5	610·0
of which:				
livestock	*52·4*	*49·3*	*31·2*	*47·9*
fresh meat	*87·7*	*106·1*	*75·8*	*44·1*
canned meat and fish	*73·2*	*66·5*	*36·8*	*12·8*
dairy produce	*152·3*	*186·9*	*136·2*	*102·3*
cereals	*140·6*	*78·6*	*48·9*	*26·6*
sugar and by-products	*198·9*	*218·5*	*192·9*	*184·2*
oleaginous products	*11·4*	*29·0*	*37·8*	*55·9*
Mineral fuels, lubricants and connected products	388·1	372·1	229·6	215·8
Other products	3,878·1	2,858·6	1,730·9	1,911·2
of which:				
chemical goods	*131·5*	*131·9*	*78·9*	*77·7*
natural and artificial textiles	*321·5*	*256·2*	*202·6*	*205·4*
iron and steel products	*534·2*	*408·4*	*202·6*	*226·4*
boilers and machinery	*456·6*	*292·8*	*165·8*	*261·8*
electrical machinery	*250·1*	*210·1*	*134·0*	*133·6*
cars and bicycles	*531·1*	*274·1*	*140·4*	*199·0*
garments (furs excepted)	*261·3*	*187·4*	*136·5*	*163·3*
Totals	5,395·2	4,376·1	2,784·0	2,737·0

Table 7

ALGERIAN STATE BUDGET FOR 1964

	Algerian Dinars (equivalent to French francs)
Presidency of the Republic	40,854,754
First Vice-President and Ministry for National Defence	493,801,104
Second Vice-President	156,600
State Ministry	156,600
Ministry of Justice	47,562,806
Ministry of Interior	264,802,120

Ministry of National Economy:
Ordinary expenditure	255,926,971
Financial services	90,684,867
Ministry of Agriculture	91,155,000
Ministry of National Orientation (Education)	622,154,060
Ministry of Social Affairs	528,529,900
Ministry of Foreign Affairs	47,107,665
Ministry of Reconstruction, Public Works and Transport	133,993,303
Ministry of 'Habus' (Religious Affairs)	14,702,900
Ministry of Tourism	20,605,163
Ministry of Posts and Telegraphs	213,218,646

The Ministry for Defence received additional resources not shown in the budget.

Table 8

SOURCES OF NATIONAL INCOME

(in million French francs)

	1959	1963
Agriculture	2,750	2,200
Industry and Public Works	2,750	2,400
Services	5,500	3,800
Totals	11,000	8,400

Table 9

STUDENTS IN DIFFERENT FACULTIES OF THE UNIVERSITY OF ALGIERS NOVEMBER 1954

	All Students	Europeans	Algerians	Foreigners
Law	1,713	1,528	179	6
Medicine	824	714	110	—
Pharmacy	427	369	34	24
Arts	1,347	1,175	172	—
Sciences	835	762	62	11
Totals	5,146	4,548	557	41

Table 10

POSITION OF THE TEACHING CORPS
MARCH 1964

	All Teachers	Algerians	French	Arab Nationals	Foreigners
Primary	27,919	16,078	9,900	1,932	9
Colleges	1,248	545	659	44	—
Ecoles Normales	101	40	54	7	—
Lycées, classical and modern	1,235	595	563	77	—
Technical schools	1,391	694	674	23	—
Arab lycées	44	18	6	14	6
Technical lycées	190	19	163	—	8
Teacher Training Schools	24	2	16	6	—
Higher education	574	325	239	2	8
Totals	32,726	18,316	12,274	2,105	31
Administration	847	755	89	2	1
Information	187	186	—	—	1
Youth and Sports	2,969	2,797	159	—	13
Grand Totals	36,729	22,054	12,522	2,107	46

Table 11

ALGERIANISATION OF THE TEACHING CORPS

	Pre-1962%	1963-64%
Primary	15	58
Inspectors, primary	5	95
Secondary	2	46
Technical	16	n.a.
Higher	5	n.a.

Table 12

ADMINISTRATIVE AND TECHNICAL PERSONNEL IN SAHARAN OIL AND GAS INDUSTRY

(Based on Jeanne Favrer's *Socio-Economie des Départements Sahariens : Eléments d'études—Problèmes Humains,* 1964)

Grade	Total Employed	French No.	%	Algerian No.	%	Existing	Posts Vacant	Left
Administrative								
Senior								
Executives	28	27	96·4	1	3·6	30	2	29
Executives	124	117	94·4	7	5·6	128	4	121
Senior Clerical	450	381	84·7	69	15·3	482	32	413
Clerical	1,255	361	28·8	894	71·2	1,344	89	450
Totals	1,857	886	47·7	971	52·3	1,984	127	1,013
Technical								
Management	69	69	100·0	—	—	71	2	71
Executive	348	348	100·0	—	—	389	41	389
Foremen	1,407	1,309	93·0	98	7·0	1,746	69	1,378
Skilled and								
Unskilled								
Operatives	4,758	1,100	23·1	3,658	76·9	4,872	114	1,214
Totals	6,582	2,826	42·9	3,756	57·1	6,808	226	3,052
Grand Totals	8,439	3,712	44·0	4,727	56·0	8,792	353	4,065

Table 13

PRODUCTION OF CRUDE OIL
(million tons)

Companies	1960	1961	1962	1963	1964	1965 (est.)
CREPS	1,927	6,702	9,941	10,486	10,986	10,100
SN REPAL	4,271	4,877	5,506	6,562	7,318	7,216
CFP (Algeria)	2,372	3,321	3,670	4,882	4,938	5,359
Sinclair			587	182	1,010	1,170
CEP		288	750	856	921	1,289
SNPA	23	466		1,116	714	800
COPEFA				11	230	420
EURAFREP			31	38	102	130
Totals	8,593	15,654	20,485	24,133	26,219	26,484

APPENDIX IV
THE ALGERIAN PRESS

All the press organs of the colonial era disappeared at independence when a 'national press' was instituted. *L'Echo d'Alger*, founded in 1911, was suppressed by a decree of April 1962, and so were the *Journal d'Alger* (also in April), *Oran Républicain* (July) and *La Dépêche de Bône* (December). On September 17, 1963, coinciding with a political crisis with France, Algeria nationalised *L'Echo d'Oran* (founded in 1844), *La Dépêche de Constantine* and *La Dépêche d'Algérie*. The suppression of this latter was not without repercussions since it was, albeit French-owned, the most widely read daily paper in the country, its better journalistic techniques putting it streets ahead of the newly established official papers. There were protests from the International Institute of Journalists but these proved of little avail because the suppression of *La Dépêche d'Algérie* aroused little popular sympathy. Its editorial policy had made a remarkable switch from being pro-colonial to supporting Ben Bella. It can now be disclosed that the French ambassador, M. Gorce, knowing of the coming nationalisation of the paper, had asked Ben Bella only a few days earlier to inform him of the move in good time so that he could 'take care of the inevitable protests which would ensue'. When it was so abruptly nationalised Gorce complained to the foreign minister, Bouteflika, not of the act itself but of his not being 'warned beforehand as agreed'. Bouteflika smilingly replied that 'this should then make the (Franco-Algerian) crisis look even more serious'. The modern premises and printing facilities of *La Dépêche d'Algérie* were handed over to the official FLN organ, *Le Peuple*: a very poor affair which was eventually abandoned after having swallowed up a great deal of money. The main gainer from the suppression was the more articulate *Alger Républicain*, a communist organ.

As was noted in chapter 5, the birth of the 'national press' in Algeria was most unimpressive, and was accomplished in circumstances which did not encourage it to conform to the minimum internationally accepted code of journalistic ethics and standards.

APPENDIX IV

APS: Algérie Presse Service; Algeria Press Service. Mohammed Yazid, minister of Information of the GPRA, found it convenient to use both French and English titles. The APS was founded in Tunis in 1961. After a year or so of interruptions, it was started up again, also in Tunis, by Mohammed Ben Mehal. At independence, Mehal managed, under extremely difficult conditions, to make a real go of it by arranging with Reuters for foreign news coverage. This was negotiated against fierce opposition from the Czech news agency, CTK, which specialises in providing journalistic material and personnel for emergent countries. Agence France Presse was also, of course, strongly opposed to the deal with Reuters. It is to the credit of British journalism that Reuters was preferred; this agency enjoys a world wide reputation for political independence in comparison with most other European news agencies. Agence France Presse in the end managed to sell its services to the APS, but only after agreeing—as Reuters had already done—that its news material would not carry its own credit-lines. Mehal, who strove to maintain some degree of journalistic independence, was eventually dismissed by Ben Bella.

DAILIES

An Shaab ('The People'; Arabic): appeared first on December 11, 1962 as the Arabic version of *Le Peuple*, though not a mere translation of the latter. It survived the closure of *Le Peuple* (*q.v.*).

Alger Ce Soir (French): initiated in 1964 by Serge Michel as an evening paper, similar in style to the old Paris communist daily, *Ce Soir*. It has had an irregular existence and its fate looked all the more uncertain when Boumedienne took over. Its editor, S. Michel, is a Frenchman who has long worked for the Algerians and was lent by them for a time to Lumumba.

Alger Républicain (Fr.): this is the organ of the Algerian Communist Party (PAC). Founded in 1938, it was suspended by the French authorities in 1940 but reappeared in 1942 with the permission of the Allied powers who had landed in North Africa. It was again banned by the French in 1955 for its role as official daily of the PAC. It saw the light again on July 18, 1962, its type set in the printery of a communist daily in Marseilles and off-printed in Algiers. Henri Alleg, Boualem Khalfa and Abdelhamid Benzine, assisted by P. Lambitte of *Humanité*, did wonders in producing this paper single-handed. While editors of *Le Peuple* were buzzing about in cars carrying the name of their paper—but nothing yet off the press—*Alger Républicain* was out on the streets, selling copies like hot cakes. At a diplomatic reception in 1963, a British diplomatist gave a bad shock to a newly arrived official of the American embassy who asked him for advice about 'what paper to read here'. The Foreign Office man without hesitation said '*Alger Républicain*, of course.' 'But that's the communist paper!' 'Yes, of course, I know. It's still the best paper!' Indeed, it was the best newspaper that has yet appeared in Algeria, with a daily circulation—a record for Algeria—of some 30,000 copies. This soared to 70,000 when *La Dépêche d'Algérie* disappeared, but sales fell as the PAC began to identify itself with Ben Bella. *Alger Républicain* survived the banning of the PAC by Ben Bella, but it had to become increasingly servile, and thereby lost much of its original appeal. In 1965 it was amalgamated with the new daily, *El Moudjahid* (*q.v.*).

An Nasr ('Victory'; Fr.): this is the main newspaper in eastern Algeria. It first appeared on September 28, 1963 following the nationalisation of *La Dépêche de Constantine*.

El Moudjahid ('Fighter for the Faith'; Fr.): the official daily of the FLN, first published on June 24, 1965. It was born from the fusion of *Le Peuple* and *Alger Républicain*. (See also the weekly paper of the same name.)

La République—El Djoumhouriya (Fr.): the main publication in western Algeria. Starting as an illustrated weekly, it became a weekly in March 1963, taking over the premises and printery of *Oran Républicain*.

Le Peuple (Fr.): the official organ of the FLN, founded on August 21, 1962. Initially it carried the Arabic name, *An Shaab*, but adopted the French title on March 21, 1963, *An Shaab* becoming a separate Arabic edition (*q.v.*). Its personnel, especially its director and editor-in-chief, was changed several times. It never attained more than 3,000 copies circulation despite its being heavily subsidised by the government and party. In October 1963 it launched a Sunday edition, *Le Peuple Hebdomadaire*, which changed its name to *Dimanche Le Peuple* in 1964. On party orders, *Le Peuple*, together with *Alger Républicain*, ceased publication in June 1965 in favour of the new official daily, *El Moudjahid*. Although the fusion of these two papers was decided on under Ben Bella, with the understanding that the personnel of *Alger Républicain* would play a leading part in *El Moudjahid*, the actual amalgamation took place under Boumedienne who made sure that the communist editors were kept away from the new official journal.

WEEKLIES

Al Djazairin ('The Algerian'; Fr.): published twice a week in Paris; the official publication of Algerian emigrants in Europe.

Hebdo-Coopération (Fr.): organ of French residents in Algeria. It first appeared as *Journal des Français en Algérie*, and than as *Coopération*.

El Hourriya ('Liberty'; Fr. and Ar.): weekly organ of the PAC, it disappeared when the latter was banned by Ben Bella.

El Moudjahid (Fr.): the official ideological organ of the FLN throughout the war of independence. It first appeared, clandestinely and irregularly, in 1956. From 1959 it was published more regularly and in June 1960 started normal weekly publication from Tunis. Its editor-in-chief was then Rehda Malek, one of the framers of the Tripoli Programme and after independence Algerian ambassador, first in Belgrade and later in Paris. During the war *El Moudjahid* was followed very closely both by Algerians and by foreign observers, but after independence its status and interest diminished. In mid-1963 it was discontinued in favour of *Révolution Africaine* (*q.v.*). The complete collection, in three volumes, of the issues of *El Moudjahid* is considered by students of Algerian affairs to be an indispensable source.

Al Mujahid (Ar.): this Arabic version continues to appear. At times, after independence, it was dominated by a group of young pro-Ba'ath socialists, including Bahi Mohammed, a Moroccan and a special correspondent of the UNFP organ, *Al Tahrir*.

Jeunesse (Fr.): the organ of the Jeunesse FLN. It first appeared in August 1964 but disappeared after the coup of June 19, 1965. Its editor, Boualem Makhouf, also head of the Jeunesse FLN, was arrested in August 1965.

Journal Officiel de la République Algérienne Démocratique et Populaire (Fr. and Ar.): since May 1964 the official gazette of the government. It appears several times a week.

Révolution Africaine (Fr.): this controversial publication was founded after independence by Jacques Vergès, a French communist lawyer who had defended Algerians during the war. Its aim was to spread revolution to the whole of the African continent. Vergès—whose position was akin to that of Rabah Bitat, then opposed to Ben Bella—had to leave Algeria for Europe where he edited the overtly pro-Chinese *Révolution*. Some confusion was created when another publication, *Revolution in Africa* (allegedly supporting China and claiming to be printed in Tirana, Albania) started to appear in Africa after Vergés *Révolution* ran into financial difficulties, due, it seems, to the Chinese deciding they no longer needed it. *Revolution in Africa* was too provocatively pro-Chinese and both Peking and Tirana denounced it as 'a fake'. *The Spark*, Nkrumah's ideological weekly, asserted in its issue of August 27, 1965 that *Revolution in Africa* was 'prepared by the CIA in Brussels'.

Révolution Africaine assumed major importance under Mohammed Harbi, for a time Ben Bella's principal, and very influential, marxist adviser. When army pressure ousted Harbi from the editorship, Amar Ouzegane took it over, making it the organ of an ill-defined 'Arabo-socialism'. The paper had already lost much of its appeal when Ouzegane in his turn was ousted by the army. Editorial control was given 'to the party' in September 1965. For a time *Révolution Africaine* published a quarterly English-language digest.

OTHER PERIODICALS

Actualités et Documents (Fr., Ar., and Eng.): published fortnightly by the Ministry of National Orientation in Algiers.

Al Jamahir ('The Masses'; Ar.): published at irregular intervals in Constantine, it ceased publication in February 1963.

Al Ma'Arifa ('Knowledge'; Ar.): muslim religious publication issued by the Ministry of Habus.

Aujourd'hui (Fr.): catholic monthly, first appearing at the end of December 1962 and published by Pierre Le Boult.

*Bulletin Economique et Juridique de l'*OFALAC (Fr.): started in 1938, it began anew in September 1963. It represents the views of the Office Algérien d'Action Commerciale; published by Guy Fethi.

*Bulletin d'Information de l'*ASFA (Fr.): organ of the Association pour l'Amitié et la Solidarité Franco-Algérienne. First published in November 1963.

Bulletin Mensuel de Statistique Générale (Fr.): published by the Statistics section of the official Direction Générale du Plan et Etudes Economiques.

Caritas Presse (Fr.): organ of the catholic Caritas Association.

Al Ahrar ('Free Men': Ar.): published very irregularly in Constantine after independence. It caused much trouble with neighbouring Tunisia since it publicised the views of Chouchon and Ben Tobbal, two prominent exiled opponents of Bourguiba. *Al Ahrar* soon disappeared.

El Djeich ('The Army'; Fr.): fortnightly organ of the ANP. It has assumed greater importance since the coup of summer 1965. Since 1963 it has been edited by the political commissariat of the ANP. Up to July 1965 it appeared monthly. Since then, reflecting army opinion, it has become a twice-monthly political and cultural review, appearing in colour on glossy paper and with many pictures.

Fichier de Documentation Berbère (Fr.): publishes linguistic studies by the Centre d'Etudes Berbères in Algiers.

Information Rapide (Fr.): social, economic and cultural news published by the Secretariat Social d'Alger.

Jeune Algérien (Fr.): organ of the Amicale Générale de la Jeunesse Algérienne in Paris.

L'Algérie dans le Monde (Fr.): published by the Bureau National pour l'Assistance Non-gouvernementale à l'Algérie in Algiers.

L'Ecole Algérienne (Fr.): organ of the Syndicat Algérien de l'Enseignement in Algiers.

Révolution et Travail (Fr.): official organ of UGTA, it appeared first on March 1, 1963, taking over from *L'Ouvrier Algérien* which had been banned by Ben Bella.

Révolution á l'Université—At Thawra fil Jamia (Fr. and Ar.); first published on November 10, 1962 by UGEMA.

Revue de Presse (Fr.): a review of Arab newspapers.

Semaines Réligieuses: official publication of the catholic diocese of Algiers, Oran and Constantine.

NOTES AND REFERENCES

Publication details of works cited, where not given here, will be found in the Select Bibliography.

INTRODUCTION

1. Serge Bromberger, *Les Rebelles Algériens*, 1958, p. 9. Rejected at the time by the left as a 'rightwing' analysis, the views of Bromberger, a correspondent of *Le Figaro*, have been justified by events.
2. Gilles Martinet, 'Les Frères Ennemis', *France-Observateur*, July 5, 1962.
3. E. F. Gautier, cited in Charles-André Julien, *Histoire de l'Afrique du Nord*, Vol. I: *Des Origines à la Conquête Arabe*, 1961, p. 28.
4. Bromberger, *op. cit.*, p. 9.

CHAPTER I

1. Cf. *L'Etat Algérien avant 1830*, Editions Résistance Algérienne: an undated pamphlet issued during the war on behalf of the Front de Libération Nationale (FLN).
2. *La Charte d'Algers : Ensemble des Textes adoptés par le premier congrès du Parti du Front de Libération Nationale;* published in 1964 by the FLN's Commission Centrale d'Orientation.
3. Cf. Charles-André Julien, *Histoire de l'Afrique du Nord*, Vol. II: *De la Conquête Arabe à 1830* (1961); and also his *Histoire de l'Algérie Contemporaine*, Vol. I: *La Conquête et les Débuts de la Colonisation 1827–1871* (1964).
4. Jean Despois, *L'Afrique Blanche*, Vol. I: *L'Afrique du Nord*, 1964, p. x.
5. *Ibid.*, p. x.
6. Abdelaziz Benabdellah, *Les Grands Courants de la Civilisation du Maghreb*, 1958, p. 47.
7. E.-F. Gautier, cited in Julien, *Des Origines* . . .
8. Cited in *L'Etat Algérien avant 1830*, p. 8.
9. Julien, *De la Conquête Arabe* . . ., p. 113.
10. Robert Mantran, 'Les Données de l'histoire moderne et contemporaine de l'Algérie et de la Tunisie: Notes pour une étude plus approfondie', *Annuaire d'Afrique du Nord*, Vol. I, 1962.

11. The author is grateful for information on this aspect given him by Othman Kaak, Attarin Conservator of the Tunisian National Library.
12. Cf. *Révolution Africaine*, July 4, 1964, for a study by Marx of this this subject; published, it is claimed, for the first time.
13. A. Khaldi, *Le Problème Algérien devant la Conscience Démocratique*, 1946.
14. Mantran, *op. cit.*, p. 244.
15. Cited in Julien, . . . *Algérie Contemporaine*, Vol. I, 1964, p. 55.
16. *Ibid.*, p. 91.
17. Khaldi, *op. cit.*, p. 12.
18. *Ibid.*, p. 25.
19. P. Chalmin, *L'Officier français de 1815 à 1870*, cited in Mostefa Lacheraf, *L'Algérie : Nation et Société*, 1963, p. 225.
20. Khaldi, *op. cit.*, p. 48.
21. Cited by Charles-Henri Favrod, *Le FLN et l'Algérie*, 1962. This book is one of the major works on the Algerian revolution.
22. *Révolution Africaine*, September 12, 1964.
23. Cited by Favrod, *op. cit.*, p. 73.
24. Malek Bennabi, *Les Conditions de la Renaissance Algérienne*, 1949, p. 18.
25. *Ibid.*, p. 23.
26. *Ibid.*, p. 13.
27. Khaldi, *op. cit.*, p. 62.

CHAPTER 2

1. Personal accounts of the events of November 1, 1954 can be found in *Révolution Africaine*, November 2, 1963.
2. Cited in Jacques Duchemin, *Histoire du FLN*, 1962. A most interesting book, quite obviously based on official French military sources.
3. Favrod, *op. cit.*, p. 102.
4. *Cf.* André Mandouze (ed.), *La Révolution Algérienne par les Textes*, 1961.
5. Cited in Favrod, *op. cit.*, p. 231.

CHAPTER 3

1. Favrod, *op. cit.*, p. 96.

CHAPTER 5

1. Malcom Kerr, *The Arab Cold War 1958–1964* (1965), p. 69.
2. Cf. *Actualités et Documents*, No. 53, April 4, 1965; an official publication of the Ministry of Information in Algiers.
3. Robert Merle, *Ahmed Ben Bella*, 1965.

CHAPTER 6

1. Jean Lacouture, 'L'après Ben Bellisme', *Le Monde*, July 13, 1963.
2. Gérard Chalian, *L'Algérie, est-elle Socialiste?*, 1964, p. 94.
3. Mostefa Lacheraf, *L'Algérie : Nation et Société*, 1963, p. 13.
4. Cited in *Economie et Politique : Revue Marxiste d'Economie*, No. 130, March 1965.
5. Mohammed Harbi, 'The Party and the State', an address reproduced in *Révolution Africaine*, November 7, 1964.
6. Cf. Harbi, 'Les Fusils de la Colère: Ceux qui soutiennent le Pouvoir veulent les Armes', *Révolution Africaine*, June 13, 1964.
7. *Révolution Africaine*, March 21, 1964.
8. Interview published in *Jeune Afrique*, July 6, 1965.

CHAPTER 7

1. Cf. *Développement Industriel en Afrique : Situations et Perspectives*, E/CN 14/INRI: a study of the United Nations General Secretariat's Economic Commission for Africa, Addis Ababa 1964.
2. This 'co-belligerence' is dealt with in a thesis submitted to the University of Belgrade in 1964 by the Yugoslav writer and journalist, Zdravko Peccar. Unfortunately, there is as yet no translation of Peccar's work available.
3. How Bourguiba and the Neo-Destour were able to create a modern state in a country where previously hardly any organised society had existed is well explained by Jean Duvigneaud; see especially his *Classes et Conscience de Classe dans un pays du Maghreb : La Tunisie*, Presses Universitaires, Paris 1964; and *Tunisie*, Editions Rencontres, Lausanne 1965.
4. Jean Lacouture, 'En Attendant le Maghreb Uni', *Europe, France, Outremer*, Paris, August-September 1963.
5. Mohammed Boudiaf, *Où va l'Algérie?*, 1964, p. 140.
6. Figures extracted from statistics in *Europe, France, Outremer*, No. 419, Paris 1964.
7. Philippe Herreman, *Le Monde Diplomatique*, January 1965.

CHAPTER 8

1. *Révolution Africaine*, October 12, 1963.
2. Seydou Badian, *Les Dirigeants Africains face à leur Peuple*, 1964, p. 10.
3. *The Times*, September 11, 1965.
4. *Humanité*, November 9, 1954.
5. Favrod, *op. cit.*, p. 298.

6. Cf. *Le Communiste*, No. 113, October–November 1965. This organ of 'La Tendance Révolutionaire du PCF'—a splinter group of French communists—denounced in considerable detail the past and present attitudes of the PCF towards Algeria.
7. Amar Ouzegane, *Le Meilleur Combat*, 1962, p. 185.
8. Statement to Prensa Latina, the Cuban news agency, reproduced by the Algerian press and radio.
9. Bachir Hadj Ali, *Qu'est-ce qu'un Révolutionnaire Algérien en 1963?*, Editions Sociales, Paris, undated.
10. Quoted from a confidential French report of 1963.
11. *Révolution Africaine*, May 23, 1964.
12. *Ibid.*
13. French report of 1963, *op. cit.*
14. Cited in David Morison, *The USSR and Africa*, 1964, p. 76.

CHAPTER 9

1. The Jeanneney Report: *La Politique de Coopération avec les Pays en voie de Développement—Rapport et Annexes;* findings of the study commission set up under the auspices of the Ministry of State responsible for administrative reform; published by Documentation Française, Paris 1964.
2. Cf., for example, the following publications of the Organisme Saharien in Algiers: *Annexes Techniques; Revue d'Information; Agriculture et Elevage*, June 1964; *Equipement Public*, June 1964; *Mines et Hydrocarbures*, June 1964; *Problèmes Humains* by Jeanne Favret, June 1964.
3. Cf. *Pétrole Information*, No. 396, July 20, 1965.

CHAPTER 10

1. *Jeune Afrique*, July 11, 1965.
2. Eric Rouleau, 'Après l'Eviction de Ben Bella . . .', *Le Monde*, July 9, 1965.
3. Colin McDougall, *Far Eastern Economic Review*, Hong Kong, September 9, 1965.

CHAPTER 11

1. *Révolution Africaine*, September 12, 1964.
2. *Ibid.*, December 12, 1964.
3. Fadela M'Rabet, *La Femme Algérienne*, 1965.
4. *Le Monde*, August 15, 1965.
5. *El Moudjahid*, September 28, 1965.
6. *Ibid.*

7. *Le Monde*, September 12, 1965.
8. 'La Question Ininterrompue', *Le Monde*, September 29, 1965.
9. *Ibid.*
10. *Journal Officiel*, December 18, 1965.
11. Cf. *Aurore*, December 15, 1965.
12. Cf. *Al Ahram*, October 10, 1965.
13. *Jeune Afrique*, December 26, 1965.
14. Cf. Jean Teillac, *Autogestion en Algérie*, 1965.
15. For an estimate of the size and equipment of Algeria's armed forces, see *Africa 1965*, July 2, 1965 (London). Edited by Richard Kershaw, *Africa 1965*—continued as *Africa 1966*—is one of the best of the specialist sources on African affairs north and south of the Sahara.
16. Cf. *Africa 1965*, October 21, 1965.
17. *Le Monde*, September 19–20, 1965.
18. French Senate debate, November 5, 1965.
19. French National Assembly debate, October 16, 1965.
20. *El Moudjahid*, November 30, 1965.
21. *Le Monde*, November 10, 1965.

SELECT BIBLIOGRAPHY

NOTE ON SOURCES

With the exception of books dealing with history, works listed below have provided the background material rather than the substance of this survey of post-independence Algeria, since the author has relied essentially on his own journalistic notes and observations. The *Annuaire d'Afrique du Nord*, published by the Centre des Recherches sur l'Afrique Méditerranéenne—a section of the Centre National de la Recherche Scientifique—is certain to prove an invaluable source for future students of North African affairs. Unfortunately, little use could be made in this study of Volumes I and II because they came late into the author's hands, and concern only the years 1962 and 1963.

Newspapers, periodicals and documents have been examined in the course of preparing the book. They are indicated in the Notes and References section or in footnotes. Particular mention should be made of *Le Monde* (no one can claim to follow or understand Algerian affairs without the aid of this remarkable newspaper) and of the various publications of the Organisme Technique de Mise en Valeur des Richesses du Sous-Sol Saharien (abbreviated to OTS). Without these it is impossible to have any proper understanding of the Algerian Sahara.

ALLEG, Henri, *La Question*, Editions de Minuit, Paris 1958. Published in English as *The Question*, Braziller, New York 1958.

Annuaire de l'Afrique du Nord, Vol. I, 1962, Vol. II, 1963, Le Centre des Recherches sur l'Afrique Méditerranéenne, Editions du Centre National de la Recherche Scientifique, Paris.

BADIAN, Seydou, *Les Dirigeants Africains face à leur Peuple*, Editions Maspero, Paris 1964.

BEDJAOUI, Mohammed, *La Révolution Algérienne et le Droit*, Association Internationale des Juristes Démocrates, Brussels 1961.

BEHR, Edward, *The Algerian Problem*, Hodder and Stoughton, London 1961; Norton, New York 1962.

BENABDELLAH, Abdelaziz, *Les Grands Courants de la Civilisation du Maghreb*, Imprimerie du Midi, Casablanca 1958.

BENNABI, Malek, *Les Conditions de la Renaissance Algérienne*, Editions En-Nadha, Algiers 1949.

BERGHEAUD, Edmond, *Le Premier Quart d'Heure*, Plon, Paris 1964.

BERQUE, Jacques, *Les Arabes d'Hier à Demain*, Editions du Seuil, Paris 1962. Published in English as *The Arabs*, Faber, London; Praeger, New York 1964.

—— *Le Maghreb entre deux Guerres*, Editions du Seuil, Paris 1962. Published in English as *French North Africa : The Maghrib Between Two World Wars*, Faber, London; Praeger, New York 1966.

BROMBERGER, Serge, *Les Rebelles Algériens*, Plon, Paris 1958.

BOUDIAF, Mohammed, *Où va l'Algérie? :* 1. *Notre Révolution*, Librairie de l'Etoile, Paris 1964.

CHALIAN, Gérard, *L'Algérie, est-elle Socialiste?*, Editions Maspero, Paris 1964.

DESPOIS, Jean, *L'Afrique Blanche :* 1. *L'Afrique du Nord*, Presses Universitaires, Paris 1964.

DRESCH, J., *et al.*, *L'Industrialisation du Maghreb*, Editions Maspero, Paris 1963.

DUCHEMIN, Jacques C., *Histoire du* FLN, Table Ronde, Paris 1962.

ESTIER, Claude, *Pour l'Algérie*, Editions Maspero, Paris 1964.

FANON, Frantz, *L'An V de la Révolution Algérienne*, Editions Maspero, Paris 1959.

—— *Les Damnés de la Terre*, Editions Maspero, Paris 1961; published in English as *The Wretched of the Earth*, Grove Press, New York; MacGibbon and Kee, London 1965.

FAVROD, Charles-Henri, *Le* FLN *et l'Algérie*, Plon, Paris 1962.

FERAOUN, Mouloud, *Journal 1955–1962*, Editions du Seuil, Paris 1962.

HARRIS, Richard, *Independence and After : Revolution in Underdeveloped Countries*, Royal Institute of International Affairs, Oxford University Press, London and New York 1962.

JEANSON, Francis, *La Révolution Algérienne*, Feltrinelli, Milan 1962.

JULIEN, Charles-André, *Histoire de l'Afrique du Nord*, 2 vols., Payot, Paris 1961;

—— *Histoire de l'Algérie Contemporaine :* Vol. I, *La Conquête et les Débuts de la Colonisation 1827–1871*, Presses Universitaires, Paris 1964.

KERR, Malcolm, *The Arab Cold War 1958–1964 : A Study of Ideologies in Politics*, Royal Institute of International Affairs, Oxford University Press, London and New York 1965.

KHALDI, A., *Le Problème Algérien devant la Conscience Démocratique*, Editions En-Nadha, Algiers 1946.

LACHERAF, Mostefa, *L'Algérie : Nation et Société*, Editions Maspero, Paris 1963.

LACOUTURE, Jean and Simonne, *Le Maroc à l'Epreuve*, Editions du Seuil, Paris 1958.

LE TOURNEAU, Roger, *L'Islam Contemporain*, Editions Internationales, Paris 1950.

MAITAN, Livio, *L'Algeria e il Socialismo*, Libreria Internazionale Terzo Mondo, Rome 1963.

MANDOUZE, André (ed.), *La Révolution Algérienne par les Textes*, Editions Maspero, Paris 1961.

MERLE, Robert, *Ahmed Ben Bella*, Gallimard, Paris 1965.

MEYNAUD, Jean and SALAH-BEY, Anisse, *Le Syndicalisme Africain*, Payot, Paris 1963.

MORISON, David, *The USSR and Africa 1945–1963*, Royal Institute of International Affairs, Oxford University Press, London and New York 1964.

M'RABET, Fadela, *La Femme Algérienne*, Editions Maspero, Paris 1965.

OPPERMAN, Thomas, *Le Problème Algérien : Données historiques, politiques, juridiques*, Editions Maspero, Paris 1961; original German ed., *Die Algerische Frage*, Kohlhammer, Stuttgart 1959.

OUZEGANE, Amar, *Le Meilleur Combat*, Julliard, Paris 1962.

ROY, Jules, *La Guerre d'Algérie*, Julliard, Paris 1960. Published in English as *The War in Algeria*, Grove Press, New York 1960.

SAUVY, Alfred, *Le Tiers Monde : Sous-développement et développement*, Presses Universitaires, Paris 1961.

SUSINI, Jean-Jacques, *Histoire de l'OAS*, Vol. I, Table Ronde, Paris 1961.

TEILLAC, Jean, *Autogestion en Algérie*, Peyronnet, Paris 1965.

TILLION, Germaine, *L'Algérie en 1957*, Editions de Minuit, Paris 1957. Published in English as *Algeria*, Knopf, New York 1958.

—— *France and Algeria : Complementary Enemies*, Knopf, New York 1961.

TOURNEAUX, J-R., *L'Histoire Secrète*, Plon, Paris 1962.

YACEF, M. Saadi, *Souvenirs de la Bataille d'Alger*, Julliard, Paris 1962.

ZIEGLER, Jean, *Sociologie de la Nouvelle Afrique*, Gallimard, Paris 1964.

INDEX